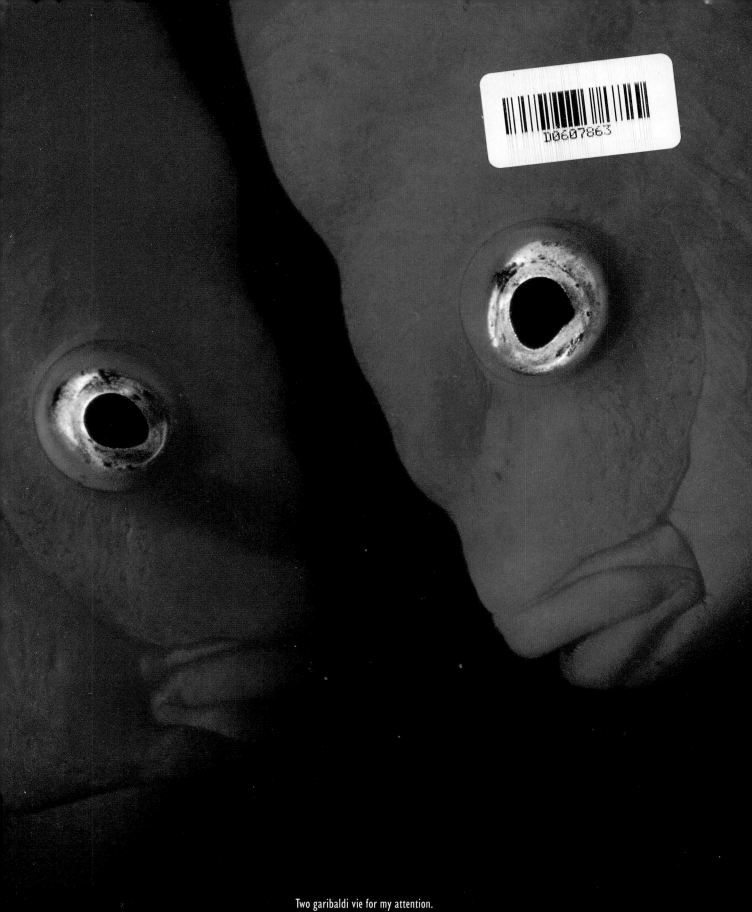

Two garibaldi vie for my attention.

The Spanish shawl is among the most resplendent of the nudibranchs that inhabit California waters.

California Marine Life

A Guide to Common Marine Species

MARTY SNYDERMAN

EDITED BY
MICHELLE BAILEY

ROBERTS
RINEHART
PUBLISHERS

IN COOPERATION WITH
MONTEREY
BAY AQUARIUM

California Marine Life

Published by Roberts Rinehart Publishers
An Imprint of Madison Books
4720 Boston Way
Lanham, MD 20706

Published in cooperation with
Monterey Bay Aquarium

International Standard Book Number 1-57098-127-2
Library of Congress Catalog Card Number 97-66387

Book and Cover Design: Ann W. Douden
Reviewers: Steve Webster and Dave Powell,
Monterey Bay Aquarium

10 9 8 7 6 5 4 3 2 1

Printed in Hong Kong

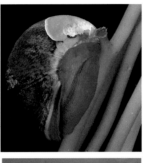

Contributing Photographers:
© Ken Bach, courtesy of Monterey Bay Aquarium:
front cover center bottom
© Ken Bondy: title page left/bottom right, pages IX,
10, 13, 16, 17, 18, 19, 23, 25, 26 bottom right, 27, 28,
29, 33, 46, 51, 55, 68, 70, 72 top/bottom, 73 bottom,
80 top/bottom, 82 top, 83 top, 85 top, 101, 107, 111,
118 top, 119 top, 129, 131 top, 132 top, 137, 151
bottom, 153, 158 bottom, 167 top/bottom, 168
© Mark Conlin: pages 12, 38, 41, 43, 45, 48, 84
middle, 86 top, 93, 104 top/bottom, 105, 112, 115,
152 bottom, 154 top, 155, 159, 169, 170
© Tom Campbell: page 145
© Gerry Ellis: page 166
© Dale Glantz: page 66 top left
© Amos Nachoum: page 160
© Dan Walsh: pages 37, 40
© David Wrobel: page 39 left
All other photographs © Marty Snyderman

Contents

About the Author

Marty Snyderman is a film producer, still photographer, author, and speaker specializing in the marine environment. Having explored California waters for more than twenty years, he has gained an intimate knowledge about the marine wildlife that inhabits the region. While Marty likes to dive anywhere, anytime, he has enjoyed unique opportunities to film sharks, whales, dolphins, manta rays, billfish, and many other large, dramatic open-ocean animals that inhabit oceans around the world.

An Emmy Award–winner, Snyderman is currently coproducing a film about the natural history of sharks and rays with his friend Rocky Strong for the PBS series *Nature*. His first film, *To Be with Sharks* (also aired under the title *View from the Cage*) premiered during *"Shark Week"* on the Discovery Channel in 1994. Over the years his underwater cinematography has been used by the National Geographic Society, the Discovery Channel, NOVA, the British Broadcasting Company, CBS, ABC, ESPN, Arts & Entertainment network, the Warner Brothers hit *Free Willy*, Home Box Office, Mutual of Omaha's *Wild Kingdom*, and many other networks and film companies around the world.

Snyderman's still photography and writing have been used by many major organizations and publications expressing interest in the marine environment, including the National Geographic Society, Nikon Inc., the National Wildlife Federation, the Monterey Bay Aquarium, Sea World, the New England Aquarium, the Seattle Aquarium, the Aquarium of the Americas, Cousteau Society publications, *Time* magazine, *Newsweek*, and many magazines in the sport diving field. He is listed on the masthead as a contributing editor for *Discover Diving* and *Scuba Times* magazines.

Residing in Solana Beach, California (near San Diego), he continues to teach underwater photography through Nikon Inc., work on film projects, and photograph, write, speak, and learn about marine wildlife and marine issues.

Commonly encountered by California divers, painted greenlings are among the most curious of reef fishes.

Preface

The first time I ever saw a gray whale underwater, I was diving in 60 feet of water off the coast of San Diego in the La Jolla Submarine Canyon. The canyon is located near the southernmost extension of a series of deep marine trenches that parallel the coast of southern California. Earlier in my dive I had been preoccupied by my efforts to film a tiny yet magnificently colored orange and purple nudibranch that is commonly called a Spanish shawl. Although common in reef communities, it is not usually seen on the sand and clay of the canyon. Nudibranchs are often described as sea slugs or shell-less snails in textbooks, but their beautiful coloration makes them virtually indescribable without an accompanying photograph.

I don't know why I looked up at the precise moment I did. I'd like to think that I have some sixth sense when I dive

that made me aware of the whale's presence, but more likely I just looked up when I ran out of film. Whatever the reason, I am glad I did. The whale was a beautiful sight, creating an image in my mind's eye that I will treasure throughout my lifetime.

At first I was overwhelmed by the whale's size. Believe me, anyone would be. Although gray whales are relatively small whales, they have body parts—the head, pectoral flippers, and tail—that are larger than a fully grown human being. The great creature was obviously big and powerful, yet it was clearly graceful and a joy to observe.

I remained motionless, standing with my fins planted on the seafloor as the whale dived down, cruising ever so slowly only 10 to 15 feet above me. I wasn't frightened and certainly never felt threatened, though I was absolutely certain that the whale knew I was there. What I did feel was a sense of awe. The whale gave me the once-over with its tennis ball–sized eye and then disappeared within a couple of seconds.

It was one of the few times in my diving career that I was glad I couldn't take a photograph. My camera would have been a burden, robbing me of the pure pleasure of watching, of just being in the wilderness next to a gray whale. Few people are ever eyeball to eyeball with a whale in the wild, and I will always treasure the experience.

When I reflect back upon twenty-plus years of diving in California, I often think back to this moment. Somehow, that dive symbolically encapsulates my experiences better than anything else. For in California we truly have the opportunity to enjoy an incredibly diverse variety of marine wildlife that ranges from inch-long, rainbow-colored nudibranchs to 40-foot-long, 40-ton California gray whales.

Being able to enjoy the amazing diversity of marine plants and animals in the majestic settings of the Pacific provides a wonderful form of relaxation and recreation for many Californians and our guests. There is a striking contrast between the densely populated metropolitan areas where trendy lifestyles can accurately be described by the phrase "life in the fast lane" and the peaceful wilderness settings of the ocean frontier. In coastal waters, less than 100 yards offshore of beaches located only a few miles from the hearts of Los Angeles, San Diego, Santa Barbara, and San Francisco, whale watchers, birders, boaters, anglers, snorkelers, and divers can escape into a marine wilderness that is rich in sea life and adventure. In a state that has a well-deserved reputation for being one of the most technically advanced areas in the world, complete with overly demanding, stress-filled, on-the-go lifestyles, spending a day at the Pacific provides a perfect escape from the harsh realities of urban pressures. Those of us who are fortunate enough to live in or visit California know the region to be a marine wilderness that is as magnificent and diverse as any wilderness area on earth.

Acknowledgments

One of the first lessons anyone will learn when they set out to write a book like this one is that it is never a one-person project. Of course, when I started this book I had no idea how much help I would need and how much I would get. I really would like to say a heartfelt thank-you to the many people who helped out along the way, though I must admit there were moments when I wasn't so sure I wanted to know anyone who encouraged me to get into this project.

The first person I want to thank was the first person I turned to, my assistant, Michelle Bailey. She helped me rewrite my original version, fact-check, organize the layout, gather images, and stay in touch with outside contributors. Thanks, Michelle, you did a great job!

But the two of us alone still wouldn't have produced this book without a lot of additional help. How many times did we pick up the phone or write a fax or an e-mail? We don't have a clue. But we do want to say a heartfelt thank-you to everyone who contributed to this effort.

That list includes Howard and Michele Hall, two of my best friends in life who also love to dive. Howard's knowledge of the sea, eagerness to share, and enthusiasm for diving and photography have been a huge help to almost every project I have ever been involved in. Bob and Cathy Cranston, Tom Campbell, and Mark Thurlow have been helpful in more ways than I can count. I have yet to be able to break something that Mark can't fix.

Images produced by Ken Bondy and Mark Conlin appear throughout this book, and I am especially grateful for their contribution. Dale Glantz generously shared information on new developments in the kelp industry, and Rocky Strong answered more questions than he realizes.

Special thanks to Steven Webster and Dave Powell for their reviews, and the gang at Monterey Bay Aquarium for their assistance and for helping me get in touch with Rick Rinehart at Roberts Rinehart. Thanks to the gang at Roberts Rinehart for working with me on this book. And thanks to Ken Loyst and the staff at *Discover Diving*, and to Fred Garth

and the folks at *Scuba Times* for helping me make diving such a big part of my life.

Longtime diving buddies Chip Matheson, Norbert Wu, Dan Walsh, Steve Earley, and Fred Fischer helped me have a lot of fun and get through the part called work. Thanks to Frank Fennell and the rest of the gang at Nikon Inc. who

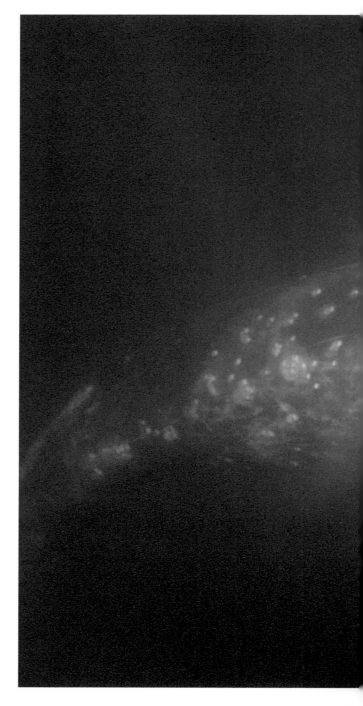

have always been ready, willing, and able to help me get whatever equipment I needed, and to Mike and Lauren Farley who published the first edition of this book in 1987. Without them there would be no new edition.

I have also received a lot of assistance from the crews of the *Bottom Scratcher* and *Sand Dollar*, the entire gang at *Truth Aquatics*, Dave Miller, and a lot of other people who have taken me diving over the years.

To all these people and to all the rest of you who helped, but whom I failed to include here, I'd really like to say a big "Thanks gang!" I couldn't have done it without you.

All the best in diving!

Majestic gray whales pass through California waters as they migrate between their Alaskan feeding grounds and their breeding grounds in Baja California.

A bat ray glides gracefully overhead.

About the Book

People are drawn to the sea for many reasons: to snorkel, scuba dive, walk, talk, run, beachcomb, play, swim, or just relax and get away from the hassles of everyday life. Whatever the reason, most people share the quest for fun, a thirst for knowledge, and a desire to enjoy the wonders of nature. With this in mind, I have written this book as both a personal guide and an entertaining reference source for anyone who enjoys spending a day at the beach or out on the water.

Although I have included some basic scientific terminology and plenty of solid information, this book is not intended to be a scientific work. Instead, the text and imagery are included to help readers acquire a practical knowledge of the natural history of many of the plants and animals of California's marine environment. After all, many of us are primarily interested in enjoying our surroundings, not in memorizing obscure facts. We want to learn when and where we are most likely to observe various plants and animals. We like knowing who is closely related to whom and why, who eats what, and who likes to eat whom. We enjoy finding out about some of the more astonishing adaptations used by various species to ensure their survival.

This type of insight helps us better understand why, for example, we are more likely to see a gray whale in California in fall or winter, a sea otter near Monterey instead of San Diego, a lobster in a crevice in a rocky reef, a halibut in the sand, and a blue shark out in the open sea. The bottom line is, the more we know about the marine environment, the richer and more captivating the setting seems to be.

Although its multiple common names (giant star, knobby star, giant-spined star)
can be confusing, this sea star has just one taxonomic name, *Pisaster giganteus*.

CHAPTER 1
CLASSIFYING PLANTS AND ANIMALS

Red crabs.

Aside from chuckling at the silly names assigned to our favorite cartoon characters (who could forget the mischievous and speedy Road Runner, *"Hot-roddicus supersonicus"*?), most of us have had very little exposure to the use of scientific names. Those who remember bits of high school biology may recall that plants and animals are given names called genus and species, the long Latin and Greek words you had to memorize even though the only living thing that knew the names, or even seemed to care, was your teacher. Although at the time, memorizing those names seemed a meaningless exercise in discipline dreamt up by a sadistic educator, be assured that the task had some merit after all. Scientific names, more properly called taxonomic names, are the foundation of a practical, simple, yet very precise system for understanding and communicating about the fascinating plants and animals that share our planet.

The use of taxonomic names is obviously critical within the scientific community, where exact and unambiguous distinctions among species are necessary. With more than 2 million living species already described and more being discovered almost daily, a standardized system of organization and naming is essential. Nevertheless, you might wonder why a nonscientist should bother with all that

Latin and Greek instead of simply using common names.

Because of the haphazard and highly regional way that common names are acquired, many species are known by several common names. To confound this problem, the same common name is often used to describe different species. In order to illustrate the potential for confusion caused by the common names of only two animals, consider two separate species of crabs, both called red crabs. You can easily imagine a conversation in which two people believe they are discussing the same crab but are not. Because one of these is also sometimes referred to as a pelagic red crab, a tuna crab, and a squat lobster, you can also foresee a conversation in which four people are discussing the same animal but believe they are not.

Of these two red crabs, one is found in northern California reef communities and is highly valued as a commercial food source; the other is much smaller, of no commercial value, and only occasionally seen near shore. The advantage of a consistent distinction between these species is obvious, and can easily be made by using the animals' taxonomic names: the commercially valuable crab is *Cancer productus*; the other is *Pleuroncodes planipes*.

To further demonstrate the usefulness of taxonomic names, consider two different species of sharks both commonly called white sharks. Imagine that you are familiar with one of these, the whitetip reef shark. While boating one day, one of your companions casually informs you that there is a white shark in the water. Knowing that whitetips are comparatively docile sharks, you naturally leap into the water to get a closer look. Now, imagine your dismay at discovering that the white shark referred to was actually a *great* white shark, infamous for its enormous size and occasional taste for surfers, swimmers, and divers. This potentially unfortunate misunder-

standing can be avoided simply by using the unique taxonomic names of the sharks: *Carcharodon carcharias* (great white shark) and *Triaenodon obesus* (whitetip reef shark).

Familiarity with taxonomy can give you an advantage in understanding the natural history of the plants and animals you see as you explore the marine environment. Because plants and animals are grouped and named according to their similarities to others, certain generalizations can be made about any given species by knowing something about the taxonomic groups in which it is described. For example, if you recognize an animal as a sea star, you can infer that it is probably carnivorous like the majority of other sea stars. If you know that sea stars are described in the taxonomic group Echinodermata, you can also infer that it is very likely capable of regenerating lost body parts, as are most other echinoderms. For convenience, the distinctive characteristics of major taxonomic groups are outlined in the "Phylum-by-Phylum Overview" section of this chapter.

It is obvious that there are important benefits of knowing and using scientific terminology. The trouble is, if you are like most people, you have long since forgotten much of the information you once had to memorize. If you fit into this group and would like a layperson's review of at least some of the basics, the information in the remainder of this chapter will prove especially helpful. It will enable you to identify specimens and gain a solid foundation of knowledge about most of the creatures you are likely to encounter in California's marine wilderness. In many cases positive identification will be possible, especially of those animals most often encountered by people who spend time in the marine environment.

DID YOU KNOW?

. . . SOME SCIENTISTS ESTIMATE THAT ON THE DEEP SEAFLOOR ALONE THERE MAY BE UP TO 10 MILLION AS-YET-UNDISCOVERED SPECIES.

Taxonomic Classification: A Quick and Easy Review

More than 2 million currently living species have been described by the scientific community. In order to study them, scientists have grouped these organisms into various categories based on commonly shared traits. This system of organization is called taxonomic classification. Introduced by Swedish scientist Carolus Linnaeus in 1758, this system is accepted worldwide as the scientific standard. (Although there is ongoing debate about the details of this system, this book will describe and use the most commonly accepted classifications.)

The broadest taxonomic division is that of kingdoms. While exploring California marine life you will notice representatives of at least two kingdoms: the plants and the animals. Most people are interested in the larger plants called kelp; although many other plants play an important role in marine ecology, smaller marine plants rarely capture the attention of recreational divers. Therefore, a discussion of California's marine plants is included in Chapter 4, but the vast majority of this book is devoted to California's marine animals.

Animals, like members of other kingdoms, are classified and named according to the following hierarchy of groups (the plural form of the group is indicated within parentheses):

HIERARCHY OF TAXONOMIC CLASSIFICATION

Kingdom (Kingdoms)

Phylum (Phyla)

Class (Classes)

Order (Orders)

Family (Families)

Genus (Genera)

species (species)

The taxonomic categories to which an animal is assigned reflect its known or assumed evolutionary relationships to other animals. Scientists describe and group animals according to similarities in a variety of traits ranging from physical appearance to genetic makeup (DNA). It is important to realize that if an animal lacks a characteristic shared by others within the group, it is the classification system that is imperfect, not the animal.

Kingdoms are the broadest group; they include organisms that are loosely related to one another. All animals, for example, are classified within the kingdom Animalia, but are subdivided among thirty-five or more phyla within that kingdom (the exact number of phyla is constantly revised and debated by scientists). The phyla are subdivided into classes, which in turn are subdivided into orders, the orders into families, the families into genera, and finally the genera are subdivided into individual species. These categories are occasionally further divided into subcategories, such as subclass or suborder, but such divisions are beyond the need or scope of this text. Species are the smallest classification groups; only animals that are nearly identical to one another belong to the same species. For example, all black-and-yellow rockfish are described as members of the same species, *Sebastes chrysomelas*. Gopher rockfish (*Sebastes carnatus*) are closely related and similar enough to black-and-yellow rockfish to be classified in the same genus (*Sebastes*), but different enough to merit their own species classification (*carnatus*).

Like your own first and last names, which describe both the exclusive group to which you belong (your family) and precisely which member of that family you are, a taxonomic name unambiguously describes where an animal falls within the taxonomic scheme. A taxonomic name consists of the two most exclusive classification groups—genus and species—and is properly written in italics with the first letter of the genus capitalized and the entire species name in lowercase. That may sound a little confusing at first, but you are probably very familiar with your own scientific name, which you share with all other humans: *Homo sapiens*.

The table below demonstrates the taxonomic classification of three species we normally refer to as the California spiny lobster, the garibaldi, and the California sea lion. It is easy to see from this chart that, in an evolutionary sense, the garibaldi and California sea lions are more closely related to each other than they are to the spiny lobster. All three are described in the kingdom Animalia, but the spiny lobster belongs to a different phylum than the garibaldi and sea lions. Garibaldi and sea lions, along with all other vertebrates (animals with backbones), are grouped together in the phylum Chordata. Because spiny lobsters are invertebrates (animals without backbones), they are classified within one of the phyla that describe invertebrate animals, phylum Arthro-

poda. Notice that you can also deduce that humpback whales, which are vertebrate animals, must be more closely related to California sea lions and garibaldi than they are to spiny lobsters. Similarly, sheep crabs, which are arthropods, must be more closely related to spiny lobster than they are to garibaldi and sea lions.

Often we are satisfied just by knowing more or less where an animal fits into nature's overall scheme. For most people this is particularly true in the case of any number of small, similar-looking invertebrates. Being able to classify a particular animal even simply to its class allows you to make some generalizations about its natural history. The more precisely you identify the animal, the more you will be able to infer about its role in the marine world.

COMMON NAME	CALIFORNIA SPINY LOBSTER	GARIBALDI	CALIFORNIA SEA LION
Kingdom	Animalia	Animalia	Animalia
Phylum	Arthropoda	Chordata	Chordata
Class	Crustacea	Osteichthyes	Mammalia
(Subclass)	Malacostraca		
Order	Decapoda	Perciformes	Pinnipedia
Family	Palinuridae	Pomacentridae	Otaridae
Genus	*Panulirus*	*Hypsypops*	*Zalophus*
species	*interruptus*	*rubicundus*	*californianus*

Phylum-by-Phylum Overview of Marine Animals

The following discussion does not include all marine phyla, but only those that recreational divers, snorkelers, boaters, and anglers are most likely to encounter and notice. In this book, phyla are discussed more or less in order of complexity or evolutionary development, beginning with the simplest of multicellular life-forms, the sponges, and ending with the most highly specialized and complex forms, the marine mammals. However, organizing the phyla strictly by complexity is difficult because evolution is not a linear process, and the general order and pattern of ancestry continue to be debated within the scientific community. At the beginning of each overview you will find the derivation of the phylum's taxonomic name, easily recognizable characteristic(s) of the group, and a list of the common names of some marine animals assigned to that phylum.

These overviews are brief general descriptions of the distinctive characteristics of the phyla, with some explanation of each phylum's placement with respect to others in the evolutionary tree. You will discover that much of what is outlined here is covered in greater detail in the following chapters. The take-home message of this section is that plants and animals within the same phylum share common physiological characteristics, and that these characteristics can be used to help you better understand species you are curious about.

Although great white sharks inhabit California waters, this fearsome visage is only very rarely encountered.

PHYLUM	MEMBERS OF PHYLUM	IDENTIFIABLE TRAITS (Not all species show all traits.)
Porifera (sponges)	sponges	Pores all over body Benthic[1] attached to substrate Asymmetrical[2]
Cnidaria (cnidarians)	corals, hydroids, sea anemones, jellyfish, by-the-wind sailors, sea fans, sea pens, sea pansies	Tentacles with stinging cells Medusa[3] or polyp[4] form Sometimes colonial[5] Radially symmetrical[6]
Ctenophora (comb jellies)	comb jellies	Sticky tentacles Eight bands of cilia line body Pelagic[7] Radially symmetrical[6]
Platyhelminthes (flatworms)	flatworms	Thin, flat body Bilaterally symmetrical[8]
Ectoprocta (bryozoans)	bryozoans	Attached to substrate Upright/encrusting colonies[5] Often resemble moss or coral
Mollusca (mollusks)	abalone, nudibranchs, sea hares, octopi, squid, scallops, mussels, oysters, clams, chitons, snails, limpets	Shell (single/double/plated) Foot or tentacles with suckers Bilaterally symmetrical[8]
Annelida (annelids)	plume worms	Featherlike gill plumes Segmented body in tube Benthic[1] Bilaterally symmetrical[8]
Arthropoda (arthropods)	barnacles, shrimp, crabs, lobster, copepods, amphipods	Jointed appendages Often clawed Hard exterior skeleton Bilaterally symmetrical[8]
Echinodermata (echinoderms)	sea stars (starfish), brittle stars, sea urchins, sand dollars, sea cucumbers	Warty or spiny skin Tube feet Benthic[1] Radially symmetrical[3]
Chordata (chordates[9])	tunicates, sharks, rays, skates, bony fish, mammals	Backbone (except tunicates) Bilaterally symmetrical[8]

1. **Benthic:** Lives on or in the seafloor.
2. **Asymmetrical:** Shape has no definite symmetry.
3. **Medusa:** A shape like a jellyfish.
4. **Polyp:** A shape much like an upside-down jellyfish.
5. **Colony:** A group of individuals that share a common skeletal casing.
6. **Radially symmetrical:** Like a wheel, symmetrical parts radiate outward on a plane from the center of the body.

7. **Pelagic:** Lives in the water column, above the seafloor.
8. **Bilaterally symmetrical:** Like a person, a shape that can be divided into symmetrical halves on only one plane through the center.
9. **Chordates:** Often mistakenly referred to as vertebrates; however, not all chordates are vertebrates.

Phylum Porifera

Derivation:
Latin for "pore-bearer."

Characteristics:
Have pores all over body.

California Representatives:
Sponges.

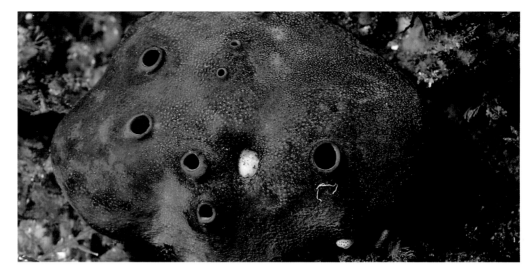

A gray moon sponge, named for its craterlike pores.

The approximately 10,000 species of sponges (5,000 of which are still living) are the sole members of phylum Porifera. Sponges are the simplest of all multicellular animals. With no organs or specialized tissues, and with cells that are only loosely associated, sponges seem to bridge the gap between colonies of single-celled creatures and truly multicellular animals. The lack of strict organization among cells results in the asymmetrical bodies so characteristic of sponges.

The name Porifera is derived from the Latin words *porus*, meaning "pore," and *ferro*, meaning "to bear." This name refers to the system of pores that perforates the bodies of all sponges. Tiny hairlike cilia line the pores, beating with no apparent synchrony but collectively creating a current of water through the sponge. With the exception of a recently discovered predacious species, sponges feed on the plankton and organic matter they trap from the water as it flows through their system of pores.

Sponges maintain their amorphous structure with an internal skeleton made of siliceous or calcareous needles called spicules, the shape of which usually allows positive species identification. Some sponges also contain stringy protein fibers called spongin. The natural bath sponges used by many people are actually the internal skeletons of sponges. Some spicules apparently taste bad to many potential predators, enabling the otherwise defenseless sponges to protect themselves. However, sponges are still a tasty meal to a variety of snails, nudibranchs, sea stars, and fishes.

Sponges, like many invertebrates, are capable of reproducing both asexually (resulting in clones) and sexually (resulting in genetic recombination). Asexual reproduction is achieved by breaking or budding off small pieces, which then develop into complete sponges. Sexual reproduction occurs when a sponge releases sperm that combine with another sponge's eggs. Many sponges are hermaphroditic, which means that the same sponge has both male and female reproductive abilities; however, even these sponges usually produce only sperm or eggs, not both, during each spawning event. Sponge larvae are free-swimming members of the plankton, while adult sponges are always attached bottom-dwellers.

Some sponges are involved in a variety of symbiotic relationships with other animals. Some larger sponges house mollusks, crustaceans, worms, fishes, and other animals. Many animals actually spend the majority of their lives inside sponges, and some feed directly on their sponge host. Some sponges actually benefit from symbiotic algae that live within their tissues; the sponges gain oxygen and nutrients produced by the algae's photosynthesis.

The simplest and most primitive group of multicellular animals, sponges have inhabited the seas for at least 550 million years. Despite their endurance, no known organisms have evolved from them. Scientists therefore consider sponges to be a "dead end" in the evolutionary road.

Reproductive Strategies
Why Have Sex?

California sea lions are polygamous animals, mating with multiple partners during their springtime breeding season.

Many lower invertebrates use a convenient method of reproduction that occurs without the participation of another animal. This method of reproduction is called asexual reproduction. Rather than bothering with eggs and sperm that must be united to produce the next generation, an asexual reproducer can simply break off bits of itself that grow into clones (exact copies) of its parent. Particularly convenient for animals that "don't get out much," such as sponges and other sessile animals that cannot travel to find mates, asexual reproduction is also used by more mobile animals—even ones that are also capable of sexual reproduction.

The nature of life is to reproduce itself. The more copies of your genetic code you successfully pass along to offspring, who will pass it along to their offspring, the more "fit" you are. Asexual reproduction results in young that are genetically identical to the parent (surely enough to satisfy any progenitor!). The asexual parent has successfully perpetuated its own genetic identity exactly, whereas in sexual reproduction, the offspring carry only half of the genetic information of each parent. In a stable or specialized environment, it is usually advantageous to the offspring to have the precise genetic makeup (genotype) that has been successful in the past. Asexual reproduction also has the benefit of speed; young can be produced quickly enough

to take advantage of times when conditions are good and food is plentiful.

"Well, then," you may logically ask, "why have sex?" Aside from the obvious, sexual reproduction has its own benefits. The basis of the advantage of sex is that it results in offspring that are genetically different from each other and from their parent(s).* Although each parent can contribute only half its genetic information to each offspring, mixing up genes can be a good thing in the long run. Occasionally, the new combination of traits results in an animal that is more fit than either of its parents. Furthermore, having offspring with a variety of traits increases the odds that at least some will survive through an environmental calamity, such as a severe change in temperature or the invasion of a virus. Having half of your genetic information perpetuated is better than none at all!

Although both methods of reproduction have their advantages, sexual reproduction has had monumental consequences for evolution. No genetic process creates diversity as rapidly or as profoundly, and the amazing variety of life we see today is in large part due to the rise of sexual reproduction.

*Just to complicate matters, some species are capable of sexual reproduction without a partner—see the sidebar "Sex in the Sea" in Chapter 5.

Although they are often mistaken for plants, these red gorgonian corals are actually animals.

Phylum Cnidaria

Derivation:
Greek for "nettle."

Characteristics:
Have tentacles that contain stinging cells.

California Representatives:
Corals, hydroids, sea anemones, jellyfish, sea pens, sea fans, by-the-wind sailors, and sea pansies.

Cnidarians (pronounced with a silent C) are a varied group of animals that includes corals, hydroids, sea anemones, jellyfish, sea pens, sea fans, by-the-wind sailors, and sea pansies. The name of this phylum, derived from the Greek word *knide*, meaning "nettle," refers to the stinging cells found in the tentacles of all cnidarians. These stinging cells, called cnidocytes, are the unique and unifying characteristic of members of this phylum; an animal with cnidocytes is a cnidarian by definition.

Cnidocytes are used for both predation and defense. Inside each cnidocyte is a hollow, coiled, harpoonlike barb called a nematocyst. When a cnidocyte is stimulated by chemicals or by touch, the nematocyst is fired into the victim with enough force to penetrate even the hard shells of many crustaceans. A potent venom is then released through the nematocyst. Because cnidarians are not actively mobile, they depend on this fast-acting toxin to deter predators and to stun their prey of small invertebrates and fish. Despite their potent arsenal, however, cnidarians are still eaten by animals ranging from nudibranchs to sea turtles.

All cnidarians are radially symmetrical, meaning that body parts radiate outward from the center of the body; they have a top and bottom but no front and back or left and right. They are gelatinous in texture, with a ring of tentacles surrounding a central mouth. Cnidarians occur in two basic forms: sessile polyps and floating medusae. You are probably familiar with medusae, in the form of jellyfish. Polyps are much like cylindrical, upside-down, attached medusae; some are solitary and others live in colonies. Some cnidarians exist only in one form or the other, while others exhibit both forms in the course of their life cycle.

Cnidarians are the most primitive animals with simple tissues and specialized body systems. They have no organs, and their nervous system consists only of a diffuse nerve net that coordinates actions and reactions among the cells. A water-filled central digestive sac acts as a skeleton (called a hydrostatic skeleton) against which simple muscles can work to allow movement. Although cnidarians have a simple digestive system, they do not have specialized systems for respiration, circulation, or excretion.

Today, there are living representatives of approximately 9,000 cnidarian species. These are divided among four classes, three of which are represented in California waters:

- **Class Hydrozoa (hydroids and by-the-wind sailors):** Hydrozoans exist in both medusa and polyp forms. Some are colonial animals.
- **Class Scyphozoa (jellyfish):** Although scyphozoans were once thought to exist almost exclusively as medusae, polyp forms are becoming more commonly recognized.
- **Class Anthozoa (sea anemones, corals, sea fans, sea pansies, and sea pens):** Anthozoans exist almost exclusively as polyps. Some are colonial animals; others are solitary.

The delicate flowerlike appearance of this aggregate anemone belies the potent sting of its tentacles.

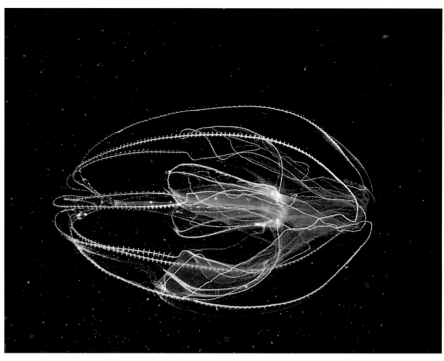

A comb jelly.

Phylum Ctenophora

Derivation:
Greek for "comb-bearer."

Characteristics:
Have eight rows of cilia on jellyfish-like body.

California Representatives:
Comb jellies.

Ctenophores (pronounced "teen-o-fors," with a silent C) are similar to cnidarians in both physiology and appearance. In fact, for many years comb jellies and cnidarians were grouped together in one phylum, Coelenterata. However, cnidarians and ctenophores were separated into different phyla when it was recognized that comb jellies lack the stinging nematocysts that are the defining characteristic of cnidarians. Other differences bring into question whether comb jellies and cnidarians are even closely related: comb jellies lack an attached (polyp) phase, have somewhat more complex bodies than cnidarians, and, more significant, are not wholly radially symmetrical.

With well under 100 living species now known, ctenophores are rarely noticed because most are very small with transparent, gelatinous bodies. However, divers who explore the waters of the open sea occasionally encounter huge numbers of ctenophores. These animals usually have long, sticky tentacles surrounding a central mouth. Eight bands of hairlike structures called cilia line their bodies and propel them through the water. Comblike in appearance, these bands of cilia are the basis for the name of the phylum—from the Greek words *cteno*, "comb," and *phoro*, "bearer."

Ctenophores prey upon larval fishes and other small animals by catching them on sticky tentacles. Once trapped, the prey is coated with mucus and carried into the digestive cavity as the ctenophore's long tentacles retract. Some ctenophores also contain symbiotic algae that provide them with nutritional by-products of photosynthesis.

Ctenophores are hermaphroditic and self-fertilization is common. Like those of most other invertebrates, their larvae are free-swimming. Asexual reproduction is not well documented among members of this phylum.

Phylum Platyhelminthes

Derivation:
Greek for "flatworm."

Characteristics:
Have very thin, flat, and often colorful sluglike bodies.

California Representatives:
Flatworms.

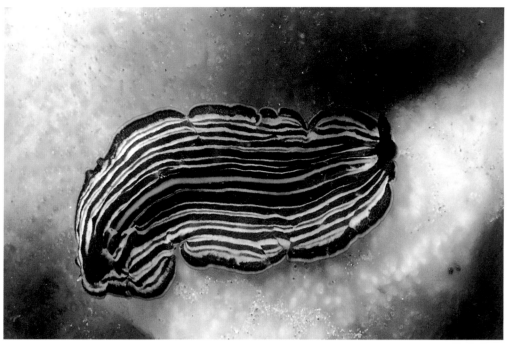

Although flatworms are rarely seen in California, it is a treat to encounter colorful specimens such as this one.

Flatworms are just that—flat. Their almost paper-thin bodies make them easily distinguishable from other worms and nudibranchs. Unlike their often repulsive terrestrial counterparts, marine flatworms are quite beautiful. Although flatworms are relatively rare in California waters (only occasionally found under rocks), they are commonly seen by divers in other areas. The phylum is discussed in this book in order to emphasize the difference between flatworms and other marine worms.

Flatworms are the most primitive animals with organs and organ systems. Although many possess a rudimentary brain, their nervous system is rather simple compared to that of more advanced invertebrates. Sensory organs allow flatworms to respond to the presence of chemicals, light, movement, and food. Most are parasitic, but some are free-living carnivores or scavengers; most of these are cannibalistic and appear quite happy to snack on each other. Unlike members of previously described phyla, flatworms are able to actively pursue their prey, sometimes swimming but usually crawling along the seafloor using cilia that line their underside.

Flatworms are the simplest animals that are bilaterally symmetrical: they have not only a top and bottom, but also a front and back, and left and right. Bilateral symmetry is a significant evolutionary advancement that allows the concentration of sensory nerves at one end of the body (the head), a development called cephalization. Because of cephalization, bilaterally symmetrical animals are often more active than radially symmetrical animals such as anemones and sea stars.

In addition to sexual reproduction, many flatworms are capable of asexual reproduction by regeneration of torn body parts—a flatworm torn in two may develop into two healthy, complete worms. Most flatworms are hermaphroditic, meaning that individuals possess both male and female reproductive organs, and sexual reproduction occurs by internal fertilization, with each partner depositing sperm into a special sac in the other. The fertilized eggs hatch into free-swimming larvae that resemble those of cnidarians, a similarity that may indicate that cnidarians and flatworms shared a relatively recent common ancestor in their evolution.

Bilateral Symmetry
The Advantage of Having a Head

Radially symmetrical animals, such as this proliferating anemone, are less complex than bilaterally symmetrical animals.

Millions of years ago, during the early stages of animal evolution, animals developed with one of two general body forms: asymmetrical bodies (like sponges), or radially symmetrical bodies (like jellyfish). Asymmetrical animals have bodies with no overall regularity of form with respect to a central point or axis. By contrast, animals with radial symmetry are, like a wheel, identical at all points at the same distance from a central axis. In other words, you can bisect the animal on any plane containing the central axis and end up with identical halves. Radially symmetrical animals have better organized and coordinated nervous responses than asymmetrical animals. Neither asymmetrical nor radially symmetrical animals have a left and a right or a front and a back. They are suited to meeting environmental stimuli equally well from any direction—but not very quickly or efficiently.

Although both asymmetrical and radially symmetrical body forms have been and still are successful (as evidenced by the multitude of representative animals in existence today), animals in these forms are limited in complexity. In order for more sophisticated organisms to evolve, another body plan had to be available. The development of bilateral symmetry was, therefore, a key advancement along the evolutionary path.

Animals with bilateral (two-sided) symmetry are identical at all equidistant points on each side of a central plane, so there is only one way to cut the body and wind up with identical halves. These animals possess right and left halves that are essentially mirror images of one another, as well as a top (dorsal) and a bottom (ventral) side. More significantly, bilaterally symmetrical animals have defined front (anterior) and back (posterior) ends—in other words, you can tell their head from their rear.

Bilateral symmetry allows greater specialization of body parts for different functions. An early effect was the concentration of sensory organs toward the front of the animal. Called cephalization, this development placed the sensory organs at the end of the body that normally is the first to encounter food, danger, and other changes in the animal's surroundings. Bilaterally symmetrical animals are much more efficient at moving around and responding to their environment than are radially symmetrical animals.

Over the course of evolution, the number and complexity of specialized organs in animals with bilateral symmetry continued to increase. Cephalization was quickly accompanied by the concentration of nerves into major longitudinal cords, called a central nervous system. Animals with a central nervous system can much more efficiently coordinate responses to environmental stimuli than can the more primitive animals that are equipped only with a system of diffuse nerves. As bilateral symmetry evolved, nerve cells also came to be concentrated toward the head, in what eventually became the brain of higher animals.

Members of all higher phyla are bilaterally symmetrical (although in echinoderms it is evident only during the larval stage). The development of bilateral symmetry, with the accompanying cephalization and subsequent development of a central nervous system and brain, was a crucial step in the advancement of the animal phyla.

Phylum Ectoprocta

Derivation:
Greek for "outside anus."

Characteristics:
Form colonies that resemble moss, coral, or worms.

California Representatives:
Bryozoans.

Like all bryozoans, this lacy bryozoan is a colonial animal, composed of many tiny individuals that share a continuous skeleton.

If you run across a delicate structure that resembles a rose or a bit of lace, it is likely you are looking at the surprisingly beautiful form of a bryozoan. Part of an obscure branch of the evolutionary tree, bryozoans are not well understood, even though the phylum contains at least 5,000 species. All bryozoans are attached bottom-dwellers that form colonies of adjoining calcareous skeletons, on substrates ranging from rocks to kelp to other animals. These colonies may be upright or may form encrusting sheets, and often resemble moss, delicately laced coral, or even worms. Each tiny individual animal within a colony is called a zooid.

The internal organs of bryozoans are enclosed in a fluid-filled body cavity called a coelom. The coelom cushions and protects the internal organs, allowing them to grow independently of the rest of the body. The coelom is an identifying characteristic of all higher invertebrates, including bryozoans, mollusks, annelids, arthropods, echinoderms, and chordates; these animals are called coelomates.

All bryozoans have a specialized feeding structure that traps plankton and detritus from the water. This featherlike organ, called a lophophore, consists of tentacles surrounding the animal's mouth. Once food is trapped by the lophophore, it is moved into the animal's mouth by cilia that line the tentacles. It then enters the animal's U-shaped digestive tract, which leads to an anus outside the lophophore. The phylum name is derived from the Greek words *ectos*, "outside," and *proktos*, "anus."

Bryozoans are hermaphroditic. Some alternate the production of sperm and eggs; others produce both simultaneously, allowing self-fertilization. Some species protect the fertilized eggs within a special area of the colony.

Phylum Mollusca

Derivation:
Latin for "soft."

Characteristics:
Have a muscular foot or tentacles with suckers and are often shelled.

California Representatives:
Abalone, nudibranchs, octopi, squid, scallops, sea hares, mussels, clams, oysters, chitons, snails, and limpets.

An octopus preys upon a small snail.

Mollusks are such a large group that characterizing them proves difficult. With over 50,000 species known, this phylum is second only to the arthropods in number of species. All mollusks are bilaterally symmetrical, most have an easily recognizable head, and all have a brain. In fact, cephalopods, a group of mollusks that includes octopi and squid, are thought to be the most intelligent of all the invertebrates. The body of a mollusk consists of three distinct parts:

- **Muscular foot:** used for movement (as in snails, nudibranchs, and octopi), attachment (as in chitons, abalone, and limpets), or digging (as in clams).
- **Visceral mass:** contains the digestive, excretive, and reproductive organs.
- **Mantle:** a flap of tissue that covers the visceral mass, encloses the respiratory system, and usually secretes a hard shell that protects the animal's soft body. The mantle is unique to members of this phylum.

The phylum name Mollusca is derived from the Latin word *molluscus*, meaning "soft," in reference to the soft bodies of these animals. The vulnerable tissues and organs of many mollusks are protected within a hard shell secreted by the mantle. Mollusk shells occur in three general forms: a single shell that is usually spiraled (like that of a snail), two shells hinged together (like those of a clam), or several overlapping shells arranged in a row (like those of a chiton). Some mollusks, such as nudibranchs and sea hares, have only small internal remnants of shell, whereas others, such as octopi, have lost their shell altogether over the course of evolution.

Most mollusks have an open circulatory system, meaning that blood flows freely through the body rather than through vessels. Their internal organs, like those of all higher animals, are protected within a fluid-filled body cavity called a coelom. Animals that have coeloms are divided into two different groups based on the way their embryos develop. Mollusk embryos develop in a pattern similar to that of annelid and arthropod embryos, while echinoderms and chordates share a markedly different pattern of embryonic development. Similarities in embryonic development are believed to reflect evolutionary relatedness, so mollusks, annelids, and arthropods are more closely related to each other than they are to echinoderms and chordates.

Feeding strategies vary among mollusks, from grazing (abalone), to filter-feeding (clams), to active predation (octopi). Most mollusks have a rasping, tonguelike organ called a radula. The structure of the radula is species-specific and depends mainly on the animal's diet. Used for scraping algae off rocks or for puncturing prey, the radulae of most species of mollusks are very hard with rows of backward-curving teeth.

In most species of mollusks the sexes are separate. Fertilization may be internal or external depending on the class or species. Some mollusks are hermaphroditic, although self-fertilization is unusual. The sexual behavior of some mollusks is astonishing, if not shocking: for example, snails called slipper shells usually live in stacks of several snails atop one another, with males on top fertilizing females lower in the stack. The snails usually begin life as males, then become females as they age and as other females become scarce. The female on the bottom of the stack carries the burdensome load of her mating group wherever she goes—so, as you might imagine, most don't move around much at all!

Mollusk larvae usually pass through two free-swimming stages: a first stage during which the ciliated larva is called a trochophore, and a second stage called a veliger, in which the larva begins to show a foot, mantle, and shell. As mollusks develop into adults, they usually become bottom-dwellers, although there are exceptions. Squid, for example, remain pelagic (living in the open ocean) throughout their lives.

Mollusks are divided into and described among seven classes. Four of these classes include members commonly seen in California waters:

- **Class Polyplacophora (chitons):** Oval-shaped with eight overlapping plates encircled by a fleshy girdle, chitons lack tentacles and eyes. They attach strongly to surfaces with their foot, and eat algae scraped from rocks.
- **Class Gastropoda (snails, nudibranchs, sea hares, abalone, and limpets):** As adults, nudibranchs and sea hares lack shells, while other gastropods are single-shelled. Both tentacles and eyes are located on the heads of these animals. Gastropods move with a rippling motion of the foot, and feed using a radula.
- **Class Bivalvia (clams, mussels, oysters, and scallops):** Bivalves are encased in two shells hinged together at the base. With no head or radula, they are filter-feeders. Most bivalves are sessile, but some use the foot to dig, and a few can swim.
- **Class Cephalopoda (octopi, squid, nautilus, and cuttle-fish):** The shells of cephalopods are reduced or absent, except in the case of nautilus, which have beautifully spiraled shells. In cephalopods the foot has been highly modified into tentacles. The head is easily recognizable, with well-developed eyes and a radula. Cephalopods are very intelligent and have keen sensory abilities, and are the only mollusks with a closed circulatory system. Both benthic (bottom-dwelling) and pelagic forms of these animals are carnivores that can move by swimming, crawling, or both.

Nudibranchs, such as this pugnacious aeolid, are shell-less mollusks closely related to snails.

Phylum Annelida

Derivation:
Latin for "little ring."

Characteristics:
Have segmented bodies often encased in a tube.

California Representatives:
Polychaete worms (including plume worms) and bristle worms.

The delicate whorls of this plume worm are feathery gills that absorb oxygen and trap planktonic food.

It comes as a surprise to many people that not all animals we normally call worms belong to the same phylum. Our inclination to consider them as closely related comes solely from our arbitrary decision to call them all "worms"—despite the fact that in many ways annelids are more similar to humans than they are to flatworms. Like humans but unlike flatworms, annelids have segmented bodies, as well as a brain, a coelom (a fluid-filled body cavity that encases the internal organs), and well-developed organ systems such as a closed circulatory system.

Annelids are bilaterally symmetrical, with a definite front and back and left and right. A well-developed brain and sensory organs are concentrated at the head of the body. Annelids have reproductive, respiratory, and excretory systems, as well as a complete digestive system. Their circulatory system is closed, meaning that blood flows through the body within specialized blood vessels. Annelids move by working muscles against the incompressible coelom in much the same way that we move with muscles working against a bony skeleton.

The bodies of annelids are composed of segments that are identical in many ways, and are often evident at the surface as a series of rings. This segmentation is the basis for the phylum name, derived from the Latin word *annelus*, meaning "little ring." The annelids are the most primitive animals to display segmentation, an important characteristic that underlies the organization of all advanced animals. Because many of the functions of one segment are repeated in others, damage to one segment is not necessarily fatal. Segmentation also allows finer control and more flexibility of movement.

Annelids may be suspension-feeders, detritivores, or carnivores. Most are bottom-dwellers, and many are permanently attached to the substrate within a tube of their own construction. These tube worms are often noticed by divers when they extend their striking, featherlike gill plumes from the tube; these gill plumes are used for both respiration and filtering plankton from the water.

The sexes of annelids are usually separate; females lay eggs that are then fertilized by the males. The pattern of development in annelid embryos is similar to that of mollusks and arthropods, indicating a closer evolutionary relationship of annelids to these animals than to others. Larvae swim freely as they grow and add segments to their bodies, until they settle out to live as benthic adults. The larvae are called trochophores, and are very similar to the trochophore stage of mollusk larvae.

Hermit crabs protect their soft bodies within shells originally inhabited by snails.

Phylum Arthropoda

Derivation:
Greek for "jointed foot."

Characteristics:
Have jointed appendages, a hard shell, and often claws.

California Representatives:
Barnacles, shrimp, crabs, lobsters, amphipods, and copepods.

Members of the phylum Arthropoda account for more than 75 percent of all living animals, making this group by far the largest of the animal phyla. Although terrestrial insects make up the majority of the arthropods, many members of this phylum are marine crustaceans. Some of the better-known marine arthropods are barnacles, shrimp, crabs, lobsters, amphipods, and copepods.

Arthropods are bilaterally symmetrical and have well-developed physiological systems, including an open circulatory system, which means that their blood flows freely through the body and is not confined to vessels. With a distinct head and a well-developed central nervous system, arthropods possess keen senses of vision, smell, and touch.

The bodies of arthropods consist of three main parts: the head, thorax, and abdomen. Many species have claws used for defense or obtaining food. Although arthropods have a segmented body, the evolution of a hard exterior skeleton (exoskeleton) has negated many of the advantages of segmentation, particularly flexibility. Apparently in compensation for the rigidity of the exoskeleton, the innovation of jointed appendages also evolved within arthropods, increasing their flexibility and mobility. The phylum name is derived from the Greek *arthros*, "joint," and *podos*, "foot."

The exoskeleton provides protection against parasites, injury, and potential predators such as fish and octopi. The exoskeleton also plays a part in an arthropod's mobility by serving as an inflexible structure for muscle attachment. Because of this inflexibility, the exoskeleton must be periodically shed and replaced with a new skeleton in order for the animal to grow. This process is called molting, and is characteristic of arthropods. Molting occurs many times before arthropod larvae even settle out of the plankton, and continues (albeit less frequently) throughout the animal's life. Because molting increases an arthropod's vulnerability, these animals face a trade-off between the benefits of faster growth and greater safety (see the section on crabs in Chapter 6).

Arthropods may be predators, grazers, parasites, or suspension-feeders. Most are free-living bottom-dwellers as adults, but some are permanently attached and many are pelagic throughout their lives. The sexes are usually separate, although some arthropods are hermaphroditic. Arthropod larvae usually pass through a succession of several stages that may be morphologically very different; this process is called metamorphosis and is another defining characteristic of arthropods.

Most marine arthropods belong to the class Crustacea. Members of this class all possess two pairs of antennae and many extensively specialized appendages. The diversity of this class is indicated by its inclusion of both attached, suspension-feeding barnacles and free-living, carnivorous lobsters.

Although its hard shell and sessile lifestyle lead many people to believe it is a mollusk, this feeding barnacle is a crustacean.

A blood star amongst entwined brittle stars.

Phylum Echinodermata

Derivation:
Greek for "spiny skin."

Characteristics:
Have spiny or warty skin and rows of tube feet.

California Representatives:

Sea stars, brittle stars, sea urchins, sand dollars, and sea cucumbers.

Echinoderms are an ancient group of invertebrates that are well represented in the fossil record. Found only in the marine environment, there are approximately 6,000 species living today. Nearly all of these species are benthic.

Echinoderms are characterized by pentamerous (five-sided) radial symmetry, a feature that is obvious in sea stars but in sea cucumbers can be seen only in cross section. Echinoderms usually have an interior skeleton made of calcareous plates and covered with a layer of skin containing thousands of neurosensory cells. The skin often has spines or wartlike projections, hence the phylum name Echinodermata, which is derived from the Greek *echinos*, "spiny," and *derma*, "skin."

Echinoderms have no brain, and instead depend on a net of nerves that runs throughout the body. Despite the lack of central control, many echinoderms are capable of surprisingly complex response patterns. Echinoderms also have distinct organ systems, one of which is the unique water vascular system that controls the movement of the animal's many rows of tiny tube feet. In addition to locomotion, the feet serve respirative, excretive, and sensory functions.

Although echinoderms cannot move quickly enough to escape most predators, they have the distinct advantage of being able to regenerate lost parts. In fact, they often voluntarily sacrifice a piece of their body in order to save themselves. If a sea star loses an arm to an attacker, the arm will eventually grow back—and because the lost appendage often distracts or satisfies a predator long enough for the sea star to escape, the sea star's temporary sacrifice has probably saved its life.

Some species of echinoderms reproduce asexually on a regular basis by breaking in two and regenerating into two animals. However, the majority of reproduction by members of this phylum is sexual. Larvae spend days to weeks as free-swimming members of the plankton before settling to the bottom as adults. Although adult echinoderms have radially symmetrical bodies, their larvae are bilaterally symmetrical, indicating that these animals probably evolved from a bilaterally symmetrical ancestor. In fact, their pattern of embryonic development reveals that echinoderms are the invertebrate group most closely related to the vertebrates. There are five modern classes of echinoderms:

- **Class Crinoidea (feather stars and sea lilies):** Although members of this class inhabit California waters, they are uncommon and rarely seen.
- **Class Asteroidea (sea stars):** The pentamerous symmetry of sea stars is usually obvious in the number of arms. The thick arms are not sharply set off from the center of the body, as are those of brittle stars. Sea stars are scavengers and predators.
- **Class Ophiuroidea (brittle stars):** Brittle stars have long, thin, fragile arms that are sharply distinguishable from the center of the body. The arms fall off easily when the animal is attacked. Members of this class include suspension-feeders, detritivores, and active predators.
- **Class Holothuroidea (sea cucumbers):** Sea cucumbers have pliable, cylindrical bodies; radial symmetry is obvious only in cross section. Some are sediment ingestors, some feed on detritus, and others are suspension-feeders. When threatened, many are able to expel their innards, an escape strategy that repels potential predators.
- **Class Echinoidea (sea urchins and sand dollars):** Most echinoids are herbivores and sediment ingestors. Their bodies are flat and disc-shaped or spherical with spines.

DID YOU KNOW?

. . . "STARFISH" AREN'T REALLY FISH

AT ALL, THE PREFERABLE TERM IS

"SEA STAR."

California sea lions are among the most playful of marine mammals that inhabit California waters.

Phylum Chordata

Derivation:
Latin for "cord."

Characteristics:
Most have a backbone.

California Representatives:
Tunicates, sharks, rays, skates, bony fish, and mammals.

Most people are aware that fishes, amphibians, birds, reptiles, and mammals are all chordates. What surprises many is that this group also includes tunicates. In order to understand how animals as varied as tunicates and whales can be included in the same phylum, it is important to realize that an animal does not have to be a vertebrate in order to be a chordate. Instead, classification as a chordate is based on characteristics of embryonic development. These characteristics are fairly technical and difficult to explain simply, but are summarized briefly below.

In order to be classified as a chordate, an animal needs to display the following traits during at least some stage of development:

- **Notochord:** a longitudinal, flexible rod between the gut and the nerve cord.
- **Hollow dorsal nerve cord:** a hollow nerve cord in the back.
- **Pharyngeal slits:** openings to the embryonic digestive tube.
- **Postanal tail:** a tail that extends beyond the anal opening.

All chordates share these structures in at least some stage of their development, but often just during the embryonic stages. For example, all terrestrial chordates possess pharyngeal slits only during early embryonic stages, and tunicates possess a notochord and nerve chord only in their larval stages. The gelatinous material of the discs between human vertebrae is a remnant of our own embryonic notochord.

All chordates are bilaterally symmetrical animals, with a distinct front and back, left and right, and top and bottom. They have a more or less segmented body, which is evident in the vertebrae of your own spine. Compared to other animals, most chordates have remarkable locomotive abilities, with muscles that work against an internal skeleton. In these advanced animals, all major organ systems are present and very well developed.

Looking as if they got the worst of nasty bar brawl, blackeye gobies sometimes set up house in discarded litter such as bottles and tires.

The chordates are subdivided into three subphyla. Members of two subphyla, Urochordata and Vertebrata, include species that are observed in California waters. Members of the other subphylum, Cephalochordata, are the lancelets: small, fishlike chordates that are not commonly seen. The cephalochordates and the urochordates (including tunicates) are invertebrate chordates. That sounds like an oxymoron, but simply means that they satisfy the aforementioned requirements to be classified as a chordate, but lack a backbone and a skull. Tunicates are usually small and often translucent. Pelagic tunicates are often called salps.

Vertebrates are the group of animals with which we are most familiar and to which we belong. Vertebrate and invertebrate chordates differ in that vertebrates have a backbone that encloses the nerve cord. Vertebrates also possess a highly specialized brain and sensory structures. Vertebrates are divided among several classes, of which three have members that are discussed in this book:

- **Class Chondrichthyes (sharks, skates, and rays):** These fish possess cartilaginous skeletons and respire through uncovered gills. They are exothermic, meaning that their body temperature is controlled by their environment. Cartilaginous fish do not have scales or an air bladder. In most of these fish the mouth is located below the head, and the tail is usually asymmetrical. Fertilization occurs by copulation and young are often born live, although some members of this class, such as horn sharks and swell sharks, lay eggs.
- **Class Osteichthyes (bony fish):** These fish have bony skeletons and respire through covered gills. They are exothermic, so they can regulate their body temperature only by moving to warmer or colder waters. They have scales and usually use an air bladder for buoyancy control. In bony fish the mouth is generally located at the front of the head and the tail is usually symmetrical. Most bony fish reproduce by spawning and the young hatch from eggs.
- **Class Mammalia (mammals):** Mammals have skeletons made of bone and are endothermic, meaning that they are able to regulate and maintain a constant internal body temperature. Mammals have hair on their bodies, breathe air into lungs, and bear live young. Females possess milk-producing mammary glands with which they nourish their young.

DID YOU KNOW?

. . . TUNICATES ARE MORE CLOSELY RELATED TO YOU THAN THEY ARE TO OTHER INVERTEBRATES.

CHAPTER 2

CALIFORNIA: THE BIG PICTURE

The wildlife of California's marine environment hinges on the physical conditions of the area. Any given animal can survive only where local conditions fall within a range it can tolerate, so California's water temperatures, prevailing weather patterns, geographical features, and water currents play critical roles in determining what creatures inhabit state waters. This chapter begins with an overview of useful concepts and terms, covers some of the general physical characteristics of the state's waters and coastline, and ends with an introduction to California's marine habitats.

The Oceanic Provinces

The seafloor from the North American coastline to a depth of about 600 feet is called the continental shelf. The bottom slopes gently from the coast to the edge of the shelf, where there is a sudden drop-off into a steeper region called the continental slope. The width of the continental shelf varies considerably: south of Monterey the shelf width is generally less than 5 miles, while north of San Francisco it extends to 20 miles in many places.

An abundance of life is found between the beach and the edge of the continental shelf, both in the water column (the pelagic zone) and at the seafloor below (the benthic zone). Animals and plants that live in close association with the seafloor are called benthic organisms, while creatures that live in the water column are known as pelagic organisms. Although big, dramatic, open-sea creatures such as gray whales and swordfish are commonly referred to as "the pelagics," an animal does not need to be large to be pelagic in the true sense of the word. The term "pelagic" refers to *all* creatures found in the water column, and distinguishes them from bottom-dwelling or benthic species.

The neritic province is the region of the pelagic zone that is over the continental shelf, while the deeper waters beyond the shelf are called the oceanic

Sculpin.

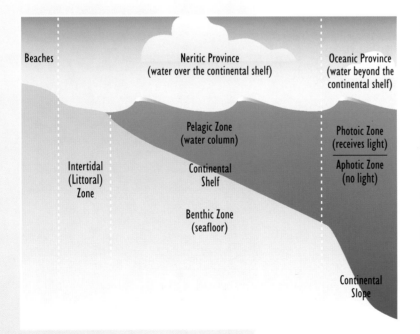

Beaches

Neritic Province
(water over the continental shelf)

Oceanic Province
(water beyond the continental shelf)

Pelagic Zone
(water column)

Photoic Zone
(receives light)

Aphotic Zone
(no light)

Intertidal
(Littoral)
Zone

Continental
Shelf

Benthic Zone
(seafloor)

Continental
Slope

province. Although the term "neritic" is not commonly used in casual conversation, it can be useful in distinguishing among different regions of the ocean. Sport diving is usually done within the neritic zone, which is relatively small in area but which supports enormous densities and varieties of life.

The shallowest part of the neritic province, the intertidal region (also called the littoral zone), is roughly the portion of the coast that is exposed at low tide and covered at high tide. As the tides advance and recede over the intertidal zone, conditions such as temperature, salinity, light, predation, and substrate vary dramatically over a limited space. These changes in conditions over a short distance are reflected in the vertical segregation of species, a configuration known as vertical zonation.

The region of the neritic zone between the mean low tide mark and a depth of roughly 150 to 200 feet is known as the sublittoral zone. Most of the plants and animals discussed in this text inhabit the sublittoral zone. Much of the sublittoral falls within the photic zone, the region of the ocean that receives enough light to support plant growth by photosynthesis. The photic zone extends far deeper in clear tropical waters than in murkier temperate waters; however, plant growth in clear tropical waters is often limited by a lack of the nutrients that are so plentiful in the temperate waters off the California coast. A region where the low level of light prevents growth by photosynthesis is known as the aphotic zone.

Benthic plants can be found off the California coast to depths of about 150 feet. Although plants are restricted to the shallower waters within the photic zone, benthic animals range from intertidal depths to oceanic trenches that can plummet to depths greater than 30,000 feet. The benthic region beyond the continental shelf, on the continental slope, is referred to as bathyal. Beyond the bathyal region, the ocean floor plunges to abyssal and even deeper hadal depths.

Like all marine plants, California's lush undersea forests of giant kelp can survive only within sunlit waters of the photic zone.

A southern California beach bordered with flowers in bloom.

Geographical Divisions of California

Because of the length and the north-south orientation of California, the water conditions and life in and along its coastal waters are much more varied than those at many other well-known, often-dived wilderness areas. Underwater California is a large, inhomogeneous region filled with a wide variety of settings and a tremendous diversity of life-forms. This great mixture of geophysical and biological phenomena contributes greatly to the allure of the state's marine kingdom.

Mainland California is commonly described as having

three geographical sectors: southern, central, and northern. With over 1,100 miles of coastline in the state, these same divisions logically extend to underwater California. Southern California is generally considered to be the region between Point Conception and

The dramatic cliffs of a northern California beach.

Like many other young animals, this juvenile wolf-eel settled far from its parents after drifting with water currents.

the Mexican border; central California is the area between Point Conception and San Francisco; and northern California encompasses the section between San Francisco and the Oregon border.

These geographical divisions roughly coincide with many, though certainly not all, differences in local marine life. Whereas some plants and animals range throughout the state, the waters of southern California support many warm-water life-forms not found farther north, and many species found in northern waters are not seen down south. Although the flora and fauna of central and northern California are more similar to each other—because both regions lie to the north of Point Conception—there are still differences in the species encountered as well as in the concentrations of specific populations.

Prevailing Currents

The California Current is a major surface current that brings cold water from the Gulf of Alaska into California waters. It maintains a generally slow southward flow throughout the year, though the intensity of the flow varies with the seasons. During late summer and fall, the current tends to hug the coastline of northern and central California more closely than in winter and spring. Another, smaller current called the Davidson Current brings warm water northward along the coast between November and February.

If you examine the map of California at the beginning of this chapter, you will notice that the entire mainland coast south of Point Conception indents sharply to the east. This indentation is referred to as the Great California Bight. The California Current more or less hugs the state's coastline until it reaches the bight; south of this point the current does not meet the coast again until just about 100 miles south of the

Many divers find that dry suits offer greater thermal protection than wet suits, allowing them to focus on the surrounding beauty rather than the water chill.

Thermal Protection

From the Oregon border to the Mexican border, throughout the year, divers need thermal protection in California waters. That means for dives of any depth and any duration, you need a wet suit or a dry suit. Which of these you prefer depends primarily upon your build, your typical underwater activities, whether you dive on windy, rainy, and rough days as well as great ones, and, of course, your pocketbook. Like a lot of slow-moving, serious underwater photographers, I typically prefer to dive in a dry suit. However, when looking for ocean sunfish or yellowtail in the open sea, I prefer my wet suit.

For a wet suit, most serious divers prefer some kind of layered farmer-john style, usually one that is $\frac{1}{4}$-inch thick. I can't tell you how many times I have heard people say that in such and such a place they only need a $\frac{1}{8}$-inch suit, and for just a day or two in California water they are sure it will do. These divers may be well intentioned, but in California, divers require more thermal protection. A thin suit may enable one to survive, but diving is supposed to be fun, not an endurance contest.

Mexican border, along the shores of Baja. Because all eight California Channel Islands lie roughly in the lee of this bight, they, along with the mainland coast south of Point Conception, are less immediately influenced by the California Current than are waters to the north of the bight.

During spring and early summer, north-northwest winds (which blow from the north toward the south) cause upwelling as they drive surface waters from the coastline, bringing colder, nutrient-rich water up from below. The upwellings, which are generally more prominent in central and northern California than they are in the southern end of the state, are the reason that coastal waters are colder than surface waters of the open sea. The nutrient-rich upwellings play a major role in the life cycle of many species and are crucial for the high productivity of California waters. Water conditions, especially visibility, are also affected by current flow and by the concentration of nutrients.

Water Temperatures

California waters are located between a latitude of 32°N, the latitude of the coastal border between Mexico and California, and 42°N, along the California/Oregon border, a distance of 522 miles as the seagull flies. California waters are described as temperate, as opposed to warmer tropical water, colder polar water, or various gradients in between. Water temperature throughout the state varies considerably from north to south on any given day. Surface water temperatures in northern California typically range from about 50°F (10°C) during the winter to 59°F (15°C) during late summer. Surface water temperatures in southern California are considerably warmer, typically ranging from 59°F (15°C) during the winter to as high as 70°F (21°C) during the summer.

Point Conception generally demarcates the warmer waters to the south from the cooler waters to the north, despite the fact that it is located well south of the center of California and is therefore not a geographical midpoint. Although water conditions vary gradually elsewhere along the California coast, conditions above and below Point Conception differ dramatically due to the shape of the coastline combined with the prevailing currents and weather patterns. Water conditions to the north of Point Conception are usually considerably rougher and temperatures are noticeably cooler than they are to the south.

In California waters, descending divers often notice a dramatic change in temperature as they suddenly pass from a warmer layer of water into a layer that can be a shocking 5°F to 10°F cooler. This phenomenon is a result of the greater density of colder water than warmer water, causing warmer water to "float" on top of colder water. The thin boundary between layers of water of different temperatures is called a thermocline, and is often visible as a murky region where rising heat creates a strong resemblance to the heat waves that rise from a desert. The presence and depth of thermoclines depend on local winds, water currents, and amount and intensity of sunlight. Thermoclines are more common and pronounced in southern California, but occur throughout the state's waters. The message for divers is, do not be misled by surface temperatures. If you want to enjoy your dive, be prepared for the cold water—where visibility is often remarkably better—immediately below a thermocline.

Many marine animals have a distinct preference for a specific range of water temperatures, and you may occasionally notice sharply delineated schools of fish or groups of invertebrates holding their positions just above or just below a thermocline. Experienced anglers and divers also know that there are differences in the life found at given depths along the state coast; members of the same species may be found at very different depths along the coast, at least partially because similar temperatures are found in shallower water in northern California than in warmer southern California. For example, in southern California ratfish and red abalone are observed only in deep water toward the limits of safe sport diving, whereas in central and northern California both animals commonly live in shallow water that is accessible even by snorkeling. Noticing such patterns enables us to better understand the importance of water temperature to the lives of sea creatures.

A surface canopy of giant kelp afloat on clear waters in the Channel Islands.

Water Visibility

Scuba divers and snorkelers use the term "water visibility" to describe the degree of water clarity. Water visibility ("the vis") is expressed in terms of feet and refers to the distance a person wearing a diving mask can see underwater. Water visibility varies from day to day in the same location, but tendencies are evident in certain areas and at particular times of the year. Visibility generally ranges from 5 to 10 feet off the beaches of the north coast to 150 feet on a great day at the southern Channel Islands.

Because visibility at the Channel Islands is almost always far better than off the beaches of the mainland, the islands are a feature attraction for California sport divers. At the southern islands (San Clemente, Santa Catalina, Santa Barbara, and San Nicolas), visibility normally ranges from 30 to 70 feet, and 150 feet is certainly not unheard of. At the four northern islands (Anacapa, Santa Rosa, Santa Cruz, and San Miguel), visibility ranges from 20 to 50 feet on most days, but 100- to 150-foot days are reported.

Water conditions are almost always considerably better to the south of Point Conception than to the north. Visibility to the south of the point is often 5 to 15 feet greater, the water is usually much warmer, and there tends to be less wind and surface chop. However, there are few absolutes when it comes to West Coast water. Water conditions in central and northern California can be superb, and when they are, areas such as the shores of Monterey offer incredible diving opportunities that match or top any site in southern California.

Because California water conditions are not as predictable or as diver-friendly as those of tropical paradises such as the Cayman Islands, the Bahamas, Fiji, and Papua New Guinea, many divers who are not familiar with California waters jump to the conclusions that California water (1) is rough, (2) is too cold to enjoy, and (3) doesn't offer much for divers to see anyway. In reality, quite the opposite is true. The bottom line on California diving is that although temperate areas are less likely to have as many great diving days annually as many of the well-publicized tropical paradises, when conditions are good the diving is superb.

Central and northern California reefs teem with brightly colored invertebrates such as this rose anemone.

Diving in Central and Northern California

If you talk to divers around the world, you will likely discover that California waters have an undeserved reputation for being somewhat drab and colorless. Because the waters are colder than those of the tropics and because the visibility is lower, many people think that the diving is subpar. California divers know this is not the case. Conditions may be tougher, but when conditions are favorable, California has plenty of color and beauty to offer.

Even within the state, many people who dive in southern California seem to think that conditions in central and northern California are too demanding and that the effort involved in diving isn't worth it. Not true. The kelp forests and reefs of central and northern California provide some incredible diving. I'll always remember my pal Jim Morgan taking me to dive in Point Lobos for the first time. We had great conditions, 70-plus-foot visibility, calm seas, and clear skies. I can still picture the towering kelp forests and spectacular colors on the reef. The kelp was as dense and majestic as any I had ever dived—golden fronds swaying in a blue-green sea. There were beautiful *Urticina* anemones, decorator crabs, sea stars, and cowries as well as some fantastically colorful rockfish. We also saw sea otters and harbor seals. It was a magical experience.

Every time I dive in Monterey I am amazed by the variety of invertebrates I want to photograph. Diving the Monterey Canyon is easily the equal of that in the Scripps Canyon in San Diego, and Scripps is one of my all-time favorite sites. Farther north there is plenty of great diving close to shore when conditions allow.

If you want a really great diving vacation, do something different. Head north and enjoy the sights that central and northern California waters have to offer.

Red Tide

"Red tide" is the name given to a potentially dangerous condition that occurs sporadically in coastal waters, usually during late spring, summer, or early fall in California. Red tides occur when certain tiny organisms are present in the water in very dense concentrations. When this happens the water visibility is often markedly reduced, and the water may take on a reddish hue.

The usual culprit in northern California waters is a protist (a one-celled microorganism) called *Gonyaulax catenella*; its cousin, *Gonyaulax polyhedra*, is usually responsible for red tides in the southern part of the state. During a red tide, these microscopic creatures release toxins into the water. Scientists aren't certain why the organisms do this, but the toxin may deter potential predators and competitors. Red tides may last for days or for months, and long-lasting ones can result in massive die-offs of local animals that become poisoned by the toxins. When the densely concentrated microorganisms eventually die themselves, their decomposition can seriously deplete oxygen levels, often killing many more local creatures by suffocation.

Although the protists and their toxins cannot be absorbed through the skin, and thus pose no known health risk to swimmers and divers, the toxins cause a serious type of paralytic food poisoning when ingested. The primary health risk to humans is through the consumption of shellfish such as mussels, scallops, and clams. These shellfish are filter-feeders that strain their food from the water, so the protists and toxins become concentrated within their tissues. Although the shellfish themselves are not killed by the toxins, eating an infected shellfish can be fatal. In order to prevent such fatalities, health officials regularly test toxin levels to determine whether shellfish taken from a given area are safe for consumption. It is imperative to realize that the name "red tide" is a misleading term: the water does not, illogically enough, necessarily turn red during one of these events. Don't fall into the potentially dangerous trap of making the assumption that it is perfectly safe to consume shellfish if the water looks normal and you don't see any red color. To determine the status of shellfish call the shellfish information line at the California Department of Health Services: (510) 540-2605.

Seasons

Changes in ocean currents, water temperatures, upwelling, and weather patterns cause conditions below the ocean's surface to be as seasonal as those above. Ever-changing communities, behaviors, and seascapes make these waters unendingly fascinating to many California divers. The more you understand about seasonal changes in the ocean, the more you will appreciate what you see beneath the surface.

During spring and summer along most of the California coast, cold, nutrient-rich water wells up from below, sparking a bloom of growth that ripples up the food chain. Fertilized by nutrients and enjoying higher light levels, populations of phytoplankton explode to densities high enough to cloud the water. Kelp and other large plants begin to grow and sprout new blades at fantastic rates. Many animals choose this bountiful time to procreate, and the ocean is enlivened with riotous mating behavior. Juveniles of many species appear soon thereafter, often very different in appearance from their parents. Unfortunately, as pleasant as spring is on land in many parts of the country, it is often the season with the toughest diving conditions.

Late summer and fall are generally the best times to

dive in California. As upwelling slows and ceases, the water warms up. Water visibility usually improves as clear water flows in from offshore and as dense plankton populations dissipate because of predation and nutrient limitation. The changing water currents bring new visitors to California habitats. Kelp forests are lush but grow much more slowly as sunlight and nutrients become less plentiful. The behavior and appearance of many species continue to shift with the seasons, in accordance with their mating and growth patterns, varying food supplies, and changing predation threats.

Wintertime often means rough conditions in California coastal waters. Limited light and nutrients slow the growth of plants and phytoplankton that are at the base of the food chain. Dying kelp provides a feast for detritivores as the fronds fall to the seafloor, overweighted with encrusting invertebrates. As the food supply of some animals dwindles, they may broaden their diets. The weather gets rougher and the water becomes colder and more turbulent, with surge that often rips off and sets adrift entire kelp plants and their inhabitants. Although winter waters in California can be rough and very difficult to predict, conditions and diving are excellent at some point during every winter. When winter conditions are good, the diving can be fantastic. Some of California's most exciting underwater phenomena, such as squid mating, typically occur in the winter.

El Niño

Every so often our planet experiences a severe dislocation of its largest and most dominant weather patterns, with dramatic worldwide ramifications. This climatic phenomenon is known as El Niño (pronounced "el neen-yo"), or the El Niño Southern Oscillation (ENSO). The name is derived from a Spanish reference to Christ ("The Child"), and refers to the fact that a dramatic increase in water temperature along the coast of South America, usually the first indication of an El Niño event, often occurs near Christmas. Interspersed with both periods of colder-than-normal temperatures (known as "La Niña") and periods of "normal" weather, El Niño events usually take place once every three to seven years and are highly variable in intensity.

During El Niño, the trade winds that normally push equatorial surface waters westward slow, stop, or even change directions. This causes warm water that is usually piled up along tropical coasts of the western Pacific Ocean to slosh back eastward toward the coast of South America. Some of this warm water then tends to move northward in a current called the El Niño Current. Water temperatures and ocean currents affect wind and rain patterns as well, so weather patterns are often drastically affected worldwide.

Because El Niño exerts so many complicated effects on the weather, the net effect in California (as well as other

El Niño conditions have been linked with beach strandings and deaths of marine mammals such as northern elephant seals.

areas of the world) can vary from severe droughts, such as those experienced during the 1976–1977 El Niño, to the torrential winter storms that inundated the state during the intense El Niño of 1982–1983. Local effects are not always negative: the El Niño that began in 1991 may have played a large part in ending a long California drought. What swimmers and divers are most likely to notice is that water temperatures are often elevated 4°F to 10°F, and can be increased as much as 14°F. That may not sound like a lot compared to fluctuations in air temperatures, but if you consider that water requires 3,600 times as much heat per volume as does air to bring about a comparable temperature change, you will begin to realize how much energy the current contains.

These dramatic changes can be devastating to California's marine life, as well as that of other parts of the world. The increased temperature directly causes two problems for marine life: (1) many plants and animals cannot withstand the stress of temperatures that rise too high or too fast, and (2) the warm layer of water places a density cap on colder deep water, cutting off the normal influx of nutrients from below. During the notorious El Niño of 1982–1983, miles of healthy kelp forests and associated kelp communities were decimated by the rise in water temperature and lack of nutrients. Two years later, many kelp beds were just beginning to reestablish themselves. These biological crises create a domino effect up the food chain; El Niño events have been linked to enormous losses in commercial fisheries,

unprecedented mortality rates among local seabirds, and even an increase in sea lion and northern elephant seal beach strandings and deaths.

An additional change in marine communities has been the invasion of species that usually are found only much farther south. As temperatures rise, these animals migrate into California waters that are normally too cold for them. Wahoo, triggerfish, butterflyfish, and angel fish were common sights at some of the Channel Islands during the 1982–1983 El Niño. Howard Hall, a well-known underwater photographer, and Jon Hardy, a well-known authority in the sport diving business, enjoyed the good fortune to film manta rays at Anacapa Island and Catalina Island, respectively. Mantas, like many of the other above-mentioned species, are seldom sighted farther north than the southern tip of Baja, nearly 1,000 miles south of the Channel Islands.

El Niño events normally last for one to two years. However, some scientists believe that effects of the 1982–1983 El Niño may have displaced part of the Kuroshio Current 200 miles northward in 1992—nine years later. Although El Niño years are believed to be part of a normal, cyclical pattern of nature, recently the incidence seems to be increasing. In fact, El Niños of 1991–1992, 1993, and 1994–1995 have been separated by a matter of only months. Scientists debate whether this unusual pattern is caused by global warming or is merely a normal extreme of global weather cycles.

DID YOU KNOW?

. . . MONTEREY AND SAN FRANCISCO AREN'T REALLY IN NORTHERN CALIFORNIA ALTHOUGH THEY ARE OFTEN REFERRED TO THAT WAY. SAN FRANCISCO IS IN CENTRAL CALIFORNIA, NEARLY 350 MILES FROM THE OREGON BORDER.

Habitats

As with terrestrial plants and animals, marine plants and animals show distinct habitat preferences. Divers encounter dramatically different bottom terrain and habitats as they explore California waters. Kelp forests, rocky reefs, open-ocean seamounts, sandy plains, deepwater canyons, the iridescent blue open sea—these diverse marine habitats each offer a unique community of plants and animals. For example, a significant percentage of the animals seen in the sand flats are rarely, if ever, observed in a kelp forest community. Likewise, the residents of a kelp community are seldom seen far out to sea.

Some animals often cross the boundary from one habitat to the next. Some species can be found in one habitat as juveniles and in another as adults; others may feed in one locale and rest or breed in another. Still other species are frequently found in multiple habitats. As a general rule, however, most animals prefer to dwell in one setting.

Although marine habitats may be classified in a variety of ways (e.g., according to the amount of light received, tidal flow, depth, or location with respect to the continental shelf), most people describe habitats according to their most conspicuous physical features. Thus the marine habitats of California are commonly described as the tidepools, the sandy beaches, the mudflats, the kelp forests, the rocky reefs, the sandy plains, and the open sea. Knowing the characteristics of these different habitats will help you gain an understanding of who you might or might not encounter as you explore each habitat, and why. It is from the perspective of these habitats that the plants and animals of California's marine kingdom will be covered in the following chapters.

California's giant kelp beds are home to an amazing variety of invertebrates and fishes, such as the sheephead, senorita, and blacksmith fishes shown here.

Springtime wildflowers bloom along the southern California coast.

CHAPTER 3
THE BEACHES

A California sunset.

Explorers of California's legendary beaches encounter at least three distinct habitat types: rocky shores, sandy beaches, and estuarine shores. These habitats provide homes, resting places, feeding areas, and breeding grounds for a wonderful variety of marine animals. The creatures that inhabit these biomes are key members of food chains involving both marine and terrestrial creatures, thus linking the ecology of the land and that of the sea.

Many animals are frequently observed in more than one habitat. For example, many of the creatures found in California beach habitats are also found in either the reef community or the sandy plains. In order to avoid repetition, each animal is discussed in detail in only one section of this book. The two groups of animals discussed in this chapter are some of the most prominent animals in beach communities, and animals that are only rarely, if ever, seen in other habitats. For example, chitons are covered in "The Rocky Shores" section of this chapter, sand crabs in "The Sandy Beaches" section of this chapter, and garibaldi in Chapter 5, "The Rocky Reefs."

Estuarine Habitats

Estuaries are semi-enclosed areas where saline ocean water is diluted by freshwater runoff from the land. Sheltering myriad invertebrates and many fishes, estuaries are particularly important to juveniles of many marine creatures that hatch and/or develop within the relatively calm and protective waters. The salt marshes that border many estuaries are also unique habitats, dominated by an abundance of salt-tolerant plants that form the basis of a thriving community. These areas are among the most highly productive habitats in the world, providing food and shelter to a disproportionate number of endangered plants and animals, including many migratory waterfowl. Of the fish and shellfish that are commercially harvested in the United States, more than half spend at least some stage of their development within an estuarine habitat—including many of our most commercially important species. The importance of estuaries and salt marshes to humans is not limited to these species; estuarine habitats also help minimize flood damage and are natural water purifiers. Unfortunately, these habitats are also prime real estate and, according to some estimates, well over 90 percent of estuaries and the bordering salt marshes and mudflats have been severely impacted or destroyed by commercial development.

Estuarine habitats are among the most productive and most threatened habitats in the world.

DID YOU KNOW?

. . . BECAUSE WETLANDS HAVE A NATURAL ABILITY TO ASSIMILATE WASTES, SOME COMMUNITIES HAVE CREATED ARTIFICIAL WETLANDS TO TREAT THEIR SEWAGE.

Mudflats are an intertidal habitat found along the shores of estuaries, developing where waves and currents are too weak to wash away particles of clay and silt. The mudflats support a diverse array of polychaete worms, crustaceans, and other creatures that thrive on organic debris trapped in the mud, forming the basis of the mudflat community. These animals face unique problems owing to the nature of the mudflat habitat: because the spaces among a mudflat's tiny sediment grains are so small, water in these spaces (interstitial water) is not efficiently flushed by the tides. In order to cope with these conditions, animals must tolerate much higher levels of their own wastes than do inhabitants of other areas. Furthermore, oxygen in the interstitial water is quickly used up and not replaced until the next tidal flushing—and usually only a very thin surface layer of mud ever contains oxygenated water at all. Below that level are darker sediments dominated by species of anaerobic bacteria, which do not require any oxygen. The decomposing activity of these bacteria is responsible for the noxious smell of sulfur that is usually associated with anaerobic sediments.

The fact that some animals live within the mud despite these daunting challenges is evidenced by the many holes, tubes, and burrows visible at the surface. One notable member of northern and central California mudflat communities is the

The exposed siphons of the geoduck clam.

California Tides

California tides are classified as mixed semidiurnal, meaning that two high tides and two low tides occur each day, but the heights of successive high and low tides are different. Tides are the result of the net gravitational pull on the Earth due to the relative positions of the sun and the moon. These factors are well understood, and although powerful storms occasionally alter the times and heights of the tides, as a general rule the tides can be quite accurately predicted. Tide tables are easily obtained from your local dive shop or other water sports store, and can be quite useful in planning your beach exploration and diving expeditions.

geoduck. This oddly named edible clam lives as deep as 5 feet below the surface and grows to an enormous size, up to a yard long (including the siphons), and weighing up to 12 pounds. Geoducks and other mudflat bivalves stretch siphons to the surface in order to draw in oxygenated water, from which they also filter their food. Similarly serving as snorkels to the surface, the tubes and burrows of worms and **ghost shrimp** allow these animals to obtain oxygen and food from the surface water. All burrowing animals are important for decomposition within mudflat sediments: the tubes and burrows bring oxygen deeper and allow fast-working aerobic bacteria to continue their work farther beneath the mudflat's surface.

A visit to a mudflat is both peaceful and fascinating. You can watch birds quietly pick their way through the mud after prey, or take along a shovel and dig up clams, if it's legal (see the "Fish and Game Regulations" sidebar in Chapter 5). Because there are usually few other people around, you can enjoy the wildlife at your leisure. If possible during your visit, be sure to notice how the mudflat changes with the tides; the activity will increase dramatically with the water level. As the tide rises, mudflats are often visited by shore crabs, shrimp, birds, fish, and any number of other animals that come to feed or spawn. Their stay is only temporary, and most depart with the receding waters.

California sandy beaches are home to many secretive creatures that are never even noticed by most beachgoers.

Many animals have inner clocks that are timed to cycles such as the rising and setting of the sun.

Inner Clocks

Hiding under debris or burrowing into the sand every day, and bounding across the beach in search of food every night, amphipods are just one of the countless animals that repeat the same behavior patterns every twenty-four hours. Even when removed from any perception of night and day, a built-in natural inner clock called a circadean rhythm causes animals to maintain their normal cycle of activity with remarkable accuracy (although most quickly adapt to new schedules of light and darkness in laboratory settings). Most, if not all, animals regulate their behavior based on a circadean rhythm. Think about it; how often have you been surprised by your ability to awaken just before your alarm screams its wake-up call?

A similar type of cycle that corresponds to tidal activity, called a circalunadian cycle, also regulates the behavior of marine animals. For example, their perception of the tides plays an important part in allowing many animals to coordinate spawning and mating—often so accurately that these events can be predicted almost to the hour.

The Sandy Beaches

Existing where waves are gentle enough to allow sand to accumulate yet powerful enough to wash away silt, mud, and clay, sandy beaches change character rapidly as they conform to the conditions imposed by tides, waves, and currents. As is the case in the mudflats, few plants are able to exist in such an unstable environment. Unlike the mudflats, however, the relatively large spaces among the coarse sand grains are regularly and efficiently flushed out by the tides. Although this means that oxygen is more readily available, the washing action also means that far less of the organic debris supporting mudflat communities is trapped by the sandy sediments. With a limited basis for either a plant-based or a debris-based food chain, the sandy beaches are desolate compared to other habitats. Amazingly, some small animals manage quite well in these demanding surroundings.

Named for their habit of leaving itchy bites on beach visitors, **sand fleas** are an irritatingly common sandy beach creature. Sometimes called beach hoppers or scuds, sand fleas are often mistaken for insects, but are actually crustaceans and are more closely related to crabs, shrimp, and barnacles than to terrestrial insects. The **large beach hopper** is a southern California species that tends to reside in areas of coarse damp sand, and can attain a length of up to an inch.

Many animals that inhabit the sandy beaches travel up and down the beach with the tides, a perpetual migration that is crucial to their existence. **Sand crabs**, or mole crabs, are a classic example, as they are often seen scurrying backward along the beach to stay close to the water's edge as the tide moves in and out. These crustaceans speedily burrow tail-first into the sand, facing the incoming ocean water, until only their eyes and antennae are exposed. Extending their long, feathery antennae as waves break over them, they catch plankton and bits of seaweed in the receding water. The species most often sighted is the **Pacific sand crab**. Its body carapace, or shell, is elongate and convex, pale blue to off-white, and up to about an inch long. Although this species is occasionally seen as far north as Alaska, those found north of California are derived from larvae that hatched farther south and were carried northward in water currents; these sand crabs are apparently unable to reproduce in colder northern waters.

Less mobile sandy beach animals depend on excellent burrowing skills to protect them from the rough-and-tumble of the waves. Such skills also come in handy during low tides, when a cover of sand can protect an animal from the life-threatening dangers of heat and loss of water. Clams are the champions of sandy beach burrowers, digging so quickly into the sand that it is nearly impossible to catch one without using a shovel.

Pismo clams spend their lives about 10 inches deep in the sand. Deriving their name from the Pismo Beach area where they once were common, pismo clams range from central California to about halfway down the Pacific side of Baja. Their shell is tan to dark brown, often with brownish stripes. A muscular tube called an incurrent siphon extends to the surface to draw in water containing food and oxygen, while water containing wastes is expelled through an excurrent siphon. The clam's gills serve the dual purposes of respiration and feeding: as water passes through the animal's mantle cavity, oxygen is extracted and food (small plankton and debris) is filtered out and trapped in a sticky mucus that coats the gills.

Pismo clams are particularly popular with seafood connoisseurs. You can find pismo clams by looking for jets of water that shoot out from their siphon tubes as you walk on the sand above them. Although the numbers of pismo clams are apparently declining because of overfishing (and in fact are no longer legal to take in Pismo Beach), as of this writing, you can dig up a limited number of legal-sized clams if: they are in season, you are not in a pismo clam preserve, and you have a valid fishing license from the Department of Fish and Game.

The only healthy fish you will ever see on a California sandy beach are **grunions**. For three or four nights following full moons and new moons between late February and early September, these small fish leave the water to squirm up onto the sandy beaches, where they spawn. Each female grunion wriggles tail-first vertically into the sand, up to her pectoral fins, and lays her eggs. One or more males then curl around her upper body and releases sperm that flow down her body to the eggs. The young grunions will hatch and be carried to sea when the next high tide reaches them.

Grunions are famous for their odd spawning behavior, and multitudes of people visit California beaches on spring and summer nights after the full moon in hopes of witnessing a "grunion run." To avoid suffering extra hours in the cold and wet, get hold of a tide table before you trek out to see a grunion run—the fish visit the beaches for only two or three hours following the high tide.

Grunions spawn with abandon on a California sandy beach.

Tidepools are oases of life in the rocky intertidal.

The Rocky Shores

With multitudes of diverse creatures living in very close proximity, rocky beaches are excellent places to see countless fascinating plants and animals in the span of only an hour or two. Tidepools, in particular, are home to an incredible variety of life. Tidepools often provide both children and adults with their first exposure to marine life, sparking an enchantment that can last a lifetime. Ranging in size from small puddles to small lakes, tidepools are located where tidal ebb and flow submerges rocks and recedes, leaving behind basins filled with enough water to sustain life. Found all along the rocky outer coasts of California, tidepools are inhabited by a variety of creatures that have successfully adapted to the rigorous conditions of this narrow band where the sea collides with the land. During a visit to a tidepool community, you can scarcely help but notice and marvel at the abundant diversity of life in this amazing habitat.

The basic needs of tidepool creatures are the same as those of others: food, oxygen, water, and sometimes shelter. This might not seem like too much to ask, but meeting these needs presents a constant challenge to rocky intertidal organisms. No other habitat is subjected to such drastic changes. Conditions vary dramatically over the course of a day, or even an hour, as tides ebb and flow. Sometimes the tidepools are completely devoid of water; at other times they are flooded. Temperatures can vary from extremely hot to below freezing. Salinity increases quickly in exposed tidepools as water evaporates into the atmosphere in the heat of the sun. Dissolved oxygen may become scarce as it is consumed too quickly. Wave after wave mercilessly pounds the rocks and their inhabitants for days, weeks, or months on end. Predation by both terrestrial and marine animals is intense, as is competition for space. And yet, as amazing as it sounds, this relatively tiny strip of land may be the earth's most densely populated region. Rocky intertidal animals

A striped shore crab poses amiably for the camera.

display an often similar, yet always fascinating, suite of adaptations that allow them to survive the multitude of threats they face on an ongoing basis.

The intertidal region of a rocky beach can generally be divided into four zones:

- **Splash zone:** the area above the high water mark that is, except in the rare event of extremely high tides or severe storms, reached only by the splash or spray of the waves.
- **High tide zone:** the area between average and high tide levels.
- **Middle tide zone:** the area between local average sea level and average low tide level.
- **Low tide zone:** the area exposed to air only during the lowest tides of the year.

Despite the physical proximity of these zones, the environmental conditions in each zone differ considerably,

and species tend to congregate within the zone most favorable to them. The resulting striated pattern of populations is called vertical zonation. Exactly where the boundaries between the zones are drawn, and whether or not these are all the zones, remain points of scientific debate. Certainly the boundaries for these zones are artificial in the sense that they are frequently crossed by their residents.

The Splash Zone

Creatures living within the splash zone are particularly subject to extreme temperature changes and to desiccation (life-threatening loss of water). Although they live part or most of their lives above the waterline, intertidal animals must remain moist in order to survive. Desiccation is the number-one killer of tidepool organisms. Amazingly enough, creatures living in the splash zone have adaptations that help them retain water and flourish even when the only moisture they receive is water spray.

Species of green and blue-green **algae** thrive in the splash zone, often growing in tarlike bands on rocks at the upper reaches of the region. The algae are especially adept at resisting desiccation because of their ability to form gelatinous masses that trap and store water. Algae are, however, much less able to defend themselves against the numerous grazers that also inhabit the splash zone, and are food for a number of snails, limpets, and crustaceans.

The **rock louse** is a scavenger that inhabits the upper splash zone, feeding primarily on organic decay. Sometimes called common rock isopods, they are usually seen scurrying along the rocks at night, when the threat of predation lessens. Rock lice look much like garden-variety pill bugs, with flat bodies that grow to about 1.5 inches long, but you'll have to look closely to find these animals since their coloration usually helps them disappear into the surrounding rocks. Rock lice have two sets of pointed appendages on their tails, which help them maneuver quickly across the rocks. More terrestrial than aquatic, these crustaceans will drown if they are submerged too long.

Periwinkle snails, such as the flat-bottomed periwinkle and the checkered periwinkle, live high within the splash zone. In fact, flat-bottomed periwinkles spend most of their lives out of water, and occupy a higher vertical position on land than any other California marine mollusk. Nevertheless, periwinkles must remain moist to survive. In order to prevent the loss of too much water, particularly during low tide when they are without water spray, periwinkles are able to clamp tightly to the rock and seal the edges of their shell to retain moisture. Visitors to the splash zone will usually see periwinkles aggregated in protectively moist pockets and rock crevices, feeding on algae and seaweed scraped from the

An acorn barnacle waves its feathery legs through the water to entrap planktonic food.

rocks. These mollusks are abundant but tiny; the whorled shells of periwinkles rarely reach as large as a quarter inch in diameter.

Limpets (including various species such as finger, rough, shield, and owl limpets) are another type of gastropod mollusk found in the splash zone. Like the periwinkles, they are extremely tolerant of temperature extremes. In order to combat the threat of desiccation, each limpet painstakingly cuts into a rock, in time creating a groove that conforms to the edge of its shell. If the rock is too hard, it twists its body back and forth until the edge of its shell is filed to fit the rock. The limpet's strong foot clamps the elliptical single shell against the rock, creating a tight fit that helps prevent water loss during low tides. Limpets leave their crevices at night to feed much as periwinkles do, using a rasplike radula to scrape algae off the rocks.

Just below the level of the snails and limpets in an area that receives a bit more water from spray, you are likely to discover populations of small **acorn barnacles,** described under the genus *Chthamalus.* Although they superficially resemble mollusks, barnacles are actually arthropods, even though the jointed, segmented bodies characteristic of their phylum are only visible during their planktonic larval stage.

These animals are filter-feeders, but amazingly are able to survive while feeding only a few hours a month, when the tides are high enough to submerge them. During periods of extremely high tides, barnacles extend red feathery feet from their volcano-like shells to filter tiny planktonic food from the water. Between feedings, barnacles seal themselves within their shells with a calcareous "door" called an operculum, thereby preventing desiccation during the long fast.

A variety of species of barnacles grow in crowded colonies on rocks, boat hulls, piers, and even on the shells of other crustaceans. Larvae are attracted to settlement sites by the presence of other barnacles, thereby increasing the probability of finding both a favorable site and potential mates. When the larva settles out of the water column to become an adult, it glues its head to a rock with a cement secreted from its antennae, surrounds itself with hard calcareous plates to protect its shrimplike body, and spends the remainder of its life upside down and stuck in place.

Most barnacles are hermaphroditic, meaning that each individual possesses both male and female organs; however, self-fertilization is rare. Although immobility is normally a hindrance to mating, barnacles overcome this difficulty by possessing the world record for largest penis–to–body size ratio. During mating, this long organ is extended to transfer sperm into a neighboring barnacle. Fertilized eggs develop and hatch within the recipient barnacle's shell, where the larvae are brooded for a short time before their release into the plankton. After a series of metamorphoses and molts, the larvae settle out to begin the cycle again.

Although the splash zone is dominated by *Chthamalus*, another species of **acorn barnacle** is more common in the lower zones. *Balanus* is able to outcompete *Chthamalus* for space under certain favorable conditions. However, because *Chthamalus* is more resistant to desiccation, it is able to survive higher in the intertidal zone than is *Balanus*. If larvae of both species settle throughout the intertidal area, the *Balanus* will normally be killed off by desiccation in the upper intertidal, but will outcompete the *Chthamalus* for space in the lower intertidal, resulting in the observed distribution. These two species demonstrate a trend that is common to all species in the rocky intertidal: in general, the upper limit of species distribution is limited by its ability to deal with physiological stress; its lower vertical range tends to be limited by its ability to compete with other species. Animals are not always found in a particular area because the physical conditions are the most favorable to them, but sometimes simply because they can survive under harsher conditions than the species that outcompete them for more favorable sites.

Goose-neck barnacles are named for their "resemblance" to a waterfowl.

The ornate shell of a lined chiton.

The High Tide Zone

The creatures that live in the high tide zone must be adept at surviving on both land and sea because they are awash twice each day. This zone is nevertheless populated by far more species than the splash zone; in fact, the farther you move down from the splash zone, the more life you are likely to discover. Crabs, snails, limpets, mussels, barnacles—a multitude of animals are found in this area, many of them also inhabitants of the splash zone and lower zones. The most significant difference between the populations of the high tide zone and the drier splash zone is that more species of arthropods and mollusks tend to be found in the high tide zone.

Striped shore crabs, also called green-lined shore crabs, are common arthropods of the high tide zone as well as other areas of the intertidal. The most common shore crab in southern California, it can be distinguished by its size (usually about 2 inches); its red, purple, and/or green markings; its large dark red to purple claws; and its abundance. Although these crabs also reside in the mud and sand, they are most common along rocky outer coasts. Striped shore

crabs are scavengers that feed primarily on algae, but also eat other plant and animal material and, occasionally, a live limpet or snail. If you startle one of these pugnacious crabs, it will challenge you by stretching and raising its claws, but will dash to shelter in a convenient crevice as quickly as possible.

Barnacles, including acorn barnacles and goose-neck barnacles, are among the dominant species of this zone and the middle tide zone. The shell of hard plates that protects the body of goose-neck barnacles is attached to the substrate by a flexible, fleshy base called a peduncle. Often found in large numbers in the upper two-thirds of the intertidal zone, the **goose-neck barnacle** is even more noteworthy for the remarkable way in which it gained its common name. Before the summer breeding grounds of a bird called the barnacle goose were known, folklore held that the young geese originated from the "barnacle trees" that grew by the seashore. Hence the common name of barnacles, and particularly of this barnacle, since (if you squint a bit and look from just the right angle) the general outline of the goose-neck barnacle somewhat resembles the head and neck of a goose.

The Middle Tide Zone

The middle tide zone abounds with life. Permanent tide-pools not normally found in the upper zones protect hermit crabs, snails, nudibranchs, anemones, and even small fish from exposure and the pounding of waves. Green, red, and brown algae are abundant, as are mussels, barnacles, sea stars, and a multitude of other animals. All these animals have flexible bodies or rounded, low profiles and methods of anchoring themselves to the substrate to minimize the threat of the pounding, ever-present surf.

Chitons are particularly common in the mid tide and lower zones. Resembling small oval mounds covered with an eight-sectioned plate of armor, their unusual shape has led to a number of other common names, including sea cradles and coat-of-mail shells. They are the only mollusks with jointed shells. This flexibility allows chitons to bend to fit readily into uneven depressions in the rocks. The chiton's foot grasps the substrate so strongly that it is difficult to dislodge the animal without harming it. The fleshy girdle surrounding the shells enables the chiton to seal tightly to the rocks in an effort to prevent desiccation. Most chitons hide under rocks or in depressions in the surface of rocks during daylight, but come out to feed on various algae at night. Although they belong to an entirely different class of mollusks, chitons have a lifestyle very similar to that of limpets.

Mossy chitons are among the most common tidepool chitons. Growing to a length of 2.5 inches, they are dark brown to green, with a fleshy girdle covered by mossy-looking, stiff hairs that often entrap seaweed. Found throughout California, mossy chitons tend to be slightly larger in the northern part of the state. Troglodyte chitons are smaller, reaching only about 1.5 inches, and vary in color from light yellow to dark brown. Troglodytes tend to permanently inhabit shallow depressions that they cut to fit their own shape. Extremely territorial, they rarely leave their pit except to feed at high tide, after which they return to the same pit. The lined chiton is among the most beautiful of all California mollusks, with a brightly colored shell decorated with zig-zag patterns. It feeds primarily on coralline algae, and can often be found beneath purple sea urchins. The predatory

A hermit crab vacates its old home en route to a larger shell.

Dense mussel beds of the lower rocky intertidal shelter a hidden community of invertebrate animals.

carnivorous chiton is unique in its feeding behavior. It holds its head flap up so that it resembles a bit of seaweed and then, when an unsuspecting tiny invertebrate passes by, snaps the trap down over its prey. The granddaddy of the California chitons is the Pacific giant chiton, also called the **gumboot chiton**. Reaching a length of up to 16 inches, it is the largest chiton in the world. Its mantle completely covers the animal's plated shell, giving the creature a soft, almost fleshy appearance. Gumboot chitons may live up to twenty years or more.

Numerous crabs scurry about their business throughout the mid to low tide zones. The **flat porcelain crab** is a scavenger that eats small dead and live animals. Distinguishable mainly by its feeding antennae, which extend to three times its body length, this small crab has a flattened, brownish body and large reddish-orange claws. Often found clinging to the underside of rocks, porcelain crabs quickly run sideways for cover when exposed. They have an amazing disregard for their own limbs, occasionally shedding legs with startling ease

when trying to escape a predator or curious human.

Mussels are among the dominant and most conspicuous members of the upper middle tide zone community. As adults, mussels attach to the rocks with strong, elastic, hairlike structures called byssal threads, which are produced by glands in the foot. Although they are capable of moving slowly about on their hatchet-shaped foot, they seldom do so once they attach. Like most other bivalves, mussels are filter-feeders, capturing their food by straining the water for tiny plants and animals. Commonly observed species include the bay mussel, also called the blue or edible mussel, and the California sea mussel. The gill chambers of many mussels contain an irritating and unwelcome guest: the parasitic **pea crab**. The tiny pea crab picks at the mussel's gills to remove food, causing considerable damage to its host. Only one pea crab is found in each mussel, and it usually leaves only to breed. Other species of pea crabs are found in various bivalves and tunicates, as well as in the burrows of worms and shrimp.

The middle tide zone is also home to many animals that live in the shelter of tidepools. In addition to the dangers faced by inhabitants of the higher intertidal zones, tidepool creatures face the threats of high salinity and depleted oxygen during low tides. Many of these animals possess large gills that increase the surface area available for oxygen absorption. Other physiological adaptations increase the efficiency of oxygen extraction from the water, as well as the efficiency of oxygen use.

Hermit crabs are common inhabitants of tidepools, busily trundling over the rocks in search of food to scavenge. Unlike other crabs, only the front of their body is armored; their soft abdomen is not covered by a protective shell. Such a build could create some serious problems, but these clever crustaceans protect themselves from potential predators by residing in a discarded snail shell. Only the well-armed claws and the front of the body remain exposed. It is quite difficult to remove a hermit crab from a shell, as the abdomen is curved to accommodate the spiral construction of most snail shells. They carry their borrowed homes with them wherever they go, and when threatened will withdraw into the shell and block the opening with one of their well-armored claws. As these crabs molt and grow larger, they are eventually forced to find a larger shell. A lot of shell trading happens among hermit crab populations, and the exchanges must occur quickly—literally within seconds because the crabs are extremely vulnerable to predation when they are between shells. Different species of hermit crabs prefer different types of snail shells; some opt for lightweight shells that allow faster and more agile movement, while other, more cautious crabs prefer larger and heavier shells that offer more protection.

Sea anemones living in the tidepools of the middle tide zone have an astonishing ability to prevent both fatal desiccation and greatly elevated body temperatures. One species that has adapted well to these conditions is the **aggregate anemone**; studies have shown that these animals can withstand internal body temperatures up to 55°F above typical ambient air temperatures. To prevent the fatal loss of water from body tissues during low tide, they retract their tentacles and cover themselves with light-colored rocks and shells that tend to reflect, rather than absorb, heat.

The clumped mats so characteristic of aggregate anemones are the result of a remarkable mode of reproduction. A parent anemone creeps simultaneously in two opposite directions, slowly pulling itself in two. Amazingly, each half then regenerates its missing part to become a new, complete anemone. This sort of reproduction results in mats of genetically identical anemones. The clonal clumps are often separated from adjacent clumps by about the width of a single anemone. Such gaps are due to an ongoing battle among the different clones; each anemone is armed with special tentacles that can wound or kill an anemone of a different clone, but will not affect individuals of the same clone. The production of new anemone groups occurs when the aggregate anemones reproduce sexually by releasing eggs and sperm into the water. (For a discussion of the benefits of sexual and asexual reproduction, see the "Sex in the Sea" sidebar in Chapter 5.)

DID YOU KNOW?

. . . ALTHOUGH THE CLONING OF MAMMALS IS A CONTROVERSIAL NEW ISSUE, SOME INVERTEBRATES HAVE BEEN CLONING THEMSELVES FOR EONS.

The Low Tide Zone

Diversity of species, rather than domination by a few, is the key to the low tide zone. Here you'll discover an incredible array of animals, including many fishes, sponges, nudibranchs, sea hares, anemones, chitons, barnacles, mussels, sponges, sea cucumbers, tube worms, limpets, shrimp, urchins, sea stars, brittle stars, hydroids, clams, crabs, snails, and more. Eelgrass, surf grass, sargassum, and red and brown seaweeds are the dominant plants.

Anemones often inhabit the tidepools in the lower tide zone, and the beautiful **giant green anemone**, or solitary green anemone, is a common resident. As its name suggests, this anemone is both large (reaching a diameter of almost 8 inches) and solitary. Its striking color is due to a mutually beneficial relationship with green algae and protists that live within its tissues: the anemone provides its tenants with protection and compounds necessary for photosynthesis, and gains oxygen and nutrients from photosynthetic by-products. Because its photosynthesizing symbionts thrive only in the light, the vibrancy of the green color varies with exposure to the sun—a giant green anemone growing in dim light is white. Mats of smaller green anemones covering the seaward walls of many pinnacles are often mistaken for the giant green anemone, which also inhabits rocky reefs, but are actually a different species called the aggregate anemone.

The population density of echinoderms—sea stars, sea cucumbers, brittle stars, and sea urchins—increases markedly in the low tide zone. These animals are highly susceptible to the threat of desiccation and salinity changes in higher tidal zones, but thrive in the low tide zone where the number of potential food sources also increases. The most commonly sighted sea star in Pacific Coast intertidal communities is the **ochre sea star**. Voracious and usually dominant predators, ochre sea stars eat mussels, barnacles, snails, and many other animals.

The intense predation that sea stars inflict on mussels is partially responsible for the high diversity of life in the lower intertidal. With space at a premium for all species in this zone, mussels and barnacles engage in a particularly ruthless competition. Patches of space open when the previous tenants are removed by predation (by

Enjoying Tidepools

Of all the places to observe marine life, no habitat is more accessible and varied than the tidepools. By observing life in the tidepools, the behaviors and interactions of many animals can be witnessed in great detail over extended periods of time throughout the year. Access to rocky beaches and tidepool communities is quite easy in many locations along the California coast. And although scuba diving and snorkeling are also great ways to observe marine life, as a tidepool visitor your time is not limited by your supply of air. A series of mornings, afternoons, and evenings leisurely spent in various tidepool communities during different tidal conditions will provide endless fascinating insights into one of the earth's most incredible biomes.

Learning about the plants and animals that inhabit tidepools and rocky beaches can be a lot of fun, but please be careful to observe only and not disturb. Thoughtless acts can cause significant harm, and even if you think you are helping, you may actually be harming. For example, the rocks you see covering the retracted tentacles of an anemone may seem to be a hindrance to the animal, but if you remove the rocks, you will actually deprive the anemone of its protection against life-threatening desiccation.

The simplest and best rule to live by is to leave the tidepool as you found it. Be very careful if you handle any tidepool creatures, and always quickly replace them exactly where and how you found them. If you move a rock, carefully put it back exactly as you found it to avoid squashing any of the animals that use it for shelter. Observe and enjoy, and try not to intercede.

This solitary green anemone gains its vibrant color from tiny symbiotic algae that live within its tissues.

sea stars and some predatory snails), dislodgment (by grazing limpets or battering waves), or seasonal mortality. The identity of the next tenants depends on chance and physical factors: chance decides which larvae reach the bare patch, and physical factors determine whether they can gain a foothold. In the initial stages of resettlement, the bare patch is usually colonized by either algal spores or barnacle larvae, or both. In suitable conditions, barnacles will normally overgrow or dislodge the algae. Sooner or later, mussel larvae will arrive, and as they grow, they will almost certainly outcompete the barnacles. This series of colonizations is called biological succession.

In the absence of any disturbances, the succession would end with a stable community of mussels. However, mussels are a favored food of sea stars, and also seem to be particularly prone to dislodgment by the grazing action of limpets and snails. These factors ensure that empty patches of space will be regularly reopened, beginning the sequence of succession all over again. The outcome or current status of this ongoing struggle affects many species because mussel beds are home to a community of animals including gooseneck barnacles, sea stars, and countless small clams, worms, shrimp, crabs, hydroids, and algae that live within the mussel bed's shelter. In this way, the disturbances caused by predatory sea stars and snails contribute to the overall health and amazing biological diversity of the rocky intertidal region.

A garibaldi hovers among fronds of giant kelp.

CHAPTER 4

THE KELP FORESTS

A kelp pneumatocyst.

California's magnificent kelp forests rank high among the world's most attractive and unusual underwater displays. During ideal diving conditions, few places on earth are as inviting. On the surface, the Pacific is warm and calm, and the sky is a vibrant blue. As you slip below the surface, you enter a magical underwater world where shimmering rays of sunlight dance through a towering forest of giant kelp. The golden hues of the kelp fronds stand out against a blue-green background as strands of bright green eelgrass ripple with the surge along the rocky bottom. Twenty to 30 feet below the surface canopy, you become aware of the rhythmic sway of the forest as it keeps time with the ocean's swells. As far as you can see, plants and animals move in perfect synchrony with the water's ebb and flow.

When diving conditions are favorable in a kelp forest, the opportunity to observe diverse marine creatures in a beautiful wilderness setting is rarely, if ever, surpassed in all of nature. In the forests of giant kelp found in southern California, bright orange garibaldi and curious sheephead often greet divers as soon as they make a splash, while schools of silvery jackmackerel flash by in the sunlight. Migratory fishes such as yellowtail, barracuda, black sea bass, and white sea bass occasionally visit the kelp to feed. Rockfish hover above the cabezon, sculpin, gobies, painted greenlings, and other colorful bottom-dwelling fishes that rest on the rocky substrate below.

Moray eels, California spiny lobsters, abalone, and a host of colorful invertebrates ranging from anemones to sea stars to brilliant sea fans and purple coral await in the recesses of the reef. These are common sights in the kelp forest, and you never know when you'll be lucky enough to swim with a harbor seal, a herd of sea lions, or a school of bonito—or glance up after photographing a tiny nudibranch and see an enormous gray whale swimming silently and gracefully overhead.

A harbor seal cruises through featherboa kelp.

Marine Plants

Other than the large brown algae that we commonly refer to as kelp, the majority of marine plants are rather inconspicuous. They do, however, play an important role in maintaining the stability of the substrate and in providing food and shelter for numerous animal species.

Two notable marine plants that are not seaweeds are **eelgrass** and **surfgrass**. These green plants are true flowering plants rather than algae. Like all flowering plants, but unlike algae, both eelgrass and surfgrass produce seeds as the result of sexual reproduction and have true root systems, leaves, and stems. The long, narrow, bright green strands of surfgrass are most often seen in shallow rocky waters, whereas eelgrass usually grows in the calmer waters of back bays and estuaries. Eelgrass is the most widely distributed sea grass in North America, growing in waters from Alaska to Baja along the Pacific Coast and from Greenland to North Carolina in Atlantic waters; its presence is an indication of a stable diverse ecosystem. In addition to its value in preventing erosion, eelgrass is a primary food source for some migratory birds as well as for a variety of invertebrates and fishes.

With the above exceptions, almost all the common species of marine plants in California are algae that belong to one of three phyla of seaweeds: the green seaweeds, the brown seaweeds, and the red seaweeds. Plants can generally be placed into the proper phylum simply by noting their color, although determining true color can be difficult at depth. Representatives from all three phyla contain chlorophyll, a green pigment essential for photosynthesis. Brown seaweeds have an additional pigment called fucoxanthin, which creates the brown hue, whereas red seaweeds contain a red pigment called phycoerythrin.

The most prominent of the green seaweeds is **sea lettuce**, which attains a diameter of about 1 foot and bears a strong resemblance to—guess what—lettuce.

Coralline algae are among the most common of the red seaweeds. The cells of these plants deposit calcium carbonate as a hard, shell-like covering, making them somewhat similar in appearance to living corals found in tropical waters. Despite this resemblance to corals, coralline algae are plants, not animals. They are usually found in intertidal and subtidal regions throughout the state.

The **brown seaweeds** are far and away the most noticed and admired of California marine plants. This group includes the giant kelp, *Macrocystis pyrifera*, which is the foundation for entire marine ecosystems.

Common Kelp Species

Kelp thrives in the cold, nutrient-rich conditions of our state waters, and twenty-one species are found off California's Pacific Coast. Of these, the following species are among those most commonly seen by recreational enthusiasts. Though in some instances these species coexist, their distributions vary throughout the various geographical and oceanic zones.

Featherboa kelp, sometimes called ribbon kelp or Venus' girdle, lines the intertidal region to a depth of about 50 feet. It grows in some reef communities between Point Conception and Ensenada. Attaining a height of only 10 to 12 feet, this kelp lacks both branches and long blades, and bears a strong resemblance to long feathery ribbons.

Elk kelp grows in the waters south of Point Conception, in depths of 10 to 90 feet. It has a very long stipe that ends in a single grapefruit-sized, spherical float, from which two rows of long flat fronds branch out. Elk kelp is often observed along the outer edges of giant kelp forests, where it is free from the domination of the larger *Macrocystis* plants and can receive sufficient sunlight.

There are three species of kelp in California waters that are commonly called **palm kelp**. That known by scientists as *Eisenia arborea* is found from Monterey to Baja at intertidal depths to 120 feet, and can be distinguished by the serrated edges of its blades and the stipe that forks just below the blades. Another species, sea palm kelp (*Postelsia palmaeformis*), is a short plant that appears intertidally in central California. Also called palm kelp or winged kelp, the species *Pterygophora californica* appears along the entire coast of California, growing from intertidal depths to approximately 120 feet. The smooth blades of *Pterygophora* spread out from the upper half of a single stipe.

Oarweed can be observed along the entire length of the coast, though it is most common in central California. The stipe of this simple kelp grows to a height of only about 1 foot before spreading laterally into a series of 3- to 6-inch-wide blades that can reach a length of 6 to 8 feet.

Growing in waters from Oregon to San Miguel Island, **bull kelp** is the most dominant species north of San Francisco. Its streamerlike blades are fastened to a tennis ball–sized float, which is in turn attached to a single ropelike, elastic stipe. The simple design reduces drag, allowing bull kelp to dominate in waters rougher than can be weathered by the closely related giant kelp. The hollow stipe of bull kelp is occasionally sliced up, pickled, and eaten by adventurous beach visitors.

Agarum is characterized by its wrinkled single blade, which reaches a length of up to 8 feet and a width of 2 to 3 feet. In rough waters the blade becomes perforated with a number of holes.

A purple-ringed top shell grazes on coralline algae.

A bat ray cruises through a forest of giant kelp.

Giant Kelp: *Macrocystis pyrifera*

Although a variety of kelp species are found in most kelp forests, the most common and dominant species in the kelp forests of southern California is giant kelp, *Macrocystis pyrifera*. Giant kelp forests are found in waters ranging from Santa Cruz, California, to Turtle Bay, Mexico.

All kelp are types of algae, which are simpler than flowering plants, lacking special tissues to carry water and food from one part of the plant to another. Nevertheless, seaweeds demonstrate a remarkable ability to survive in conditions too harsh for flowering plants. Forests of giant kelp are excellent examples, thriving in areas where water motion and currents are too strong for many other plants. The relentless water flow is actually advantageous to the kelp, providing a continuously renewed supply of vital nutrients such as nitrogen and potassium. Giant kelp rarely grows from deeper than 130

feet, yet individual plants often reach lengths of up to 200 feet as the golden fronds extend straight up from the bottom to the surface, where they stretch out to form a floating surface canopy. This canopy can be up to 10 feet thick in a healthy kelp forest, and sunlight filtering through the fronds creates a stunning cathedral effect for divers below.

The buoyant fronds of a mature giant kelp plant are composed of three parts: a stemlike stipe, leaflike blades, and gas-filled spheres called pneumatocysts. The fronds are anchored to the seafloor by the kelp plant's holdfast. Although the holdfast resembles a tangled mass of roots, kelp plants have no root system; the holdfast's thin, sturdy, spaghetti-like structures, called haptera, do not penetrate the substrate as do the roots of flowering plants. Also unlike terrestrial plants, which take in most of their nutrients through their roots, kelp plants absorb nutrients through all their parts (holdfast, stipe, pneumatocysts, and blades).

The largest plant in the marine environment, giant kelp is also the fastest growing. Under ideal conditions, giant kelp is capable of increasing in length by up to 2 feet per day. This rapid growth is due in part to a design that enhances the kelp's ability to turn sunlight into energy. Although kelp is quite heavy on land, in water the plant's gas-filled pneumatocysts buoy the fronds upward, maximizing the blades' exposure to sunlight. Unlike leaves of terrestrial plants, kelp blades have no top or bottom side, so photosynthesis can continue even when the blades are flipped over by water action. In fact, the entire frond takes part in photosynthesis, further assisting the kelp plant's speedy growth.

Healthy beds of *Macrocystis* exist only where the water stays between 50°F and 68°F, making this kelp particularly vulnerable to the warm-water invasion of El Niño. With few exceptions, giant kelp is found in areas with a rocky substrate to which the plants can attach. The holdfasts are well designed for gripping the substrate to resist the constant shock and pull of wave action, surge, and current, and can withstand surges equivalent to winds of over 120 miles per hour. However, severe winter storms can rip the holdfasts loose, and if you have ever visited a southern California beach after a winter storm, you probably noticed enormous mounds of giant kelp piled up on the sand. Storms are the greatest natural threat to kelp forests. In the calm waters off the shores of Santa Barbara, which is sheltered from the brunt of bad weather by Point Conception and the Channel Islands, a unique community of *Macrocystis* is able to thrive in the sand. Rather than attaching to rocks with their haptera, these giant kelp plants anchor themselves to sturdy worm tubes, becoming increasingly stabilized as sand accumulates around them.

The haptera of giant kelp are, however, incapable of attaching directly to sand, mud, or even silt-covered rocks.

During the 1950s to 1970s, when sewage outfalls near major metropolitan areas covered the seafloor with a layer of silt, many miles of healthy kelp forest communities were destroyed. Not only were new haptera unable to attach to any surface, but many existing plants were killed by high concentrations of phosphates and other chemicals in the sewage. Californians have since become much more aware of the impact of sewage on marine communities, and most towns have taken responsible actions to prevent a recurrence of this destruction. Nevertheless, to protect the health of our marine environment we must continue to monitor and improve sewage treatment processes, reduce sewage treatment costs, and work toward preventing raw sewage spills, especially after heavy rains.

Kelp species reproduce through a cycle known as alternation of generations. The complete reproductive cycle consists of two generations of plants: a sexually reproducing generation and an asexually reproducing generation. The large kelp plants we are familiar with are the asexually reproducing form, called sporophytes. Sporophytes release one-celled spores that develop into male and female gametophytes—the microscopic, sexually reproducing form of kelp we never see. After a gametophyte egg is fertilized, it will eventually develop into a mature sporophyte, thus completing the cycle.

The juvenile sporophyte, if it is lucky enough to find a favorable place to attach, first develops into a tiny one-bladed plant. When it reaches 3 or 4 inches in height, the blade begins to split in two from the base to the tip. Before the split is even complete, the two new blades begin to split as well. As the process continues, fronds begin to develop and pneumatocysts (gas bladders) appear at the base of the blades. A special blade called an apical blade at the tip of each frond continuously produces new blades as the plant grows upward.

DID YOU KNOW?

. . . GIANT KELP CAN GROW AN AMAZING 2 FEET LONGER IN A SINGLE DAY.

Oceanic Food Chains

Plants and animals are grouped and classified in many ways: vertebrates and invertebrates, benthic and pelagic, planktonic and nektonic, algae and flowering plants. They can also be classified according to trophic relationships. Commonly called food chains, trophic relationships describe "who eats whom and is eaten by whom."

Plants are primary producers; they harness the sun's energy to grow by photosynthesis, using only simple raw materials. The energy that sustains nearly all living creatures is ultimately derived from the sun, but is made available to animals only through the primary producers. Primary producers are therefore at the base of a food chain and are considered to be the first trophic level. Herbivores (animals that eat plants) are at the second trophic level because they eat the primary producers of the first trophic level. Carnivores (animals that eat other animals) that eat herbivores belong to the third trophic level. Predators that eat the carnivores of the third trophic level belong to the fourth trophic level, and so on.

It is important to distinguish between the flow of nutrients and the flow of energy in an ecosystem. The flow of nutrients is circular, generally going in various forms from plants to consumers to decomposers and back to plants. Energy transfer, on the other hand, is essentially unidirectional; some energy is lost with each transfer from one trophic level to the next. This loss occurs because each animal uses up part of the energy it gains; some is lost through metabolic activity and some is simply excreted. Laboratory and field studies indicate that energy is transferred from one trophic level to the next with an average efficiency of only about 10 percent. That means that if you start with 100 percent of the energy of primary producers, only

about 10 percent is available to support herbivores, and only about 1 percent to support carnivores of the third trophic level, and so on, with a drastic reduction of energy available to each successive trophic level.

This inefficient transfer of energy explains why there are so many more animals and so much more biomass at lower trophic levels than at higher ones. Less of the original energy from the primary producers has been dissipated at lower trophic levels, so there is more energy available to animals at these lower levels. Inefficient energy transfer also explains why so many of the large predators at higher trophic levels are solitary hunters. Large predators need not school for safety, and it is more advantageous for them not to compete with others for the limited food available to satisfy their huge appetites.

Another fascinating effect is that so many very large animals, such as blue whales, humpback whales, and whale sharks, are plankton-eaters, placing them at only the second or third trophic level. One might think that such large animals should be formidable predators, rather than going to all the apparent trouble of straining microscopic creatures from the water. However, these huge animals require an enormous amount of energy to live and grow, and thousands of times more biomass and energy are available to them in the form of plankton at the lowest trophic levels, than in the form of larger fish, which are at higher trophic levels.

The paths through which the transfer of energy among trophic levels takes place are called food chains, or more accurately, food webs. Straight and orderly chains of energy transfer from one well-defined trophic level to the next simply do not exist in nature, and most creatures occupy more than one trophic level with respect to dif-

A white-spotted rose anemone engulfs a limpet.

ferent prey. For example, a blue shark can eat an anchovy (and thus be operating in about the fourth trophic level), or it can eat a yellowtail that ate a mackerel that ate the anchovy (and thus be operating in the sixth trophic level). Other animals, such as lobster, may act both as predators (when they feed on small animals) and as detritivores (by feeding on organic decay). The lobster may consume the dead body of, or waste from, one of its potential predators, thereby further intertwining the threads of energy transfer in the food web.

These trophic relationships are not limited to a particular area. There are no completely impermeable boundaries in the ocean, and trophic relationships link marine organisms the world over. The interconnectedness of the food web means that when any portion of the web is altered, the reverberations may affect creatures throughout the web. It is important to remember that over-exploitation of a particular species, or local pollution problems, can have ramifications that extend far beyond a single species or small area.

Palm kelp is named for its resemblance to the trees that grace many California beaches.

The Kelp Community Ecosystem

Charles Darwin first noted the ecological importance of kelp forests when he proclaimed:

> The number of living creatures of all orders, whose existence intimately depends on the kelp is wonderful. A great volume might be written, describing the inhabitants of one of these beds of seaweed . . . I can only compare these great aquatic forests . . . with terrestrial ones in the intertropical regions. Yet, if in any country a forest was destroyed, I do not believe nearly so many species of animals would perish as would here, from the destruction of kelp.

Although recent discoveries of many previously unknown insects and birds in tropical rain forests have brought Darwin's last statement into question, his recognition of the biological importance and diversity of kelp beds was well founded.

Kelp beds are truly the lush forests of the ocean. It is not only the foliage that makes the analogy an accurate one, for healthy kelp forests are home to an estimated 800 species of marine life. So many marine organisms use the kelp forest for food, protection, and substrate that the sheer number of individuals is difficult to calculate. Long ago it was documented that a single mature kelp plant may support more than a million organisms, most of which are microscopic, but many of which are wonderfully visible. More than 175 species of crabs, nudibranchs, brittle stars, isopods, worms, and other creatures have been shown to inhabit the holdfasts alone, and more than 100 species of motile invertebrates have been documented in and around the fronds. The presence of a kelp plant in a water column can increase the amount of life supported in that column by a factor of thousands.

Divers frequently notice kelp blades encrusted with dense clusters of sessile animals. Most of these animals are either **hydroids** or **bryozoans**, all of which are filter-feeders that establish colonies on the blades of kelp plants. Bryozoans are often so numerous that the kelp blades appear to be white rather than their true golden hue. Blades dominated by hydroids, tiny cousins of sea anemones, have a furry yellowish appearance. The presence of hydroids and bryozoans on the fronds attracts numerous hungry fishes, crustaceans, and mollusks.

Although kelp plants often live for several years, the individual blades fall off and decay after only a few months.

This short life span prevents encrusting colonies of bryozoans and hydroids from overburdening and killing the kelp plant by dragging it to depths where there is too little light for photosynthesis. The constant sloughing of blades and fronds feeds a healthy detrital community of sea cucumbers, bat stars, lobsters, crustaceans, and other animals. Detritivores (animals that eat dead and decaying organic material) recycle the energy harnessed from the sun by the kelp back into the community; they eat dead parts of the plant and are in turn eaten by animals that are eaten by still other animals in the detritus-based food chain.

Animals that eat living parts of kelp plants are links in a second food chain of the kelp forest ecosystem. Grazers such as kelp snails, abalone, crustaceans, gastropods, and fish are

Lion's mane nudibranchs use their large oral hoods to prey on tiny crustaceans.

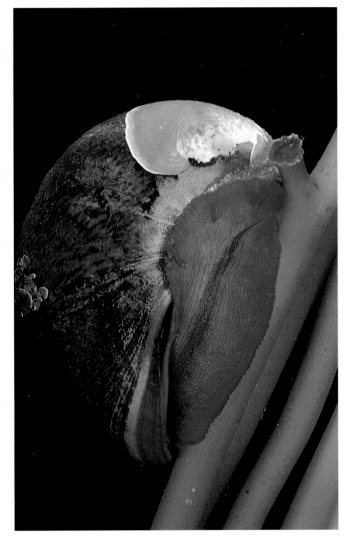

The brilliantly colored foot of a Norris' top shell carries the snail up a stipe of giant kelp.

direct links from the living kelp plant to higher trophic levels. Because some animals (like sea urchins) are both grazers and detritivores, and because some predators consume both grazers and detritivores, all animals in the kelp forest ecosystem are actually part of one large, complex food web, rather than different isolated food chains.

The **Norris' top shell** is a beautiful inhabitant of giant kelp forests. Growing up to 2 inches in diameter, this colorful snail has a handsome chestnut-brown shell and an orange to deep red foot. Although occasionally seen on the rocky substrate, these snails spend the majority of their lives grazing upon the kelp plant. Starting on the holdfast, they slowly work their way up the plant. If they fall off the plant and crash to the bottom, they simply locate a nearby holdfast and begin the process over again. Kelp snails are often covered by a number of mollusks called slipper shells, which are filter-feeders, not parasites.

Magnificent nudibranchs of all colors explore the kelp forest communities. The **lion's mane nudibranch** perches atop kelp blades and casts its large oral hood netlike through the water in order to snare its prey of small crustaceans. When attacked or startled, the lion's mane abruptly ceases

A northern kelp crab perches defiantly on the holdfast of a giant kelp plant.

longer than it is wide, with an obviously pointed rostrum. The shells of **foliate kelp crabs**, also called mimicking crabs, are frequently encrusted with camouflaging organisms such as sponges and algaes. Seventy-three foliate kelp crabs were once found in a single square yard of holdfast.

Numerous species of fishes inhabit kelp forests, consuming the plants and smaller animals. **Halfmoon** and **opaleye** feed directly upon giant kelp, while the **rainbow surfperch, striped surfperch,** and **kelp surfperch** are planktivores,

fishing, drops off the kelp plant, and swims away in search of safer hunting grounds.

As you might suspect, **kelp crabs** are most commonly sighted on kelp plants, where they hide among the stipes and holdfasts. **Northern kelp crabs** are among the most pugnacious of California crabs, and have been known to pounce on unwary divers. They vary from olive green to brown, and attain a width of 6 inches including their legs. The diameter of their claws is much larger than that of their legs. **Southern kelp crabs** can be distinguished from their northern counterparts by their claws, with a diameter smaller than that of their legs and a body

An anemone growing on the blade of a giant kelp plant.

which feed on small planktonic animals. Like other midwater fishes, including jackmackerel and smelt, perches are sometimes called "picker fish" because they pick food out of midwater as they feed.

Almost perfectly camouflaged to match the coloration of kelp, the **giant kelpfish** and its close relative, the **striped kelpfish,** hide in the fronds and mimic the kelp as it moves back and forth with the surge. The giant kelpfish reaches a length of 2 feet, is shaped much like a blade of kelp, and even has white spots that resemble the bryozoans that cover kelp blades. Although both males and females are able to alter their colors somewhat to match their surroundings, females seem to be more adept at camouflage. The smaller striped kelpfish is reddish to light brown, and is usually seen in either shallower depths where the kelp has a warmer hue or in red seaweeds along shore. **Kelp rockfish** employ a similar method of camouflage, often hanging upside down and motionless among the blades of a kelp plant.

Kelp clingfish blend in well with kelp and eelgrass, using the plants' protective fronds as a place to hide. The camouflage allows the clingfish, which can change its color from brown to emerald green, to remain undetected until it captures its prey. Their pelvic fins are modified into suctionlike discs that enable them to hold onto kelp blades, a feature from which the fish derives its common name. These small fish cling tightly to the blades and are well hidden against the plant, so you must look closely and carefully to find one. Kelp clingfish are most common in northern California, although the very similar southern clingfish and slender clingfish inhabit southern California waters.

Although **senorita fish** don't feed specifically on kelp, these cigar-shaped

wrasses often incidentally ingest some kelp as they pick at the surface of the blades for tiny invertebrate prey. Senoritas are frequently seen cleaning blacksmith fish, garibaldi, and other fishes at midwater cleaning stations. In this mutually beneficial behavior, they gain food in the form of small parasites and dead skin, while the fish being cleaned are happy to be rid of the irritants. When startled, senorita fish dive headlong into the sand and bury themselves. They also sleep snugly buried in the sand.

Swirling schools of **jackmackerel** race through kelp forests and reefs throughout the state, glistening like silver kaleidoscopes in the sun. Large schools are truly a beautiful sight on a sunny day, as thousands of fish cruise the kelp in synchrony. Individual jackmackerel are generally less than 10 inches long, but are reported to reach a length of up to 32 inches. Jackmackerel are usually observed to feed on plankton and juvenile squid and fishes near the surface, but they are also known to probe into the sand for food. Their presence is often a tip that yellowtail and other predatory game fish are nearby.

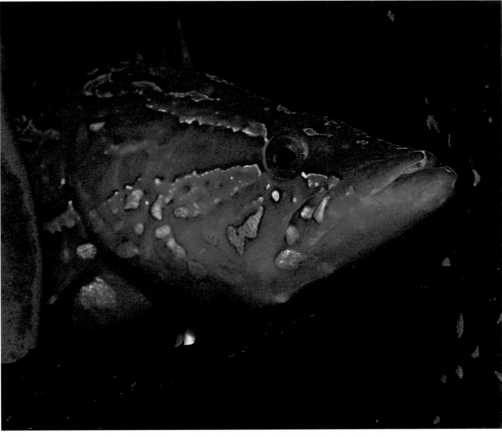

A giant kelpfish camouflages itself within the fronds of a giant kelp plant.

Another silvery inhabitant of the reefs and kelp forests is the **California barracuda**, or Pacific barracuda. Their distinctive long, slender body and protruding jaw full of sharp, daggerlike teeth make them easy to recognize. These fish are known to reach a length of up to 4 feet, although most grow to no more than 3 feet. Enormous schools of barracuda cruise around kelp beds and reefs in coastal areas ranging from Point Conception southward into Baja, but are occasionally seen as far north as Alaska. Unlike their sometimes aggressive Caribbean cousins, California barracuda are not known to attack humans. Although the long sharp teeth can be unnerving, California barracuda prey on small fishes and squid, not on divers. These fish are relatively fearless, but slowly retreat upon a diver's approach and usually shy away from scuba exhaust.

A diver descends into a sunlit kelp forest.

Gas-filled pneumatocysts buoy giant kelp fronds toward sunlight.

Swimming, Snorkeling, and Diving in Kelp

In Hollywood lore, kelp often plays the role of a man-eating monster with the ability to reach out and entangle any intruder who as much as blinks while swimming through a kelp forest. Such a reputation makes for good, cheap, late-night entertainment (or at least cheap and late), but it is a long, long way from the truth. With only a little common sense you can generally avoid the slightest entanglement, and even if you do become caught in kelp, it is quite easy to get free.

Preventing entanglement in the first place is the best approach, and is easy even in dense kelp beds. If you swim under the canopy and around the fronds, the plant will not—because it cannot—reach out and grab you. Knowing this, you should be able to relax and enjoy a swim through a kelp bed. If you do get hung up, don't worry; the stipe of the plant is easy to break.

It is important to realize that a kelp plant is highly elastic. It must be so to survive the thrashing it takes from wave action and surge during winter storms, otherwise the stipes would break. Elasticity allows the stipe to give with the pull of water motion and prevents healthy plants from being torn free of the bottom except in cases of severe storms.

An awareness of kelp's elasticity is important because you will rarely, if ever, be able to tear the plant by stretching it. If you do become slightly entangled, or if a fin buckle gets hung up in a stipe and you find yourself towing an irritatingly heavy, 30-foot-long strand of kelp, simply snap the stipe in two in much the same way that you would snap a pencil. Bending the stipe back and forth a few times should enable you to break even the sturdier plants. At that point you can easily remove any remaining strands without the fear of being done in by a mythical monster of sea lore.

If you do somehow manage to become really engulfed in the stuff, a knife can help. But be careful—you won't be the first diver who has cut through a pressure gauge hose that was hidden in a clump of kelp. Swimming back to a boat full of friends can be awfully embarrassing after you have just sliced your own gear into pieces. I recommend trying to sneak back onboard.

Kelp as a Commercial Resource

Beyond the purely esoteric value of its beauty, giant kelp has many practical uses. In 1911 the U.S. Department of Agriculture sponsored a study of the kelp beds, and since that time, numerous industrial uses for kelp have been developed. During World War I, kelp was harvested and processed into potash and acetone for use in the munitions industry. Shortly thereafter, researchers discovered that algin, a colloidal substance found in kelp, has many commercial applications. Available only from certain sea plants, algin has a strong affinity for water and is therefore extremely useful as a suspending, stabilizing, emulsifying, gel-producing, and film-forming additive. Algin is added to hundreds of commercial and household products, including some brands of ice cream, beer, fruit drinks, eggnog, candy, cake mixes, paint, paper sizing, medications, toothpaste, and hand lotions.

In 1996, researchers at NutraSweet Kelco Co. (a unit of Monsanto), the largest commercial harvester of kelp on the West Coast, began development of an innovative use for algin. Scientists have been able to purify algin to such an extent as to eliminate all trace compounds detectable by the human body's immune system. Although further research is required, the potential for biomedical applications is tremendously exciting. For instance, it may be possible to reduce rejections of donated and artificial organs by coating them with ultrapure algin prior to transplantation. Because research as of this writing indicates that the recipient's immune system should not recognize the ultrapure algin as a foreign substance, the new organ may be much more readily accepted. If ongoing studies and tests continue to be promising, this is only one among countless examples of future potential uses of ultrapure algin in saving and improving human lives.

DID YOU KNOW?

. . . YOUR TOOTHPASTE PROBABLY CONTAINS AN EXTRACT FROM A KELP PLANT.

California Marine Life

A kelp harvester at work.

Commercial harvesting of kelp is regulated by the California Department of Fish and Game. Modern techniques employ ships that work much as wheat combines, cutting through the top 3 or 4 feet of the surface canopy. The strands of kelp are then collected on large conveyor belts and taken to industrial plants for processing. Kelp-related industries provide jobs for many state residents. In fact, recent estimates indicate that commercial harvesting of kelp generates well over $100 million annually for southern California's economy.

Protecting Our Kelp Forests

Human invasion of the kelp forest ecosystem has placed many kelp beds in great jeopardy. Overzealous hunting of sea otters during the seventeenth century is a classic example. Along with the plummeting sea otter numbers came a meteoric rise in the population of sea urchins, a favorite prey of otters. The unchecked and hungry urchins destroyed kelp forests at an alarming rate. (See the sidebar on page 171.)

Schools of jackmackerel dart through a giant kelp forest.

A diver and senorita fish among giant kelp.

In addition to the assault by sea urchins, many kelp forests were further damaged by human and industrial pollution. Waste effluents decrease water clarity, which limits the amount of light available to the kelp for photosynthesis, thereby threatening the kelp's ability to survive. Furthermore, as the waste settles, it can bury and kill tiny young kelp plants before they have a chance to establish themselves. The layer of silt sometimes makes it difficult for new haptera to gain a grip on the substrate, and therefore easier for the kelp to be torn from the seafloor. Thus human activities, in the forms of pollution and unregulated hunting, severely threatened the existence of a great many kelp forest communities as thousands of square miles of kelp vanished from the sea.

In 1913, sea otters in California waters became fully protected by law, and by the 1950s and 1960s were numerous enough to again control sea urchin populations in many areas. During the same period, conservationists began planting healthy kelp in deteriorating forests to supplement the natural regrowth of kelp. In some endangered kelp beds where natural predators of sea urchins were rare, quicklime was applied to reduce numbers of grazing sea urchins. As urchin populations declined and as waste treatment procedures improved and became better regulated, many kelp forests began to make a remarkable comeback.

If anything positive is to be gained from this chain of events, it is an understanding of the vulnerability of the kelp forest habitat. Although they appear quite rugged, kelp forests can be quickly destroyed by overexploitation of kelp or of other vital members of the kelp community. Loss of the kelp forests would not only be a tragic waste of a beautiful habitat, but would also deprive the state of uncountable revenue. Only if we protect this valuable ecosystem will California kelp forests continue to enrich the waters.

The nooks, crevices, and surfaces of a rocky reef support an amazing diversity of colorful invertebrate animals.

CHAPTER 5

THE ROCKY REEFS

An orange puffball sponge.

Hosting an incredible array of animals ranging from dime-sized anemones to 3-foot-long horn sharks, the rocky reefs are a diving destination not to be missed. Unlike most tropical reefs, which are built from the skeletal remains of corals, the reefs in California's temperate waters are composed of rocks. Much like tropical reefs, however, the surfaces, cracks, and crevices of these rocks provide ideal living quarters for a bewildering variety of species. In fact, most of California's commonly observed marine life is found in its rocky reef communities. It is easy to understand why most California dives are reef dives.

Brightly colored anemones, sea stars, sea cucumbers, sea hares, keyhole limpets, abalone, and scallops cover the rocks of reef communities. Kelp forests, often associated with rocky reefs, hide multitudes of creatures within their fronds and holdfasts. Blackeye (or nickeleye) gobies, Catalina (or bluebanded) gobies, painted greenlings, rockfish, island kelpfish, and moray eels inhabit crevices of the reef. California spiny lobsters are plentiful as well, but divers still need quick hands to bag a limit.

A red gorgonian adds a splash of color to a rocky reef.

debris from the plants is consumed by animals such as mollusks, urchins, sea stars, worms, and crustaceans. The abundance of these lower trophic–level animals in turn supports many carnivores that further enliven the reef communities.

As a general rule, the more irregular the bottom contour, the more life you will find per unit area. Many species of small marine invertebrates, such as barnacles, rock scallops, anemones, and worms, find attachment sites within the crevices of the rocks. Although life is found everywhere on the reef, the smooth ledges are remarkably barren compared to convoluted areas where there is considerably more surface area for attachment. When you visit the rocky reefs, it often seems as if every crack, crevice, and convoluted surface you examine is teeming with life of all kinds.

Rocky Reef Invertebrates

There are approximately fifty species of **sponges** found in California reef communities, but even a specialist needs a microscope to tell many of the species apart. Sponges occur in a variety of shapes and a spectrum of colors, but all sponges have numerous pores on the surface of their bodies. In some species of sponges, large pores (called oscula) are distributed in a regular pattern, while in other species they are more irregular. Sponges are always attached to rocks or other hard surfaces, and most are quite flexible and resilient.

Tiny hairlike cilia within a sponge's pores beat independently to collectively create a current of water through the sponge. Oxygen and food (plankton and organic debris) are extracted from the incurrent water as it flows through the pores and into an internal cavity called a spongocoel; waste products are removed as the water flows out through other pores. Some large sponges are able to filter 50 or more gallons of water per day. In tropical areas where sponges are large and numerous, their combined filtering efforts contribute to water clarity.

In many respects, creatures found in and around the rocky reefs are very different from those found in the sandy plains or the open sea. Their habitat is uniquely characterized by a rocky bottom, a lot of surge, and usually plenty of food. Because many rocky reef creatures cannot keep themselves afloat in the water column, the relatively shallow seafloor acts as a safety net for animals that would perish if they were to sink to the abyssal depths of the open sea. The rocky substrate is also a perfect site for plants and animals to rest on, burrow in, or attach to in order to survive the sometimes violent water motion. Food is plentiful in this habitat, as plankton and detritus collect on the rocky surface and support a thriving community of grazers, scavengers, and detritivores. Grazers also feed directly on kelp and other plants, and

Sex in the Sea

Sex in the sea runs the gamut of hot talk-show topics. Sexual reproduction first evolved among marine organisms, and they've had time to develop a range of variations that could make the most open-minded sodomite blush. But every odd-sounding behavior has evolved because it in some way enhances the animal's reproductive success.

There are two general approaches to reproduction, each with its own advantages and disadvantages. An animal can produce hundreds or thousands of tiny offspring, and with little energy cost to the neglectful parent, a few will manage to survive due to the sheer number of offspring. For example, sponges release millions of sperm and eggs, and never have an instant's concern about the welfare of the offspring; only a tiny fraction will survive to grow into adult sponges. An alternate reproductive strategy, resulting in larger and more highly developed offspring, requires the investment of much more energy by one or both parents, and usually far more parental care. However, each offspring has a much greater chance of surviving to reproduce itself. For example, a pregnant female dolphin endures a gestation period of a year or more, then devotes many months more to nursing and caring for her single offspring. Although it is time- and energy-consuming, such intense care greatly increases the odds of her young's survival.

Many marine invertebrates never even have to meet in order to produce offspring; sperm and eggs are released directly into the water column, where union occurs. This would be an extremely inefficient way of making babies if each animal haphazardly released eggs or sperm now and then. The eggs and sperm would be rapidly depleted and diluted as they were eaten and dispersed in the water currents, and even the few eggs that were successfully fertilized would probably be snatched up immediately by hungry predators. Animals can overcome this problem by coordinating reproductive behavior; for example, in some populations of corals all individuals simultaneously release packets of eggs and sperm on a single orgiastic night. Such coordination is accomplished by the excretion of chemicals called pheromones, which stimulate other members of the same species to release their own eggs or sperm, increasing the likelihood of successful fertilization.

Of course, another solution would be not to depend on other individuals at all. Some animals achieve this independence by asexual reproduction (see the first sidebar in Chapter 1), but others simply have sex with themselves. Many invertebrate species are hermaphrodites (simultaneously possessing both male and female reproductive organs) and, although cross-fertilization is more common, self-fertilization is certainly not unheard of. Besides the convenience of not requiring a partner, self-fertilization allows genetic recombination without diluting one's own genes.

Hermaphroditic animals aren't always self-fertilizing, but some of their other behavior may be even more shocking. For example, certain particularly promiscuous hermaphrodites called sea hares join in orgiastic mating circles. Each sea hare simultaneously acts as a male with one partner and a female with another. Other hermaphroditic animals may be males during one reproductive event and females the next. These sex-changers may alternate their sex regularly, or may switch at some point during their life span, as do sheephead. The flexibility afforded by this odd ability ensures that an appropriate partner will always be available.

Orgies are everyday events in the marine world. The common market squid reproduces in yearly orgies, albeit with a tragic ending. Thousands of squid gather together to mate with frantic abandon, then die, grossly disfigured, among their egg casings.

And you thought your own sex life was confusing. . . .

A red encrusting sponge camouflages the carapace of this masking crab.

Sponges have astonishing regenerative abilities. When a mature sponge of one species was completely broken apart by being forced through a cloth sieve, the bits quickly reassembled themselves into near replicas of the original sponge. This ability is used for asexual reproduction in some species that break off bits of themselves to form new sponges. Most sponges are also capable of sexual reproduction by spawning; the larvae produced in this way spend a short time in the plankton, then turn themselves inside out as they settle to the seafloor to begin their sessile existence.

Sponges are often named according to their usual color or shape. Divers call various species of sponges purple, cobalt, red, yellow, sulphur, vanilla, and gray moon sponges. However, true color can be difficult to determine at depth without the use of an artificial light, so color can be a misleading means of identifying a sponge. Shape is another method of differentiating between species, and in California waters there are urn sponges, crumb-of-bread sponges, finger sponges, gray puffball sponges, and orange puffball sponges. Unfortunately, shape can also be misleading, as the same species will often take on different shapes through competition for space.

Bearing a strong resemblance to small bushy plants, **hydroids** are tiny colonial cnidarians that usually grow in small, 2- to 8-inch-high, feathery clumps attached to the surface of a kelp blade, rock, or other hard surface. Most are whitish in color and rather innocuous, but do not be fooled—the sting from the nematocysts can be painful. The pain does not usually last more than thirty minutes or so, but your skin may itch for several days. Among the commonly encountered hydroids in California waters are the bushy hydroid; the

Like all cnidarians, this hydroid contains venomous stinging cells used for feeding and defense.

A blood star on California hydrocoral.

in southern California and is typically found in deeper, flowing waters. In northern California the hydrocoral is much more common and is even seen at intertidal depths. Although it was once commercially harvested for use as decor, it is now illegal to collect California hydrocoral in state waters.

No less brilliantly colored is the **encrusting hydrocoral**, which forms encrusting sheets of red, pink, and purple on rocks and other hard surfaces. Growing in the low inter-tidal to depths of 100 feet, sheets of encrusting hydrocoral sometimes extend 3 feet across.

ostrich plume hydroid, whose stems have a feathery appear-ance; the pinkish-colored hedgehog hydroid; and the orange hydroid.

Although California waters, like all temperate waters, lack reef-building corals, the state is blessed with brilliantly colored **California hydrocoral**, which ranges from purple to pinkish-red. It may be difficult to remember that colonial corals are animals, and that each flowerlike polyp is an indi-vidual creature. Like other corals, the branches of Cali-fornia hydrocoral are con-structed by colonies of individual animals encased in a common calcareous skele-ton. Clumps of this slow-growing hydrocoral rarely exceed 2 feet in diameter, but even smaller clumps add a pleasant splash of color to any reef.

On seamounts, clumps of hydrocoral are often sur-rounded by colorful straw-berry anemones and other invertebrates. California hydrocoral is somewhat rare

There are also several species of **solitary corals** (or stony corals) in California. One that deserves special men-tion is the attractive orange coral that is frequently found on rocky reefs. Commonly called **orange solitary corals** or orange cup corals, when fully expanded, they are about 1 inch in diameter. Although the orange solitary coral is not a colonial animal (it does not share a skeletal casing with other individuals), several specimens are often seen within only a few centime-ters of one another. Close neighbors are usually related—in their larval stage these corals crawl a short distance from the female coral that produced them, then attach and grow into new polyps.

Sea fans, sometimes called gorgonians, are closely related to anemones and corals. Although they have a bushlike appearance,

California golden gorgonians.

they are colonies of living animals. Like corals, each individual polyp of a sea fan shares a common skeletal casing with the others. Depending upon currents to bring them food, sea fan polyps capture plankton with their extended tentacles, which are well armed with stinging cells. Sea fans tend to maximize their feeding opportunities by orienting themselves perpendicular to the prevailing current, so all sea fans in a given area usually face the same direction.

Mats of strawberry anemones color expanses of current-swept reefs.

anemones living on a sea fan. This species of anemone is bioluminescent and usually less than a half inch in diameter. Despite their attractive appearance, when present in dense concentrations, these parasitic anemones can kill a host sea fan.

Closely resembling jellyfish flipped upside down and attached to the bottom, **sea anemones** are common inhabitants of California's rocky reefs. Anemones attach to rocks

Sea fan polyps are quite sensitive to light, and often retract during the day or at the touch of a diver. When the polyps are retracted, sea fans resemble leafless twigs; it is only when the polyps are extended that the gorgonians take on their lush, bushlike appearance. Distinguishable primarily by color, the most common gorgonians in California are the orange, purple, red, brown, and California golden sea fans. **Red gorgonians** are common at the Channel Islands and at offshore pinnacles, and are found as far north as Monterey Bay. **Brown gorgonians** vary between off-red and brown, but

with the bottom of a strong, tubelike base, which has no skeleton and is remarkably flexible. The upward-facing mouth of anemones is surrounded by tentacles armed with the stinging nematocysts characteristic of cnidarians.

Anemones are able to move slowly and bend their bodies in an effort to find food, but normally depend on tiny animals to stumble into their tentacles. Touching a tentacle triggers an instant firing of the poisonous, harpoonlike nematocysts. Using water pressure to discharge, the firing of a nematocyst occurs within a time span of only three

are much less vividly red than true red sea fans and are easily distinguishable with a little practice. All these gorgonians are more common in the southern part of the state.

A number of species of nudibranchs prey upon sea fan polyps. Unharmed by the sea fan's stinging nematocysts, these amazing nudibranchs are able to transfer the unfired barbs into their bodies for use in their own defense. Divers also occasionally encounter golden yellow, parasitic **zoanthid**

The beautiful rose anemone eats fish and other small animals that come into contact with its stinging tentacles.

milliseconds and at a speed of 2 meters per second, making this one of the fastest cellular processes in nature. When the barb of the nematocyst penetrates its prey or its attacker, venom is injected through the hollow filament to stun or kill it. The tentacles may then envelop the prey and carry it to the anemone's mouth. The stinging cells can fire only once and are absorbed by the body after use. Although some anemones can inflict painful stings, the nematocysts of most California species will not penetrate human skin and feel only slightly sticky.

Some anemones are solitary, while others live in groups called clusters or aggregations—clusters of anemones do not share a common test or skeletal case, and are therefore not called colonies. Several species of California anemones are particularly striking. One of the prettiest, the **white-plumed anemone** (*Metridium giganteum*), is most commonly sighted in the bays of northern California, though it is frequently observed in deeper waters as far south as the northern Channel Islands. These snow-white anemones grow to about 20 inches in height. Another closely related anemone, *M. senile*, is very similar in appearance and is sometimes also called the white-plumed anemone, although it varies in color from pure white to orange to brown. Both *Metridium* anemones are easily identified by the feathery, frilled appearance of the tentacles. These striking anemones are associated with the most beautiful seascapes in central and northern California.

Bright red *Urticina* anemones decorate many rocky reef communities and become more common the farther north one explores. The **painted anemone**, *U. crassicornis*, has a column mottled with red and olive green, whereas the **white-spotted rose anemone**, *U. lofotensis*, is red with white spots, and the fish-eating anemone or **rose anemone**, *U. piscivora*, usually has no spots. Though they are found in southern California, none of these species becomes prevalent until the northern Channel Islands. These anemones are commonly called strawberry anemones, but so are the much smaller *Corynactis* anemones—even in conversation with fellow sport divers you need to be careful to avoid confusion and misunderstanding.

If you encounter an anemone that appears to have small growths protruding from its column, look again. It may be a **proliferating anemone**, in which case the "growths" are actually the anemone's tiny offspring. Larvae of a proliferating anemone crawl out of their mother's mouth and onto her column, where they settle and grow into juveniles in the protection of her stinging tentacles. Most proliferating anemones begin life as females; as they age they become hermaphroditic and are able to fertilize their own eggs or those of others.

White-plumed anemones are considered to be among the most beautiful of California anemones.

Certainly no discussion of California anemones should omit the aggregate strawberry anemones, even though they are not actually anemones at all. These cnidarians are actually corallimorphs, and are more similar to corals than to anemones. Strawberry anemones are much like corals without a hard casing. Large aggregations often cover patches of current-swept reefs so densely that the superstructure of the reefs appears to be a lush carpet of dime-to quarter-sized strawberry anemones rather than rock. Their vivid coloration varies from bright red to pink, to brilliant orange, to light brown, creating an array of potentially superb photographic subjects for underwater photographers. A strawberry anemone often reproduces by the painful-sounding method of fission, slowly crawling in opposite directions until its middle section stretches and tears in two. Each half then grows and heals, and soon it is impossible to see where the division occurred.

Divers often encounter orange masses that resemble a lacy imitation of the petal of a rose. The 2- to 6-inch-wide, flowerlike structure is actually an upright colony of animals called bryozoans. Two commonly observed bryozoan species are the **fluted bryozoan**, which is yellow to orange and has a curly leaflike shape, and the **lacy bryozoan**, which has a distinctive lacy look and is orange to orange-brown. Both species are filter-feeders that thrive on current-swept reefs where plankton is abundant.

Almost all California divers have admired **tube worms** such as feather-duster worms, plume worms, fragile tube worms, and Christmas tree worms, all of which are types of

The glorious plumes of tube worms belie their close relationship to terrestrial earthworms.

some have a colorful mantle that is exposed when covering the shell. Mantle secretions maintain the shell and give it a lustrous quality. The snail's body is normally completely hidden from view within its shell, but if you approach cautiously, you may also be able to see the foot, eye stalks, and tubelike mouth (the proboscis).

Of all the snails in California waters, perhaps the most striking is the chestnut cowry. Although their range extends throughout California, these snails are much more abundant in southern California than in central and northern California. Attaining a length of just over 2 inches, the surface of the shell is a combination of white, tan, and chestnut brown. The shell of a healthy animal has a highly polished, glossy appearance caused by secretions from glands in the golden mantle, which is highlighted by many black spots. If you wish to take a closer look at the exposed mantle of a chestnut cowry, be careful not to disturb the animal since it quickly retracts its mantle when threatened. Although all gastropods have a mantle, this soft tissue is either unexposed or not as beautiful in many species as it is in the chestnut cowry.

annelids called polychaete worms. Divers usually first notice the brilliant, featherlike, red or orange gills that are extended when the animal is feeding. These plumes play the dual roles of trapping food and extracting oxygen from the water. To observe the plumes from close range you must approach slowly and be careful not to alarm the animal, because once disturbed, it will instantly retract its plumes. The rest of the worm is protectively hidden in a tube that it constructs from sand, debris, and its own secretions.

Another species of polychaete worm, the **colonial sand castle worm**, lives in large, honeycomb-like colonies on rocks in shallow water near sand bottoms. The colonies depend heavily upon a constant wash of sand in order to build and maintain their tubes. These worms feed by trapping drifting organic matter in a net of mucus, or by catching smaller particles of food in tiny, purple, hairlike structures that protrude from holes at the top of the tubes. Divers usually spot these worms by noticing their large colonial construction rather than any extended plumes or feeding apparatus.

Snails are abundant in California reef areas. Many species are drably colored and rather inconspicuous, but

Other impressive shells of California reef snails are the beautifully sculpted Kellet's whelk and leafy hornmouth, the streamlined, darkly colored Ida's miter and California cone shell (which subdues its prey with a poison-injecting tooth), and the brilliantly colored, spiraled blue top snail and purple-ringed top snail.

Limpets are actually species of snails, members of the class of gastropods. Their shells are quite simple and lack the spiral design of

A chestnut cowry with a partially exposed mantle.

A Kellet's whelk laying eggs.

limpets do not possess similar markings, and giant keyhole limpets are not as heavy or as hard as abalone, the similarities in their overall shape and habitat preference make it easy to understand how divers mistake them for abalone. Although eaten in Japan, limpets are not usually considered a food source by Californians, and many new divers have experienced an embarrassing moment when asking an old pro what to do with their limpets.

Several species of **abalone** are common in state waters ranging from tidepools to at least 150 feet deep. Abalone are relatively slow-moving, reclusive animals that prefer to seek cover in the crevices of the reef during the day, and rarely leave its protection except to feed at night. They attach strongly to the rocky substrate with their muscular foot, which is bordered by a circular fringe of skin called the epipodium. Abalone feed by trapping algae under their foot, then scraping off portions of the algae with a toothed, tonguelike organ called a radula.

Abalone are gastropod mollusks with a single shell that covers the entire body. Properly preserved and finished abalone shells are an attractive decoration, especially the colorful, lustrous inner shell, called mother-of-pearl. A number of holes in the shell, called apertures, help to circulate water over the gills and serve as an excurrent opening for getting rid of waste. Most shells have an overall caplike shape, and appear much like the rocks upon which they live—many are even encrusted with worms. Because abalone blend in well with rocky bottoms, they are easy to overlook, though they become easier to find with practice. The shell varies considerably with species; some species have a shell that is thin, flat, and smooth, while the shell of others is thick and corrugated. The color and number of apertures also vary with species.

many other gastropods. These herbivorous animals are usually seen on rocks, where they graze upon algae. Some common limpets include the tiny **kelp limpets** (often seen on the stipes of featherboa kelp), and the rough, volcano, and giant keyhole limpets. **Rough keyhole limpets** often thwart hungry sea stars by extruding their slippery mantles over their shells and leaving no bare surface the sea star can grasp. **Volcano limpets** (recognizable by their pink shell with darker rays) instead try to outrun sea stars.

The largest of California limpets, **giant keyhole limpets** attain a shell diameter of up to 5 inches. The mantle extends over the shell and can be black, white, gray, or a mottled combination. The keyhole-like design created by the opening at the apex of the shell explains the origin of its name. These limpets are the bane of many beginning divers, who often mistake them for abalone. Although abalone and

An amazing variety of animals prey on abalone whenever the opportunity arises, including cabezon, sheephead, bat rays, sea lions, crabs, moray eels, and octopi. Like many mollusks, abalone are

Novice divers often mistake the giant keyhole limpet for an abalone.

Fish and Game Regulations

A spearfisher descends into a kelp forest.

As a responsible sportsman or sportswoman, you should familiarize yourself with the California Department of Fish and Game's sport fishing regulations before taking game of any sort. The first step is to make sure that you have purchased the appropriate fishing license. Licenses must always be carried along when you are taking game, and are available for a reasonable fee from most sporting goods stores. As of this writing, annual licenses for California residents are $25.70, while those for nonresidents are $69.55; other options, such as one-day licenses and discounts for eligible individuals, are also available. For questions about licensing, contact the Department of Fish and Game's License and Revenue Branch at:

Department of Fish and Game

License and Revenue Branch

3211 South Street

Sacramento, CA 95816

(916) 227-2244

You should be aware of the limits placed on taking the type of game you are interested in. These may include limits on:

- Species (some may not be taken).

- Size (there is often a minimum).

- Sex (e.g., sometimes reproductive females may not be taken).

- Number (there is often a maximum).

- Area (some places are protected and off-limits).

- Time of day and time of year.

- Methods and tools (there are often strict guidelines).

These limits are clearly outlined in a pamphlet entitled "California Sport Fishing Regulations," published by the California Department of Fish and Game. You can pick up a free copy at sporting goods stores or by contacting the Department of Fish and Game. Check the government section of your phone book for a local branch, or write or call the main office at:

Department of Fish and Game

P.O. Box 944209

Sacramento, CA 94244-2090

(916) 653-7664

Fish and game regulations have been set up to prevent overexploitation and depletion of marine resources. In order to protect your own right to continue to take game in California waters, and the rights and abilities of future generations, respect these regulations and report violations to California Department of Fish and Game officials at (800) 952-5400.

also considered a delicacy by humans. The taking of abalone is regulated by the California Department of Fish and Game. Size restrictions and bag limits are well enforced, and abalone hunters should familiarize themselves with any special restrictions that apply to their particular location—for example, scuba gear currently may not be used in the taking of abalone north of Yankee Point in Monterey County.

Of the seven common species in California—black, green, white (also called Sorenson), pink, pinto, flat, and red abalone—only red abalone may be legally harvested in California as of this writing. Attaining a diameter of more than 11 inches, **red abalone** are the world's largest abalone. These gastropods are characterized by their thick, dark black tentacles and the bright red margin along the growing edge of their shell. Red abs usually have three to five slightly elevated apertures, though as with most species, some older specimens possess fewer apertures. Inhabiting waters from Baja to Oregon, reds are normally encountered at depths of 20 to 100 feet south of Point Conception, while they are commonly found in the intertidal zone to the north. They are rarely taken in water warmer than 60°F, so the farther south you dive, the deeper you normally have to go to find them.

In order to be a legal "take," a red abalone must be at least 7 inches in its largest shell diameter; it takes a red ab about fifteen years to reach this size. Responsible divers take only abs that they have first measured with a calipered device, thereby never taking a "short." You are legally obligated to carry a measuring device with you in the water any time you are taking abs or any other game with size restrictions. Because abalone are hemophiliacs and will bleed to death if cut while being pried off rocks, it is illegal to take abalone with any instrument other than an approved tool called an abalone iron. Even when using an ab iron, which has rounded edges, take care not to accidentally cut the animal.

Fish and game laws become stricter when the animals become scarce. For example, the recent ban on the harvesting of green, pink, and white abalone was enacted because the numbers of these abalone have been seriously depleted by a combination of overharvesting, habitat disruption, and a poorly understood disease called withering syndrome, which causes an abalone's foot to atrophy and eventually results in the animal's death. These harvesting restrictions are necessary to protect surviving abalone and to allow the populations to recover. You should always make sure that you are familiar with and abide by current restrictions.

Nudibranchs are shell-less mollusks that are sometimes called sea slugs, an unappealing name that seems inappropriate for these attractive gastropods. Trying to describe a nudibranch to anyone who has never seen one underwater is a nearly impossible task, especially without the use of an accompanying photograph or drawing. Words alone simply do not do them justice, as many nudibranchs are considered to be among the most beautiful of marine animals. Ranging in length from less than a half inch to almost 2 feet, nudibranchs occur in an incredible diversity of striking shapes and colors. There are more than 160 species in California waters alone.

Nudibranchs can usually be distinguished by the presence, placement, or design of certain structures. "Rhinophores" are stalked sensory organs usually present as a pair at the top of or just behind the nudibranch's head; although their purpose is unclear, many scientists believe rhinophores are important for locating food and mates. "Cerata" are fingerlike or club-shaped respiratory structures on the back of many nudibranchs. In some species they are easily lost, apparently as a means of distracting potential predators. However, from the nudibranch's perspective there is good news: not only

An abalone grazes algae from the side of a rock.

A rainbow dendronotid climbs the shaft of a tube anemone, its favorite meal.

ing marine sponges; their radulae are broad with many teeth, and they lack strong jaws.

• **Dendronotid nudibranchs (suborder Dendronotacea):** Characterized by their highly branched cerata (hence the derivation of their name, which in Greek means "tree-back"), dendronotids also have long rhinophoral sheaths.

• **Aeolid nudibranchs (suborder Aeolidacea):** Aeolids have groups or rows of long, fingerlike, smooth cerata on their backs; the beautiful colors of these cerata often allow positive identification of species. The long rhinophores of aeolids are not retractable and occur in a number of shapes. Aeolids usually have long, graceful oral tentacles and very strong jaws, and most feed on hydroids and stalked bryozoans.

• **Arminid nudibranchs (suborder Arminacea):** Arminids are a difficult group to define, but they are very different from nudibranchs in the other suborders. Arminids have no sheaths to protect the rhinophores, nor do they have oral tentacles.

has it possibly escaped the jaws of death at the price of a few cerata, but in many cases the lost cerata can quickly be regenerated. The cerata of some nudibranchs contain stinging cells they have stolen from sea fans or other cnidarian prey. Many nudibranchs have graceful oral tentacles that extend forward from the front of their head. The structure of a nudibranch's radula, a tonguelike organ containing rows of teeth, is often indicative of the animal's feeding methods and diagnostic of the species; however, it is not a very useful distinguishing characteristic outside of a laboratory. The order Nudibranchia is subdivided into four suborders.

• **Dorid nudibranchs (suborder Doridacea):** Dorids possess rhinophores that, in many species, can be retracted into their body when threatened. Lacking true cerata, they instead usually have a circlet of gill plumes on their back; typically they are therefore much smoother in appearance than other nudibranchs. Many feed on encrust-

Thick-horned aeolids prey primarily on hydroids.

Nudibranchs are slow crawlers and generally poor swimmers, making one wonder how they survive in the sea. Some disguise themselves from predators by blending in with their surroundings, while the vivid coloration of others is thought to warn would-be predators of the nudibranch's defenses. Many nudibranchs simply do not taste good to most potential predators. The navanax, a close relative of nudibranchs, feasts quite readily on its nudibranch cousins—but then again, navanax also prey upon each other.

The species-specific structure of the radula helps each type of nudibranch secure its favorite foods. Some nudibranchs have a taste for cnidarians such as corals, anemones, and sea fans; amazingly, they are immune to the potent stinging nematocysts of these animals. These crafty nudibranchs often augment their own defenses with those of their cnidarian prey: the nematocysts migrate, somehow unfired, through the nudibranch's digestive system into the cerata. A predator foolish enough to take a bite of one of these animals gets a mouthful of fiery pain and quickly learns its lesson.

Most species of nudibranchs are hermaphroditic throughout their lives, whereas other species change from

The lacelike egg mass of a nudibranch.

male to female with age. Each species of nudibranch has a characteristic egg-laying pattern and color, often resulting in surprisingly beautiful lacelike or flowerlike egg masses.

While there are a great many beautiful nudibranchs, several common species are especially striking. These include the Spanish shawl, thick-horned aeolid, pugnacious aeolid, Macfarland's dorid, Hopkin's rose, California dorid, white-lined dirona, three-color polycera, Santa Barbara nudibranch, and rainbow dendronotid. One of the largest and most commonly seen species is the sea lemon or speckled sea lemon, whose color varies from burnt orange to deep yellow. This short list scarcely does justice to the multitude of magnificent nudibranchs.

Sea hares possess only a thin internal remnant of the shells characteristic of the gastropod class. This sometimes leads to confusion among nonscientists, but sea hares are descended from the same ancestors as other gastropods. Like

A sea lemon searches the reef for sponges to feed on.

octopi, sea hares are mollusks that have lost their shells over the course of evolution. Although sea hares are not closely related to octopi, both eject a purplish ink when threatened or roughly handled.

Like their close cousins the nudibranchs, sea hares are hermaphroditic. They are, however, incapable of self-fertilization and often mate in large groups. Living up to the reputation of their terrestrial namesakes, sea hares are incredibly prolific. They lay their eggs in huge quantities as an entangled mass of long yellow strings that is often as large as a basketball. Studies have shown that some sea hares produce as many as 95 million eggs a month for months on end. In fact, scientists have calculated that if just one adult laid its normal load of eggs and all were to survive and reproduce without predation, and their offspring were to survive and reproduce without predation, and so on, in just over a year the surface of the earth would be more than 6 feet deep in sea hares.

The two most commonly observed species are the California sea hare and the black sea hare. The California sea hare is characterized by its splotchy purplish or reddish body, and is usually smaller than the black sea hare, which is the world's largest gastropod, growing up to 3 feet long and weighing up to 30 pounds.

Often mistaken for large nudibranchs,

Santa Barbara arminid nudibranchs in southern California waters have cerata with bright blue tips, while those in northern California have white-tipped cerata.

California sea hares can eject a dark ink to confuse attackers.

Navanax are actually a type of sea hare. In fact, they are sometimes called bay sea hares. Navanax are carnivores that prey on nudibranchs, bubble shells, and other Navanax. Their eggs are laid in long, white, threadlike gelatinous strings, wadded up like a tangled ball of yarn; these egg masses are commonly sighted in reef areas throughout the year. Navanax reach a length of up to 7 inches, and vary in color with combinations of white, yellow, blue, and brown.

Many people are familiar with **scallops,** offered by their favorite seafood restaurants. No question about it, scallops are a culinary delight—but they are also a visual treat for divers. Many rocky reefs from Baja to British Columbia are home to rock scallops. These mollusks are bivalves, meaning they have two shells (called valves) that are hinged together and joined by a tough flexible ligament. The animal's soft body is protected within these shells, which can be tightly clamped together when the scallop senses danger.

Juvenile **rock scallops** are planktonic, but after they reach about 1 inch in diameter they settle down to a benthic existence. Young scallops then secrete a limestonelike substance that secures the lower shell to the rocky substrate where the animal will live its entire adult life. Adult rock scallops feed upon drifting plankton,

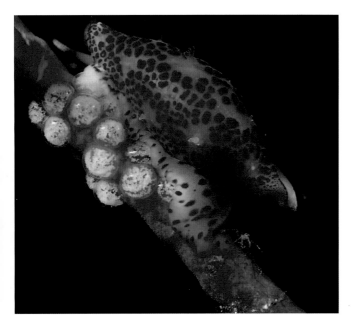

A simnia cowry lays pockets of eggs on its primary food source, a red gorgonian.

Two species are particularly notable in California reef communities. (Octopi are among those animals found in more than one type of habitat; also see Chapter 6.) They are the smaller and much more common two-spotted octopus and its larger cousin, the giant octopus. **Two-spotted octopi** rarely grow larger than 2 feet across, and are distinguishable by the prominent dark spot under each eye. They probe the reef at night for their prey of clams, crabs, and an occasional small fish. When a two-spotted octopus captures a clam, it will try to either forcefully open the shell to reach the meat, or bore a hole into the shell with its strong beak and inject a paralyzing venom.

The **giant octopus** is occasionally seen in northern California, but is only rarely encountered as far south as the

and are usually found in areas where heavy current and strong upwellings bring a steady supply of food. They are almost always horizontally oriented and strongly prefer areas that are shaded from direct sunlight. Rock scallops can be found from the intertidal zone to depths of approximately 180 feet, and usually attain diameters of 5 inches or more.

When adult rock scallops feed, they expose their colorful mantles and eyes. Scallops with bright orange mantles are males; those with brown to green mantles are females. The shell is almost always encrusted with both plants and animals. If you look closely at the edge of a scallop's shell, you will notice that it is lined with a row of dots. If you look even more closely, you'll realize that the dots are actually primitive eyes. These eyes are well developed and serve as a defense mechanism by sensing changes in light intensity; a scallop will quickly close its shell if it senses your shadow.

Although there are at least eight species of **octopi** reported in state waters, positive identification in the field is extremely difficult. In fact, even specialists have problems distinguishing among the various species, because different species have remarkably similar characteristics as adults. This similarity is interesting because their juvenile stages can be so different: some octopi have a planktonic stage that lasts several weeks, while other species are benthic immediately upon hatching.

A navanax laying strings of eggs.

Channel Islands. While giant octopi commonly attain a weight of up to 150 pounds in the waters of the Pacific Northwest, in California they rarely grow larger than 30 or 40 pounds. Although once called "devilfish," these octopi are very docile animals, and are not at all like the monsters of Hollywood sea lore. In fact, octopi tend to be extremely shy, and will typically withdraw into their den or a nearby crevice upon sighting a diver.

Octopi are nocturnal animals and are most frequently seen by night divers. However, upon a thorough examination of the cracks and crevices of the reef, a diver can often locate an octopus resting at the mouth of its den during daylight. The den is usually surrounded by a mound of empty shells, which are the discarded remains of prey. This pile of debris is called a midden, or midden heap.

Octopi normally move by crawling along the seafloor on their tentacles. The underside of each of the eight tentacles is lined with two rows of sucker cups. An octopus can draw up the centers of these cups, resulting in a vacuum that creates suction. The suction is quite strong—a 40-pound pull is necessary to release the suction grip of a 3-foot octopus. In addition to grasping, the

The brilliant color of a male rock scallop's mantle rivals that of surrounding *Corynactis* anemones.

A two-spotted octopus spreads out over a bed of brittle stars.

A giant octopus curiously observes a diver.

suckers have sensory functions and are used to distinguish taste (sweet, sour, and bitter) and texture (rough or smooth), but do not seem able to determine the size or shape of an object.

When in need of speed to escape a predator such as a moray eel, an octopus can create a jet engine–style thrust by opening its mantle and contracting it forcefully, blowing water out of its siphon. The siphon is highly directional, so the animal can control where it goes. An octopus can also emit a cloud of ink when threatened by a moray or other predator. This ink serves not so much as a visual smoke screen as an attempt to dull the olfactory sense of the eel as the octopus swims away—a moray relies heavily upon its sense of smell, and when this sense is blocked, the moray is severely hindered.

Masters of camouflage, octopi are also capable of melting into the background by rapidly changing their coloration, the texture of their skin, their shape, or any combination of these. Aided by the lack of an internal skeleton, octopi can mold their body into almost any background. These Houdinis can easily squeeze through any opening large enough for the only hard part of their body, the beak. A 30- or 40-pound octopus can easily crawl through an opening the size of a half dollar.

Octopi and other cephalopods, such as squid and cuttlefish, are the most advanced invertebrate animals. Their vision is highly developed and may be as sensitive as the vision of many vertebrates. By far the most intelligent invertebrates, in captivity some species have demonstrated an ability to learn and possibly even to reason.

For many years **barnacles** were thought to be mollusks, but in 1830 a British biologist pointed out their many similarities to crustaceans. Barnacles develop from an egg into a larval stage, similar to lobsters, crabs, and other crustaceans. They also have the jointed appendages that are characteristic of crustaceans. Displaying the typical features of its class only during the larval stage, once it is an adult a barnacle is permanently hidden within its shelled fortress.

Barnacles live in habitats ranging from intertidal areas to the skin of whales. **Giant acorn barnacles** are often found on exposed, current-swept seamounts. This species can be distinguished from its close relatives both by its habitat (it is not found in intertidal areas) and by its bright orange "lips," which are especially colorful in young specimens. Like other barnacles, the giant acorn barnacle cements itself to the substrate when it settles to the bottom after its free-swimming larval stage; as an adult it therefore depends on currents to carry food within its reach. Food is captured with the barnacle's feathery feet (cirripedia), which are extended out of the shell through the mantle opening. The feet are repeatedly drawn through the water in a rhythmic sweeping motion to catch food particles, then

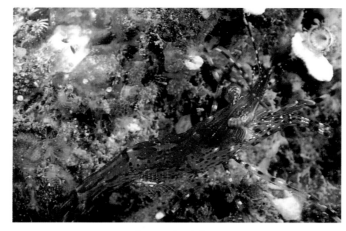
A coonstripe shrimp.

drawn into the shell where the food can be ingested. To the boating crowd, barnacles are usually no more than a major nuisance. But to divers their delicate feeding behavior can be fascinating to observe and photograph.

Lobsters, like crabs, shrimp, and barnacles, are crustaceans. But whether the **California spiny lobster** is, in fact, a lobster is a point of some debate. Unlike the Maine lobster, the California spiny lobster lacks a large pinching claw, although the female possesses a small pincer on the last pair of walking legs. Oddly enough, many people refer to the spiny lobster as a crayfish because of its lack of claws—despite the fact that freshwater crayfish *do* possess claws.

Known to inhabit the cracks and crevices of rocky reefs from Point Arguello to Baja, the California spiny lobster is believed to live up to 100 years or longer. To reach sexual maturity, it must survive a minimum of seven years. During spawning, which occurs from May through July, males deposit strings of sperm packets on the abdomen of females. When a female lays her eggs, she digs a hole in the packets to fertilize the eggs. She carries the eggs (which hatch in about ten weeks) in grapelike clusters on small abdominal legs called swimmerets. The larvae are planktonic for up to eight months before settling to the bottom, where they spend the rest of their lives seeking food such as snails, sand dollars, shellfish, and detritus.

Exactly where the best place is to find lobsters of legal size is hotly debated by California divers. At different times over the course of most years, legal-sized "bugs," as they are often called, can be found at depths ranging from tidepools to water much deeper

A California spiny lobster ventures from a protective crevice.

California Marine Life

than sport divers go. During daylight hours, lobsters are usually found in holes with only their antennae projecting past the opening. At night they leave the recesses of the reef to scavenge. Finding them is not the same as catching them; by rapidly tucking their tails, lobsters can propel themselves backward for short distances at a rate much faster than many divers realize.

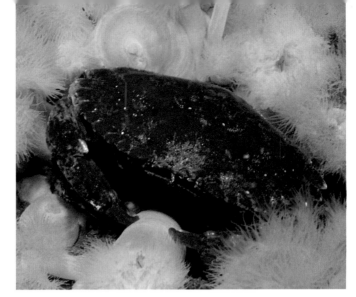

A red crab amongst snow-white *Metridium* anemones.

Whether gaming or filming, you'll probably want to wear thick durable gloves if you decide to handle a lobster. Both the antennae and the body are well armed with sharp spines. You will also want to avoid the severe pinch a lobster can deliver by curling up around your fingers; avoid placing an idle finger too close to its mandibles (jaw) or grabbing its antennae. Novice bug hunters often make the mistake of grabbing a lobster by the end of an antenna. Unfortunately, the antennae break off easily, resulting in a frustrated diver and a lobster without a vital component of its defenses. Grabbing or pinning the body is a much more reliable method, though it isn't always easy to do.

Like other crustaceans described in the order Decapoda, such as lobsters, crayfish, and crabs, shrimp possess ten legs, which are attached to their thoracic region. **Red rock shrimp** are the most commonly encountered species of shrimp in southern California. These bright red shrimp aggregate around moray eels and rid the eels' skin of harmful creatures and dead tissues. Red rock shrimp are usually seen scurrying about the skin of the eel, and if you are patient and lucky, you may even see one dart inside the mouth of an eel to clean the eel's

teeth and inner mouth. the shrimp will not enter until the moray opens its mouth quite wide in a display that is believed to be a message to the shrimp saying, "Now is the time I want my teeth and mouth cleaned, and I won't eat you." A classic case of symbiosis, both the eel and the shrimp benefit from their relationship: The shrimp gain both food (in the form of parasites and dead tissue they find on the eels) and protection (by the mere presence of the eels), while the eels benefit from the removal of potentially harmful creatures and dead tissues.

Noticed by divers for their colorful patterns, **coonstripe shrimp** are also popular among seafood connoisseurs. Inhabiting intertidal areas from Monterey northward, they have a red body decorated with a series of blue stripes. Coonstripe shrimp reach a length of nearly 3 inches.

For many years, divers, submarine operators, and scientists were puzzled by certain rapid-fire popping noises that originated underwater. The culprits were eventually discovered to be **snapping shrimp**, the noisiest of the California shrimp. With massive claws cocked, they lie in wait by their rocky burrows, snapping their claws shut when small fish pass nearby. The resultant shock wave is not only powerful enough to stun and bring down the fish, it can also shatter a scratched piece of glass. If a shrimp loses its trigger claw, it will not starve; the other claw simply grows larger to replace it. Usually living in pairs, snapping shrimp inhabit rocky intertidal burrows as well as sponge cavities and kelp holdfasts.

Red rock shrimp prepare to clean a pair of moray eels.

Crabs are essential members of California rocky reef communities, readily feeding on a wide variety of foods, including small invertebrates and fish, plants, and dead animals. In turn, the crabs are preyed upon by octopi and many species of fishes, including moray eels and bottom-dwelling sharks such as horn sharks and swell sharks. Among the many species of crabs that inhabit rocky reefs, some of the most noticeable are hermit crabs (discussed in Chapter 3), porcelain crabs, red crabs, and lithoid crabs. **Porcelain crabs** can easily be recognized by their flat, smooth body, the one pair of antennae between their eyes, and the porcelainlike appearance of the body carapace. These crabs have the useful ability to detach their own claws during a battle, leaving behind a pincer that keeps pinching the opponent as the crab makes a getaway. Different species of porcelain crabs with overlapping ranges can be distinguished by their different colorations: for example, one (*Petrolisthes eriomerus*) has mouthparts and claws with patches of brilliant blue, another (*P. cinctipes*) is marked with reddish-orange, and a third (*P. manimaculis*) has blue mouthparts and red on its claws. It is thought that these bright colors help the crabs avoid wasting time trying to mate with the wrong species; during courtship males wave their mouthparts and claws at attractive females, flashing the colors that denote their species and suitability for mating. In addition to filter-

A knobby sea star near a golden gorgonian.

feeding, as most porcelain crabs do, *P. eriomerus* uses large tufts of fur on the bottom of its claws to mop up food from rock surfaces.

Red rock crabs are distinguished by their red color and claws with black tips. As in all cancer crabs, the front margin of the carapace has many serrated, toothlike projections. Red rock crabs, sometimes called red crabs, reach a diameter of 6 inches and are a valuable food source. This nocturnal species is sometimes confused with *Pleuroncodes planipes*, also commonly called a red crab. *P. planipes* is a deepwater species that is usually found far out to sea. However, at times (often when sea surface temperatures are unusually high), innumerable crabs of this species gather in reef communities and on sandy plains, shortly after which they are often washed up onto beaches by the thousands. Exactly when and why they come into shallow water are questions that are not well understood in the scientific community.

The odd-looking **hairy lithoid crab**, also called the furry crab, can sometimes be found clinging to the underside of rocks in shallow waters. These flattened crabs are covered with thick, short, brownish hair that may actually help the crabs stick to rocks by forming a slight suction. Hairy lithoid crabs grow less than an inch long. They feed by straining plankton from the water using the long hairs near their mouth, and sometimes also graze on plants or animals.

A hairy hermit crab.

Courting bat stars.

Numerous species of **sea stars** in a rainbow of colors inhabit California's rocky reef communities. Radially symmetrical in their adult stage, as are all other echinoderms, most sea stars have arms in multiples of fives radiating out from the central disc. Many have tiny plierslike organs called pedicellariae that help protect the animal by keeping the warty skin free of debris. Like other echinoderms, sea stars move on rows of tiny tube feet by the action of a water vascular system unique to this phylum.

Sea stars are key predators in the rocky reef ecosystem, consuming bivalves at a particularly voracious rate. Two somewhat contradictory theories describe their method of getting to the meat of a bivalve. One theory suggests that the sea star grasps opposite sides of the bivalve's shell with its tube feet, eventually forcing the shell partially open as it overpowers its victim. The second theory claims that the sea star forces the bivalve closed, preventing access to oxygenated water; eventually the victim must force its own shell open or suffocate. Placing the stomach against the ligament that joins the bivalve's shells will further weaken the animal, eventually allowing the sea star easy access to the meat within. Alternatively, the sea star may be able to insert its stomach through a tiny opening between the shells, secreting digestive enzymes that begin to digest the soft tissues of its prey. When eating, the sea star may turn its own stomach inside out to reach into the shell.

Perhaps the best-known California sea star is the **knobby star**, sometimes called the giant star or giant-spined star. Each white spine of the knobby star is surrounded by a bright blue circle. Reaching a diameter of 18 inches, the knobby sea star resembles the **ochre star**, but the colors of the spines of ochre stars range from yellow to orange, brown, blue, purple, and red. Ochre stars are the more common of the two species, especially in intertidal areas. They are known as a keystone species because as a predator they play a key role in structuring the ecosystem. Their absence quickly leads to visible changes, including shifts in the numbers, types, and dominance of other species found there.

Several species of sea stars possess more than five arms. The **six-rayed star** has, as its name suggests, six arms. A group of sea stars commonly called sun stars has eight to twenty-four arms. The species of sun stars most often encountered are the orange sun star, the sunflower star, the morning sun star, and the rose star. Sun stars are relatively fast-moving sea stars that crawl quickly across the bottom, devouring prey— including other sea stars—as they go.

Other reef community sea stars are bat stars, red stars, fragile stars, and vividly colored blood stars. **Bat stars** have a thick body and webbing between their short, thick arms. Usually red on the upper surface with a yellowish underside, their coloration varies from

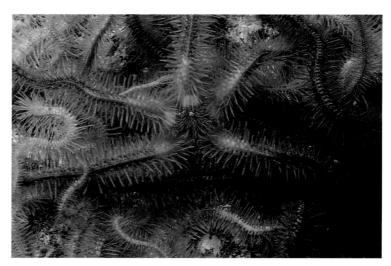

Some species of brittle stars display a rainbow of colors.

purple to green to red to a mottled combination. A bat star will eat almost anything; while crawling along the bottom it will commonly extrude its own stomach to absorb and digest organic debris.

Red stars are bright red with a series of small plates bordering the arms. They are easily distinguishable from red-colored bat stars because they lack the webbing between the arms that is characteristic of bat stars. The arms of red stars are also considerably thinner. Red stars prey on sponges, bryozoans, and sea pens, and occasionally scavenge dead animals.

Fragile stars are a mottled red and gray, and are unusual in that their thin, round arms are often of different lengths. Although all sea stars are able to regenerate lost parts, the fragile stars are by far the fastest to do so. A lost arm may develop into a complete animal, though perfect symmetry is rarely obtained. In most species of sea stars, at least one-fifth of the central disc must be attached to the arm before regeneration is possible, and even then the process can take up to a year.

Blood stars are a vivid orange to red, although smaller specimens are occasionally gray, tan, or purple. Their slender, smooth arms lack both spines and pedicellariae. Blood stars feed on bacteria, detritus, and other tiny particles that become trapped in the mucus on their arms. Unlike most species of sea stars, female blood stars carry their eggs until the young are hatched.

Brittle stars are so named because their rather delicate arms tend to break off at the slightest disturbance. This wonderful defensive adaptation allows the brittle star to escape a predator with the loss of only an arm or two, and the arms are quickly regenerated from the central disc. Brittle stars are also sometimes called serpent stars because of the characteristic snakelike motion of their arms. Although these names are used interchangeably, those species with arms

that are shed more easily are generally called brittle stars, whereas those with less fragile arms are sometimes referred to as serpent stars.

Brittle stars resemble sea stars, but they belong to a different class of echinoderms. Brittle stars can be distinguished from sea stars by (1) their long, thin, flexible arms that radiate from a small central disc, and which are waved about in a snakelike fashion; (2) the fact that their arms are not "webbed" and are instead sharply set off from the small central disc; and (3) the lack of an ambulacral groove on the underside of each arm. (An ambulacral groove is a channel on the underside of each arm in sea stars that contains the tube feet.)

Many species of brittle stars are found in California, but telling them apart underwater is rather difficult, as individuals of the same species are often different colors. Colors typically vary from a wide range of solid colors to mottled combinations.

Some brittle stars are detritivores that feed upon particulate matter that collects on the bottom, while others are suspension-feeders that capture microplankton with their long arms; some are also active carnivores. Sensitive to both sunlight and the artificial lights used by divers, many brittle stars spend their days in well-secluded areas, buried in the sand or hiding under rocks until nighttime, when they emerge to

Sunflower stars may grow up to 3 feet in diameter.

At times, brittle stars become so numerous in the Channel Islands that they seem to cover every surface, including this bat star.

feed. It is unusual to see many species of brittle stars out in the open during daylight hours, although there are exceptions, such as in the California Channel Islands.

Every now and then, brittle star populations grow explosively in areas such as the California Channel Islands. In places where brittle star sightings during the day are normally rare, thousands upon thousands of brittle stars dominate the reefs. Golden sea fans and red sea fans become transformed into homes for dozens of brittle stars, and dense aggregations of brittle stars of all imaginable colors carpet the seafloor everywhere you look. Such mysterious population explosions are yet another example of the highly dynamic, ever-changing nature of the marine ecosystem.

Sea urchins are echinoderms that are described in the class Echinoidea, as are sand dollars. In addition to the five-sided (pentamerous) symmetry displayed by other echinoderms, echinoids are characterized by their highly movable tube feet and spines. Five species of sea urchins are frequently seen in California waters, three of them in rocky reef communities. Generally distinguishable by color, they are the giant red urchin, the green urchin, and the purple urchin. (The other two species of commonly seen sea urchins are sand-dwellers; see Chapter 6.)

Green urchins inhabit the waters of northern California

and are very easy to recognize because of their short spines. The **giant red urchin** varies in color from bright red to black, and is the largest, reaching a diameter of up to 7 inches. **Purple urchins** are smaller, rarely attaining a diameter of more than 3 inches. The most abundant of the urchins, they frequently occur in dense populations in kelp forests and on large boulders on exposed coasts in the intertidal zone.

Urchins are predominantly grazers, feeding on a variety of algae. They eat using a complex five-toothed structure in their mouth called Aristotle's lantern, which comes together in a manner similar to the way a bird's beak closes. The teeth can be extended or withdrawn into the mouth and are quite strong, allowing the urchin to scrape algae off rocks and to capture small fragments of organic matter. Purple urchins can use their teeth and spines to burrow into solid rock, sometimes growing so large over time that they cannot escape through the original opening and must resort to suspension-feeding instead of grazing.

Sea urchins play a significant role in the ecology of the kelp forest and reef communities. In healthy kelp forests, they feed primarily on the shed of kelp, but when the urchin population outgrows its normal food supply, they begin to feed upon the holdfasts of living kelp plants and can ultimately destroy entire kelp forests (see Chapter 4). Urchin

California moray eels often hide within recesses of the reef.

Where to Look

Just because an animal is known to be common and to live in a given ecosystem doesn't mean that all you need do to see it is fall off a boat and land in the habitat with your eyes open. The frustration of never having sighted a given species such as a lobster, moray eel, wolf-eel, or octopus is especially common to new divers who often have to endure sour feelings as they listen to old salts discuss all the animals they saw that the new divers missed. The ability to find a particular species on any given dive is a matter of knowing where to look and having a bit of luck. Of course, the more you know about the habits of a particular creature, the better your luck will be.

One of the biggest differences between old salts and new divers is that the former know how helpful it is to get down low to the bottom and look under ledges and back into crevices in the reef matrix when they are searching for animals like lobster, octopi, abalone, and others. Many new divers tend to hover above the reef. There's no question there is a lot to see from above, but there is often far more to see if you look under, between, behind, and inside. The matrix of the reef is filled with creatures that are difficult to see when you are hovering above the reef.

Take your time: look low, in, around, beneath, behind, and under, and be all eyes. Odds are that you will make lots of new and exciting discoveries for yourself.

populations are controlled mainly by their predators, including sea otters and several species of fishes. These predators bump the urchins off the rocks and then bite into the vulnerable, exposed tube feet.

Swimmers and divers tend to think of urchins as animals to be avoided whenever possible. Urchins are well known and intensely disliked for the pain caused by their long, sharp spines. These spines are coated with mucus, and wounds often become infected. Fortunately for those who frequent California waters, the spines of urchins found here are not as sharp as those of many tropical urchins, nor do they tend to cause as much pain.

A relatively new diver will often ask, "What are those things that live on the bottom and look like cucumbers? I must have seen at least twenty-five." The answer to this question is "Sea cucumbers." **Sea cucumbers** are echinoderms that belong to a different class than sea stars, brittle stars, or urchins: class Holothuroidea. Sea cucumbers are important detritivores, meaning that they eat primarily dead and decaying organic material. In California reef communities they feed primarily on kelp shed.

Sea cucumbers are elongate and sausage-shaped, and their skin is often covered with warty projections or soft spines, or both. Unlike that of other echinoderms, the skeleton of a sea cucumber is extremely reduced and the body is generally soft and flexible. When threatened, however, cucumbers can contract their muscles and eject water from body tissues, becoming shorter, thicker, and much harder. In

Purple sea urchins graze on an algae-covered rock.

an even more fascinating defense tactic, some species of cucumbers can expel their sticky internal organs to distract potential predators, then crawl away to hide and grow a new set of innards.

Three common species of sea cucumbers in California waters are the warty sea cucumber, the California cucumber, and a smaller species called the white sea cucumber. **Warty sea cucumbers** are chestnut brown with black-tipped "warts" all over their body, and reach a length of up to 10 inches. **California cucumbers** are brown or reddish-brown and covered with pointed, cone-shaped projections. Growing to 16 inches long, these are the largest sea cucumbers found in state waters. Like warty sea cucumbers, California cucumbers use the modified tube feet that surround their mouth to ingest large amounts of sediment, extracting nutrients from the detritus as it passes through their guts. **White sea cucumbers** are light orange to white with long, nonretractable spines covering their bodies, and resemble centipedes. They reach a maximum length of about 4 inches. Unlike California and warty sea cucumbers, white sea cucumbers are nocturnal filter-feeders, feeding on tiny plankton and detritus trapped within their mouth tentacles.

Tunicates are invertebrate chordates. This may sound confusing, but it simply means that although tunicates display the defining characteristics of chordate development,

A sea cucumber rejects its innards in a surprising self-defense ploy.

they do not have a backbone. Tunicates can be either solitary, such as the stalked tunicate, or colonial, such as the light-bulb tunicate. Other commonly seen species are the sea pork, sea peach, glassy, and elephant ear tunicates. As these common names imply, tunicates occur in a variety of shapes. Most California species are white, yellow, or orange. Tunicates feed by pumping water through their bodies and removing small particulate matter. Their ability to shoot streams of water from their siphons has earned them the common name sea squirts.

Fishes

At least 550 species of fishes inhabit California's coastal waters. These are divided among three major classes: Agnatha (lampreys and hagfishes), osteichthyes (bony fishes), and Chondrichthyes (sharks and rays). Agnathids are the most ancient of the fishes. For many years it was believed that their development was first followed by that of the Chondrichthyes fishes, and that members of the class Osteichthyes had only relatively recently appeared on earth. However, newer discoveries of ancient fossilized Osteichthyes fishes have cast doubt on whether Chondrichthyes fishes did, in fact, evolve before the Osteichtheids—demonstrating once again that what appears to be scientific fact is rarely a certainty, and there are often unexpected discoveries awaiting.

The ancient agnathids are quite rare in California and generally inhabit very deep waters. Members of this class include hagfishes, slime eels, and lampreys. Ancestors of extant agnathids were the first vertebrates. Agnathids have a cartilaginous skeleton, but lack the jaws and paired fins of more advanced fishes.

The class Chondrichthyes includes approximately 850 species of sharks, rays, and skates, found in waters around the world. Many people don't realize that animals as different as bat rays and great white sharks are

A warty sea cucumber grazes on algae and detritus.

closely related. United primarily by the fact that their skeletons are made of cartilage (very similar to the cartilage found in our own ears and nose), fishes in the class Chondrichthyes are commonly referred to as cartilaginous fishes. No matter how large a whale shark or how small a bat ray, Chondrichthyes fish have not a single bone in their entire skeleton.

Although agnathids also have a cartilaginous skeleton, they are not commonly referred to as cartilaginous fishes. More advanced than agnathids, cartilaginous fishes possess both jaws and paired fins. Most have several unprotected gill slits on both sides of the head. Sharks, rays, and skates lack scales, but modified toothlike structures called dermal denticles cover and protect their skin. Unlike those of bony fishes, the mouths of most cartilaginous fishes are located below their head, with teeth that are not firmly attached to the jaw. The tails of cartilaginous fishes are generally asymmetrical, with vertebrae that extend into the upper lobe of the tail. Cartilaginous fishes have internal fertilization, reproduce by copulation, and juveniles are usually born live.

The class Osteichthyes (called bony or teleost fishes) includes all fishes with a bony skeleton. With more than 17,000 species worldwide, the vast majority of fishes are bony fishes. This group includes the bright orange garibaldi

Despite their appearance, these light-bulb tunicates are chordates.

and other familiar and frequently seen fishes, such as gobies, rockfish, sheephead, and lingcod.

Bony fishes have jaws, paired appendages, and a bony skeleton. Their single gill slits are covered and protected by a bonelike operculum, used to pump oxygenated water over the gills. Their skin is protected by true scales that are usually somewhat rounded and larger than the dermal denticles of cartilaginous fishes. Owing to the development of an air bladder (a gas-filled sac), bony fishes are able to adjust their buoyancy, allowing them to hover at whatever depth they choose. Their body design usually includes a mouth at the front of the head (the terminal position), teeth that are firmly attached in jaw sockets, and a symmetrical tail with vertebrae ending before the tail starts. Most bony fishes reproduce by spawning, and the young generally hatch from eggs.

	BONY FISH	**CARTILAGINOUS FISH**
Scales	Scales.	Dermal denticles.
Gills	One on each side of head. Protected by operculum.	Five to seven gill slits on each side. Uncovered.
Air bladder	Usually present.	Absent.
Reproduction	Spawning. Young hatch from eggs.	Copulation. Most are born live (some hatch).
Anatomy	Mouth at front of head. Tail symmetrical. Backbone ends at tip of tail. Teeth in jaw sockets. Segmented skull.	Mouth usually below head. Tail usually asymmetrical. Backbone extends into tail. Teeth not firmly affixed. Nonsegmented skull.

Cartilaginous Fishes of the Rocky Reefs

Of the more than 370 species of sharks found worldwide, only a few are commonly sighted in California reefs. However, these offer enough diversity to provide interesting insights into the mysterious world of sharks. One species often seen resting on rocks ranging from Baja to Point Conception is the **horn shark**. Horn sharks are named for the horny ridges over their eyes and the white spinelike appendage that protrudes from each dorsal fin, discouraging potential predators. Horn sharks are also characterized by their short blunt heads, pursed lips, and distinct ridges above the eyes. A horn shark is tan with black spots and grows up to 4 feet long.

Horn sharks are docile, bottom-dwelling creatures that feed upon crustaceans, mollusks, echinoderms, and small reef fish. They are equipped with two distinct types of teeth: front teeth with sharp cusps used for grasping prey, and rear teeth with rounded cusps used for crushing. You may occasionally notice a horn shark with a slightly purple tinge to its dorsal spine and/or teeth. This coloration is due to the shark's diet, as the dorsal spine and teeth of a shark that feeds heavily on purple urchins take on the purplish hue of the prey. Primarily nocturnal feeders, during daylight hours horn sharks are usually seen resting on the bottom, often with their heads comically stuck under a ledge or blade of kelp as they shield their eyes from the light.

Divers often find horn shark egg casings resting on the rocky bottom or slightly entangled in kelp. The dark brown, corkscrew-shaped

DID YOU KNOW?

. . . THE PLURAL FORM "FISH" USUALLY REFERS TO A BUNCH OF INDIVIDUAL FISH, WHILE THE FORM "FISHES" REFERS TO MORE THAN ONE SPECIES OF FISH.

A young horn shark emerges from its egg casing.

eggs are about 5 inches long and have a leathery look. They typically hatch in the early spring.

Found from Monterey southward, **swell sharks** are named for their ability to swallow large amounts of water and/or air when threatened. This dramatically increases the sharks' size and helps them wedge into cracks, making it difficult or impossible for their natural predators to dislodge them.

Like horn sharks, swell sharks are docile, bottom-dwelling, nocturnal animals. Although they are generally thought to be solitary creatures, they occasionally congregate in some areas. Preferring to spend the day nestled away in caves or crevices, swell sharks pursue a diet of small reef fish at night. Reaching a maximum length of about 3 feet, they can be distinguished by their yellowish-brown body covered with brown spots, their flattened head, and their wide mouth. Beware: just because swell sharks are small doesn't mean that they are not well equipped to defend themselves. It is not a good idea to harass these sharks in order to make them inflate their bodies. More than one diver has lost a fingernail or fingertip to the teeth of an agitated swell shark.

Among the most handsome of sharks, **leopard sharks** are the largest of the commonly seen reef sharks in California. Both sexes have a slender, brownish-gray body speckled with prominent black crossbars and black spots. Females reach a length of nearly 6 feet, while males rarely exceed 3 feet. Leopard sharks prey on some small fish but primarily on benthic invertebrates, nipping off clam siphons and sucking up buried worms.

Like other California reef sharks, these animals are extremely docile, and usually flee upon sighting a diver. When breeding, concentrations of fifty or more of these sharks are occasionally found in shallow water just beyond the surf zone and in some protected coves. During such times the sharks are easily observed because they show little, if any, reaction to the presence of swimmers or divers. Leopard sharks breed in back bays and estuaries.

People are often surprised by the beautiful face of a leopard shark.

The **great white shark**, or white shark, is referred to as the white pointer or white death in Australia and New Zealand, and known as *Carcharodon carcharias* in scientific circles. No matter what you call it, the name alone conjures up an image of terror in the mind of expert and layperson alike. And yes, it is true, great white sharks inhabit California waters. Relatively little is known about these mysterious animals; despite a growing body of research, there are huge gaps in our knowledge of their natural history. It is likely that our fear of white sharks is more closely related to media exploitation and our natural fear of the unknown than it is to the true nature of an animal that is not well understood. Given some fear to play upon, there seems to be no limit to the extent the entertainment industry will go in distorting the true nature of animals so long as the end result increases box office appeal and the accountant's all-important bottom line.

Of twenty-seven unprovoked great white shark attacks that have occurred in North Pacific waters between 1985 and 1996, only one attack was fatal, and the majority (56 percent) of victims suffered only minor wounds, if any. Considering that despite their presence here, there are very few attacks on divers, surfers, and swimmers, it seems that far too much has been written about great white sharks' predatory capabilities. However, in light of their size alone, it is equally fair to say that one could never really write enough. The large size attained by great white sharks certainly contributes to Hollywood's ability to create and perpetuate their menacing reputation. Taken in waters off the coast of Cuba, the largest reported great white was 21 feet long and weighed 7,100 pounds (although there is some controversy over the accuracy of these measurements—the largest well-documented great white shark was just under 18 feet long). While those numbers are certainly impressive, it is their girth that makes white sharks so overwhelming. It is no exaggeration that a very large person with exceptionally long arms could not reach around the record-sized shark, or even one half that size, and join hands either 1 foot behind the snout or 1 foot in front of the tail.

Great white sharks have a heavy, spindle-shaped body with a moderately long, conical snout, and look roughly like enormous overpressurized footballs. Their back and sides are black to slate-gray, while their underbelly is white, hence their name. This color pattern is known as countershading and is

The face of a swell shark.

Great white sharks are perfectly designed for their role as apex predators that prey on marine mammals.

period of time, and a well-designed circulatory system that allows them to keep their muscles, brain, and eyes warmer by retaining the body heat they produce through metabolism.

The physiology and behavior of great white sharks indicate that they are primarily visual hunters, although they also use their highly developed sense of smell. Recent research has shown that, when given a choice between two different decoys with no odor or electrical field, white sharks will preferentially

common among many species of pelagic fishes. Counter-shading allows animals to blend in with the surrounding water colors, a competitive advantage that helps them remain undetected by both predators and prey. When viewed from above, white sharks are colored to blend in with the darker seafloor, whereas when viewed from below, they blend in with lighter water colors toward the surface. This is not to say that a white shark will go completely undetected by potential prey, but it will probably go unnoticed a little longer than it might without this color pattern. In many cases, it is likely that the prey of a great white shark never sees its predator until after a strike has been made.

Great white sharks are built for rapid bursts of speed that help make them formidable predators. Although it can be difficult to focus your attention on the tail end of a great white shark in the wild, if you do so you will notice that the tail is nearly symmetrical and that it seems disproportionately large. The shape of the tail (called homocercal) is like that of many of the fastest swimmers in the ocean, including mako sharks and mackerel, and the size of the tail is another indication that white sharks are capable of rapid acceleration. Other adaptations for speed include large gill slits that enable white sharks to metabolize a lot of oxygen in a very short

approach a seal-shaped object before they will approach other decoys at the water surface. This gives credence to the well-known hypothesis that surfers and kayakers are attacked because of their resemblance to seals from below. However, the sharks were observed to approach, investigate, and often "taste" objects of all shapes and sizes. This may explain why white sharks rely on the element of surprise for successful attacks, and therefore can afford to waste little time examining their targets before attacking. It may be for this reason that many apparently unpalatable victims, including inanimate objects, sea otters, birds, and humans, are often bitten once or twice and then abandoned rather than eaten.

It is difficult to imagine that an animal as huge, dangerously dentured, and built for speed as the great white shark would need to rely on surprise for a successful attack. However, observers have noticed sea lions ignoring, or even harassing, a great white shark once its location was known. These bold mammals must be confident of their safety in teasing a great white shark, for they are counted among the shark's preferred prey. While juvenile white sharks are known to prey upon rays and a wide variety of bony fishes such as sturgeon, salmon, halibut, hake, rockfish, lingcod, cabezon, mackerel, and tuna, adult white sharks prefer to dine on marine mammals and an occasional shark. White sharks seem to have a taste for the energy-rich fat layer that insulates many marine mammals. They have been observed feeding on the blubber but avoiding the muscle layer of whales, and often prey on fatty mammals such as seals and sea lions while rarely eating (although sometimes attacking) leaner animals such as sea otters and birds. It may be our relative leanness that makes human fatalities due to white shark attacks so rare.

Films showing white sharks biting objects such as swim steps and shark cages have given many people the false impression that white sharks will eat anything. A more accurate analysis of the facts indicates that the biting is directly related to the electrical field given off by the metallic swim steps and shark cages when they are submerged in saltwater. Scientists know that some sharks can detect electrical fields that are 10,000 times fainter than those that can be detected by any other known group of animals (although the electrosensory organs of great white sharks are poorly developed compared to those of many other sharks). All animals, which obviously includes potential prey, constantly emit an electrical field. For millions of years the response of biting anything that produced an electrical field has produced food for sharks. In essence the sharks, expecting food, are confused or tricked into biting inanimate objects that emit electrical currents in seawater. In nearly all the shark attack sequences you see in films, the sharks have been aroused not only by the electrical field but also by plenty of bait to encourage them to display their "vicious" behavior.

Watching a great white shark engulf bait 2 feet in front of your face is the experience of a lifetime.

The underside of a great white shark is lightly colored, helping this predator disappear into the light waters above when seen from below.

Great white sharks range throughout tropical and temperate waters around the world, although they are believed to prefer the waters of coastal areas and offshore islands of continental shelves in temperate seas. Some large specimens have been taken in gill nets miles from the nearest land, but it is generally accepted that though some white sharks venture forth into deep ocean basins, breeding populations exist only close to shore. There is evidence that some white sharks travel along migration routes, returning to certain locations at regular intervals. Some great whites apparently also occasionally choose a home site, where they stay for a few days or weeks before moving on. White sharks usually roam singly, although they are occasionally observed in pairs and are known to congregate near offshore islands that have large populations of seals and sea lions. Smaller white sharks are generally observed to reluctantly give way to larger animals when they are competing for food, but injurious battles and bloodshed among great whites are rare.

Like many other species of sharks, whites appear to be sexually segregated at certain times and in certain places. Exactly when, where, and how they mate are a matter of some speculation. Females are often marked by mating scars, the result of biting males during copulation. In many species of sharks, the male is believed to bite the female on or near the pectoral fin in order to get a grip on her before twisting underneath in an effort to insert a clasper. The skin of female white sharks, like that of

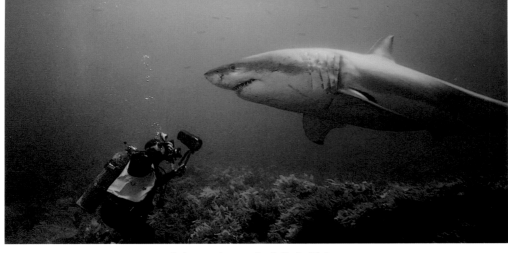

A photographer gets the thrill of a lifetime.

indicate that the immature sharks will stay in temperate waters as juveniles, and may travel to tropical waters and venture into deep water as they mature.

Great white sharks do not do well in captivity. In fact, it is rather difficult for major aquaria to keep whites alive even for a week. This is one major reason why we know so little about them, and finding them in sufficient numbers in the wild has also proven difficult. Some specialists believe their numbers may be declining because of the popularity of killing sharks for sport and for their valuable fins and jaws. In 1993 it became illegal to fish for great white sharks in California, effective through 1998. It is hoped that by the end of this ban period, we will have a better understanding of white shark populations and be in a better position to decide what measures, if any, are necessary to protect these magnificent animals from extinction. It is highly unlikely that a diver in California waters will ever see a white shark, but just knowing they are there can give all of us a greater appreciation of nature's grand scheme.

In California, **ratfish** are observed much more often the farther north you explore. Once purported to be a missing link between cartilaginous fishes and bony fishes, ratfish are one of the few members of the Chimaeridae family, a group of fishes with cartilaginous skeletons. Unlike most cartilaginous fishes, ratfish possess a gill cover called an operculum, and they do not breathe through a spiracle as do many bottom-dwelling rays, skates, and sharks. Ratfish may be common at depths beyond sport diving limits, but they are only rarely seen in less than 100 feet of water in southern California. However, they are sighted rather frequently in relatively shallow

many female sharks, is up to three times thicker in the pectoral region than over the rest of the body. This adaptation is believed to protect the females from injury while mating.

White sharks are considered to be ovoviviparous, which means that pregnant females produce shelled eggs that develop and hatch inside the body of the mother. It was once suspected that great white sharks, like some other sharks, practiced intrauterine cannibalism—meaning that though several eggs hatch inside the mother, one of the young sharks devours its brothers and sisters before birth. However, recent discoveries have revealed that the hatched but unborn white shark pups receive nourishment in a much less shocking manner: from their own yolk sac and by eating undeveloped eggs produced by their mother. Although observations of pregnant white sharks are rare, females have been found with near full-term litters of up to fourteen pups.

At birth, white sharks are thought to be between 4 and 5 feet long, weighing between 40 and 70 pounds. Small white sharks are caught by fishers in certain shallow backwaters and bays on a predictable basis, leading scientists to believe that defined pupping grounds do exist. Along this coast, pupping usually takes place in southern California, although pups are sometimes found much farther north during El Niño years. Preliminary studies

A female spotted ratfish drags her egg casings behind her.

Great white sharks are both magnificently powerful and incredibly graceful.

water in the northern part of the state. Ratfish also tend to move inshore at night, and inhabit shallower water during spring than they do the rest of the year.

Attaining a maximum length of just over 3 feet, ratfish can be distinguished by the lack of scales on their body, weak bones that are quite pliable, and a strong venomous spine at the origin of the dorsal fin. The upper side of the body is usually a metallic bronze with white spots, while the underbelly is silver. In overall shape, ratfish more closely resemble common reef fish than they do sharks or rays. However, a pair of claspers are evident upon close inspection of the males. Claspers are reproductive appendages present in the males of all cartilaginous fishes, and a characteristic that distinguishes cartilaginous fishes from bony fishes. At each spawning a female ratfish produces two eggs. It takes her many hours—up to thirty—to extrude her eggs, which hang from her body on long filaments for up to six days.

DID YOU KNOW?

. . . EELS ARE FISH AND WOLF-EELS AREN'T EELS.

Bony Fishes of the Rocky Reefs

California moray eels are common residents of many shallow reef communities south of Point Conception. Surprisingly, the dark green eels are classified as bony fish, even though several significant differences between eels and other fishes are readily apparent even to the novice biologist. Moray eels lack the large gill covers used by other fishes to pump water over their gills for oxygen extraction, and instead have only a small, round gill opening. This lack of gill covers requires morays to use their mouth as a billows-type pump to continuously circulate a fresh supply of oxygenated water across their gills; morays are constantly opening and closing their mouth as they respire. This has led to a lot of bad publicity in the media and scary scenes in movies. Almost always photographed with mouths agape, exposing their fanglike teeth, morays are often portrayed as monsters of sea lore. Nothing could be further from the truth; in fact, upon first sensing a diver, morays usually retreat into their holes. Although once they are baited they can be rather aggressive, in normal settings they are shy and reclusive.

Reaching a length of nearly 6 feet, morays are primarily nocturnal feeders, preferring to prey upon small reef fish, octopi, and crustaceans. They rely heavily on an extremely well-developed sense of smell to detect prey. The lack of gill covers or large paired fins enables them to quickly back up without getting stuck as they skillfully maneuver about the reef in search of food. Another significant adaptation is their mucus-coated skin, which is considerably different from the scale-covered skin of most reef fish; this layer of lubrication adds to their maneuverability in tight quarters and to their skill as reef predators.

Morays are often surrounded by, and at times covered by, shrimp that clean their skin of parasites and dead tissue (see the section on shrimp earlier in this chapter). Bluebanded gobies and zebra gobies are also known to provide cleaning services to morays.

It is believed that the morays found in California waters do not hatch there, probably because the waters are too cold for them to reproduce. Instead, they hatch in Baja California, and some drift north as planktonic larvae that settle and mature in California waters.

All **rockfish** belong to the family Scorpaenidae, which contains more species than any other family of fishes found in the Eastern Pacific. More than fifty species of rockfish live in California waters. The common name for rockfish, as you might suspect, comes from the fact that they usually frequent rocky habitats. Many species that are seen only near the deeper reefs of southern California are commonly observed in less than 30 feet of water in the central and northern parts of the state. Most species of rockfish are fairly sedentary and rarely

A moray eel peers curiously at the camera.

move from reef to reef.

Rockfish are basslike in appearance, characterized by a pronounced projection of the lower jaw, large eyes, prominent spines in front of the dorsal fin, and the bony support extending down from the eyes and gill slits. Individual rockfish can be difficult to identify in the field because they undergo so many color phases, especially as adults. To further complicate matters, the color patterns, shape, and number of spines in some species change markedly with age. When fully grown, most rockfish are less than 18 inches long, though some exceed 2 feet.

Unlike the eggs of most bony fishes, rockfish eggs remain within the female until just before they hatch. For the first few weeks of life the tiny hatchlings swim near the surface in the open sea, often miles from the closest reef

Copper rockfish are typically found much deeper (below safe diving limits) in southern California waters than they are farther north.

Jackmackerel schooling among kelp fronds.

Why Some Fish School

Approximately 75 percent of all marine fishes travel in groups called schools. Scientists have developed many nonexclusive theories for this behavior. One is simply that there is safety in numbers. If a single fish runs into a predator, it's a good bet that the poor guy's days are numbered. But if an entire school of fish encounters the same predator, Fred fish may be eaten, but Frank and Fanny fish stand a chance of escaping while their pursuer is busy with Fred. By schooling, each fish may increase its own odds of reaching sexual maturity and reproducing.

A second theory centers on the idea that schooling fish may confuse a predator, which is particularly advantageous when the predator is a better swimmer. The overwhelming number of fish in a school may make it difficult for the predator to single out an individual to pursue, even if it manages to focus on the kaleidoscope of flashing fish. A moment of hesitation can cost the predator its meal as the potential prey use the extra time to make an escape. In one recent experiment, scientists colored a few fish blue and returned them to their school; as hypothesized, these hapless blue fish stuck out like sore thumbs in the school of otherwise silver fish, and were quickly targeted and eliminated by predators.

Schooling fish move in incredible synchrony, with apparently simultaneous changes in direction. To a predator with limited visual abilities a school of fish may therefore appear to be a single large animal. Since the general rule is that bigger fish eat smaller fish, the predator may see itself as potential prey and leave the school alone.

Schooling behavior may not be based solely on protection from predation. Schooling keeps individuals of the same species in close proximity, so spawning activity is more easily coordinated. Whatever the reason or reasons behind schooling behavior, the advantages it provides are apparent from its prevalence among so many different types of fishes.

community. Juvenile rockfish are heavily preyed upon in mid-ocean, and sometimes seek refuge in patches of free-drifting kelp. As adults they feed on a variety of mollusks, crustaceans, and smaller fishes. Mature rockfish are preyed upon by rays, seals, sea lions, and bottom-dwelling sharks, and also rate highly with fishers.

Not only do rockfish taste great, they make excellent photographic subjects as well. Framed against a colorful reef, their dramatic faces and rich color patterns create strong photo opportunities. Some of the most photogenic species are vermilion rockfish, black-and-yellow rockfish, gopher rockfish, rosy rockfish, starry rockfish, treefish, and china rockfish. The juveniles of many rockfish are especially striking. Getting just the right photographic frame can be difficult, but as a rule rockfish are not especially wary, so they are much easier to work with than many other fishes.

Often called convict fish for the jailbird pattern of stripes along their body, **painted greenlings** inhabit rocky reefs throughout the state. Generally cigar-shaped with a comparatively small mouth, painted greenlings reach a maximum length of 10 inches, but most are 6 inches or shorter.

A juvenile treefish.

Males are usually more colorful than females, except during spawning season, when they turn almost black. Males often inhabit higher reaches of rocky reefs, whereas the red-colored females and juveniles seem to prefer the boundaries between sand and rock. These fish are highly territorial, and males aggressively defend their nests—although they may snack on a few of their own eggs. During the winter, painted greenlings are inactive and shelter in protective holes and crevices.

Painted greenlings are highly territorial, chasing off intruders several times their size.

Painted greenlings have a curious nature that will often lead them to examine divers who remain still. When approaching an object of their curiosity, these fish tend to dart about the reef, pausing only momentarily before changing their position again. In this comical scene, they generally move closer in the long run, but it appears as if they don't want the object of their attention to perceive their interest.

Although they are members of a different family (Hexagrammidae), **lingcod** are sometimes mistaken by novice divers for cabezon (also discussed in this chapter). Both cabezon and lingcod have an elongated body and a rather large head. Cabezon, however, lack scales, while lingcod lack the frilled facial appendages of cabezon. Lingcod vary in color from gray-brown to green or blue, usually with spotted or mottled patterns on their upper body. Found from intertidal depths to 1,400 feet, they are bigger the farther north you go. The largest lingcod ever documented in California weighed 41.5 pounds, while in British Columbia the record is 105 pounds.

Lingcod are extremely territorial, benthic animals that are often found on rocky ledges. The males are particularly vigilant in guarding their nests, which contain egg masses that may be more than 2 feet across and weigh up to 15 pounds. The eggs are initially pink, and turn white over the course of their eight- to ten-week development.

Lingcod are ambush predators with large appetites, feeding on squid and octopi as well as small fish—including, when the opportunity presents itself, younger lingcod. Their major natural predator is sea lions, but they are also the second most popular sport fish (next to salmon) between northern California and Washington. Although it is green prior to cooking, the meat is excellent.

A sculpin in its golden phase.

There are more than forty-five fishes in California waters that are properly called **sculpin**. These fish are included in the family Cottidae. One fish *not* included in this family is *Scorpaena guttata*—the fish most commonly called a sculpin by laypeople. *S. guttata* is actually a member of the family Scorpaenidae, which also includes all rockfish. Commonly seen species of the Cottidae family include the tidepool sculpin, cabezon, longfin sculpin, snubnose sculpin, sailfin sculpin, coralline sculpin, rosy sculpin, woolly sculpin, and red Irish lord. All these species vary in coloration, with splotches of red, purple, yellow, orange, white, green, and brown. Most are less than 7 inches long, and distinguishing one from the next is often difficult at first. Sculpin are typically extremely cryptic, with camouflage colorations that help them blend remarkably well into their surroundings.

Of all the sculpin, **cabezon** (Spanish for "large head") are particularly notorious for their unusual shape: they have a bulbous head, stumpy tail, goggle eyes, tufted "eyebrows," and very large, fanlike pectoral fins. The females are nearly always a mottled gray-green, while the males are usually a splotchy reddish-brown. Cabezon are a favorite of many fishers. The blue tint of the flesh disappears when the fish is cooked, but be aware that the roe is poisonous.

After fertilizing the female's eggs, a male cabezon guards the nest until the eggs hatch. It is quite common to encounter a vigilant male sitting right in the middle of a big dark green patch of eggs. After the eggs hatch, the hatchlings drift with currents for several weeks until, by chance, the young fish settle in shallow water and begin their bottom-dwelling life. As adults, cabezon are known to reach a length of 3 feet and weigh up to 25 pounds, but most are considerably smaller.

The vermilion scales of this red Irish lord stand out brilliantly against *Metridium* anemones.

Cabezon catch their prey by stealth, and are referred to as a lie-in-wait predator. They blend in well with rocky surroundings, so they simply rest on the bottom and wait for unsuspecting prey to come too close. When the prey, usually a crab or a small fish, wanders within range, the cabezon darts out and engulfs its victim with its oversized maw. Cabezon also prey on abalone, and have the rather amazing ability to dislodge an abalone, swallow it whole, and later disgorge the shell.

Kelp bass, also commonly called bull bass or calico bass, inhabit almost every kelp forest community in southern California. They are readily distinguishable by their markings, distinct coloration, and basslike shape. Kelp bass are brown to olive-yellow above, yellow to off-white underneath, and usually mottled with white patches. The largest known specimen was over 28 inches long and weighed just under 15 pounds. (Catching a kelp bass this size would be a feat, because the larger they are, the more wary they tend to be.) Kelp bass usu-

A kelp bass rests among brittle stars.

ally hover in the kelp, subtly maneuvering to keep some kelp between themselves and a diver without totally obstructing their own view. Despite their name, kelp bass are not only found in kelp beds; they also inhabit rocky reefs, oil platforms, and almost any other area with some sort of structure.

Small kelp bass feed on plankton and tiny invertebrates, whereas larger specimens prey on algae, large invertebrates, and fishes. Some studies have indicated that kelp bass feed particularly intensively twice a year, gorging themselves just before spawning season and just after. They sometimes join in cooperative hunting ventures, attacking a school of smaller fish from all angles. They occasionally even leap out of the water in zealous pursuit of their prey.

Black sea bass are by far the largest bony fish seen in California reef communities. Reaching a length of over 7 feet, a full-grown black sea bass can weigh in excess of 500 pounds. Mature black sea bass prefer rocky bottoms along the deep outside edges of kelp beds, whereas juveniles are often seen over sandy bottoms. The stunning brick-red juveniles have six irregular rows of black dots on their sides. These dots are still evident in some adults, but quickly disappear when the fish is removed from the water. Black sea bass prey on fishes, crustaceans, and squid, and for short distances are fast enough to catch speedy swimmers such as bonito.

A black sea bass cruises majestically through a kelp forest.

For years black sea bass, also commonly called giant sea bass or jewfish, were considered the ultimate prize by California sport fishers, but heavy fishing pressure reduced the population so drastically that they are now a threatened species. It is no longer legal to take a black sea bass, and seeing one underwater in its natural setting is a special treat. Fortunately, in recent years this majestic sight has become increasingly common, and divers are reporting numerous encounters with curious black sea bass.

Ocean whitefish are frequently encountered in southern California, though they are rarely seen north of Monterey. Reaching a length of up to 40 inches, ocean whitefish are yellow-brown above and paler below. Many of these attractive fish have blue and yellow edging on the fins, especially the tail fin. Ocean whitefish are usually seen schooling along the outside edge of a reef, and will curiously approach divers over time. Usually cruising just a few feet above the seafloor, they feed on small fishes and benthic invertebrates.

Sargo are similar in appearance to perch, but are actually members of the family Haemulidae, commonly called grunts. The common name comes from the piglike grunting noise these fish make when caught by fishers, a threat response produced by grinding their well-developed pharyngeal teeth together and amplified by their swim bladder.

Commonly observed in kelp beds and along rocky coasts, sargo tend to gather in loose schools and can be found from the shallows to depths of 130 feet. Their body is silver with a dark vertical band behind the pectoral fin, and some have other, less conspicuous dark bands near the tail. Sargo are difficult to distinguish from perch, but have only nine to eleven soft rays on their anal fin, while perch have at least thirteen.

Sargo weigh up to 6 pounds and reach a length of 17 inches or more. They feed on small crustaceans, mollusks, and worms, and are preyed upon by sea lions and some dolphins. Because these fish are able to tolerate salinities up to 20 percent greater than ocean water, sargo thrive in the Salton Sea, where they were introduced in 1951. A favorite of sport fishers and spearfishers alike, thousands of sargo are taken annually.

White sea bass are not really bass or sea bass, but members of a family of fish commonly called croakers. Considered to be among the most tasty of California fishes, white sea bass are almost never seen except by top-quality free divers, as they are extremely wary fish and seem to be frightened away by scuba divers' bubbles. When encountered, whites are usually cruising the deep outside edges of kelp or rocky reefs. Larger adults sometimes migrate to deeper waters during the winter.

Not only are white sea bass not bass or sea bass, they are not even white. Instead, these fish are named for the white color of their flesh. Adults are actually blue-gray, bronze, or yellow above with dark speckling, and silver to white on the underside, whereas juveniles display several dark vertical bars on their sides. Reaching a length of up to 5 feet, a full-grown white will weigh close to 80 pounds. White sea bass prey primarily on small pelagic fishes.

Opaleye, also commonly called button bass or opaleye perch, are members of the sea chub family. As the name implies, their eyes are a striking opalescent blue. Opaleye are also characterized by their light gray-green to dark blue color, and one or two white spots on each side of the body under the dorsal fin. The largest opaleye ever recorded was approximately eleven years old, 25.5 inches long, and weighed 13.5 pounds. However, these fish typically weigh only 3 to 4 pounds.

Although opaleye range from San Francisco to Magdalena Bay on the Baja Peninsula, they are observed year-round only south of Point Conception. As adults these schooling fish are usually seen near rocky bottoms, especially in areas where there are kelp beds. Inhabiting depths from 5 to 80 feet, they are most often observed in waters between 20 and 40 feet deep. Juvenile opaleye usually inhabit tidepools, with the youngest fish in the highest pools.

Opaleye feed heavily upon algae and eelgrass, but are believed to gain most of their nutritional benefit from the mollusks, crustaceans, and other small animals that reside on the plants, rather than from the plants themselves. Opaleyes are among the fortunate few fish that lack a known major predator, although they are a prized catch among sport fishers.

Halfmoons are also commonly called Catalina perch or Catalina blue perch. These fish usually travel in large schools, inhabiting inshore reefs as well as kelp forests, and are extremely abundant along the mainland and at the Channel Islands. Halfmoons are dark blue on top, fading to lighter blue on the sides toward the bluish-

A male garibaldi cares for his nest.

Courting Garibaldi

The adult male garibaldi cultivates a nest site by clearing a carefully selected area on the rocks and then gathering and cultivating specific species of red algae, tirelessly removing all other algae and debris. Once the nest is complete, he is ready to mate, but he has that age-old problem: he needs to attract a partner. Female garibaldi are as picky about their partners as any other females. Of course, this pickiness aids a female in mating with the best males, helping to ensure the perpetuation of her genetic code and the long-term survival of her species.

The male garibaldi entices a female by performing an elaborate courtship dance, in which he swims a series of circles around the nest site. When he is prepared for the female to come to the nest and lay her eggs, he announces his readiness with several clucking sounds that can be heard underwater if you are quiet and listen closely.

Females are extremely choosy when selecting a nest for their eggs; they prefer larger nests that already contain eggs, and may visit several nests before making their final choice. Upon being seduced by a persuasive male, the female swims over and deposits her eggs on the nest site. Once she is done, the male quickly chases her away so she doesn't eat her own eggs. The male then fertilizes the eggs and vigorously defends the nest from all intruders until the young are hatched.

white underbelly. Adults reach a length of 19 inches and weigh up to 4 pounds.

Halfmoons feed on a wide variety of creatures such as sponges, bryozoans, and red, green, and brown algae, including giant kelp. Like many other fishes that inhabit the reef community, halfmoons are preyed upon by kelp bass, sand bass, large rockfish, and a variety of seals and sea lions. They are also popular with sport fishers.

Three of the most notable species of **surfperch** seen in California waters are the rubberlip surfperch, the walleye surfperch, and the barred surfperch. **Barred surfperch**, which are silvery or brassy with yellow to rust-colored vertical bars on their body, tend to stay just beyond the breakers off sandy beaches, while rubberlip surfperch and walleye surfperch prefer rocky reefs. Surfperches are an exception among the bony fishes in that their young are born live after hatching and further developing inside the mother. Young males are sometimes able to mate immediately after birth.

As the name suggests, **rubberlip surfperch** can easily be identified by their thick, fleshy, whitish-pink lips. Abundant in kelp beds, around jetties and piers, and just outside the surf along open coasts, rubberlips often school in groups of up to about fifty fish. These remarkable fish use their flexible lips to clamp onto rocks and suction up their small invertebrate prey. They are the largest surfperches, growing up to 18 inches.

Walleye surfperch, as one would suspect, possess very large eyes, as well as a large upturned mouth. Their steel-blue upper body fades to white on the lower body, and reaches a maximum length of about a foot. These fish typically form dense schools of up to thousands of individuals over sandy bottoms during the day, then disperse onto reefs at night, where they feed on plankton and small fishes. Walleyes are considered valuable game by both commercial and sport fishers.

A member of the family of damselfishes, **garibaldi** is the California state marine fish. Garibaldi are also, appropriately, among the most attractive of all California fishes. Especially appealing as juveniles, the reddish-brown body of the young is decorated with brilliant blue iridescent spots and stripes. The blue coloration disappears in the adult stage, though some specimens retain a faint blue border along their fins. The blue patterns may serve to prevent territorial adults from attacking the juveniles; in one study, adult garibaldi that were painted with the iridescent blue patterns of juveniles were

California's state marine fish, the garibaldi.

not attacked by other adult garibaldi. Both the males and females are an unmistakable brilliant orange.

Garibaldi are sighted on almost every dive in the kelp communities of southern California, but are not often seen at Santa Rosa Island, at San Miguel Island, or north of Point Conception. Reaching a length of 15 inches, garibaldi seem to know they are protected by state law, and often display an intense curiosity about divers. If a diver cracks open a sea urchin, he or she is likely to be surrounded by a dozen or more swarming garibaldi within a matter of minutes.

Adult garibaldi, both male and female, are highly territorial and will fearlessly defend their expanse of the reef from intruders. By making clacking noises and aggressively charging, they are able to chase away even surprisingly large

Garibaldi are amazingly bold fish and often curiously approach divers.

Blacksmith fish are blue-gray damselfish with numerous small black spots along the back, dorsal, and tail fins. They are very similar in color to halfmoon, and the two fish are sometimes confused in southern waters where both are common. However, blacksmiths are much smaller than halfmoon, only rarely growing as long as 12 inches. Schooling around reefs and feeding on zooplankton during the day, they tend to rest under ledges and in crevices between sunset and sunrise, often in gregarious groups of a half dozen or so. During late spring and early summer in the Catalina Islands, divers sometimes notice dead blacksmiths with sores on their sides littered around the bottom. The deaths are caused by a bacterial infection that seems to affect only the unfortunate blacksmiths.

Blacksmith fish form loose schools that tighten when the fish are being pursued or when they are being cleaned by senorita fish. While being cleaned, they gather into a tight ball, hanging upside down in the water column as they wait patiently for the senorita to do its work. If the senorita tries to leave before all the blacksmith fish are cleaned, the uncleaned ones will often try to block the senorita's path of escape. Young adult blacksmiths are, in turn, often observed cleaning other fish. Unfortunately, the fascinating cleaning behavior of blacksmiths and senoritas usually ceases when a diver approaches too closely.

Sheephead are abundant in almost every rocky reef and kelp forest community throughout the Channel Islands and along the coast from Monterey south. They are one of the larger members of the wrasse family, attaining a length of up to 3 feet and weighing as much as 36 pounds. These are unusual fish, their most outstanding characteristic perhaps being their ability to change sex in midlife. Born females, all sheephead become males in later years. Sheephead first reach sexual maturity as females at four or five years of age, and usually transform into males between the ages of six and eight. If there is an insufficient number of males in a given area, the dominant female will change into a male. With the change in gender comes a distinct change in appearance: both the head and the tail of males are deep blue to solid black, the lower jaw is

invaders of their territory. Males are particularly vigilant in defending their nests.

Although most Californians have long believed garibaldi to be their state fish, until only recently that honor belonged to the golden trout. Popular opinion finally won out, and in 1995 the golden trout became California's state freshwater fish, while garibaldi became the official California state marine fish. Though juvenile garibaldi are popular aquarium fish in Japan, they are protected by California state law. Sport fishers and sport divers should be aware that it is illegal to catch, spear, or collect garibaldi.

DID YOU KNOW?

. . . GARIBALDI DID NOT BECOME CALIFORNIA'S OFFICIAL STATE MARINE FISH UNTIL 1995.

white, and the midbody region is pinkish, whereas females are all red and their head is much more rounded.

These wrasses begin their lives during the summer as eggs afloat in the pelagic environment. Upon hatching, the young fish spend several months at the mercy of open-ocean currents. During this stage of their lives, the hatchlings are almost translucent, although some have several tiny black dots. After a few months, those juveniles that have survived the perils of the open sea and happen to drift over a reef will settle into life in a reef community. For a few weeks the fish undergo dramatic changes in coloration. Within just a few days they become a beautiful bright red or orange, with a white lateral line and black spots. In only a few weeks, the vivid colors fade, and the white lateral lines and dark spots disappear. The fish take on a reddish hue in their upper body, while the belly tends to be white.

Sheephead sleep in protective crevices during the night, sometimes surrounding them-

A juvenile sheephead.

This female sheephead will transform into a male at the age of about eight years.

Male sheephead in a territorial dispute.

selves with a mucus envelope that seems to prevent their predators from detecting them by smell. During the day they feed heavily on hard-shelled prey such as sea urchins, crustaceans, and mollusks, including abalone. Large teeth and strong jaws enable them to crush the shells of their prey. Sheephead are known to use their hard head to bump sea urchins off rocks in order to get to their vulnerable tube feet, and are often seen swimming about with a number of sea urchin spines stuck in their bony head and gill covers.

In addition to the sheephead, two other species of wrasse are often seen by snorkelers and sport divers in California: the **senorita fish** and the **rock wrasse**. The female rock wrasse and both the male and female senoritas have golden-colored, cigar-shaped bodies, but the senoritas lack the black spots of the female rock wrasse. The male rock wrasse is gray with a black bar just behind its yellowish pectoral fin. Senoritas industriously rid blacksmith fish, kelp bass, garibaldi, and other fishes of parasites in a flurry of activity that is always fascinating to watch.

As do many other wrasses, both senoritas and rock wrasse bury themselves several inches deep in the sand at night. Ichthyologists believe they do so for two reasons: to hide from potential predators, and to use the coarse quality of the sand to knock parasites off their own mucus-coated body. The lubrication provided by the mucus is an adaptation that helps these fishes penetrate the sand.

Despite their physical appearance, **wolf-eels** are not really eels, and are more closely related to blennies than they are to moray eels.

Sharing a shelter among anemones, these wolf-eels will mate for life.

Wolf-eels inhabit many reefs, but are more commonly seen in central and northern waters. The largest recorded wolf-eel was over 6 feet long.

Wolf-eels apparently mate for life, each pair sharing a shelter. The male is typically more aggressive, while the female tends to demurely withdraw when disturbed. In courtship the male butts his head into the female, then wraps himself around her and fertilizes the eggs as she lays them. Both the male and the female protectively wrap their bodies around the egg mass, and only one parent leaves at a time to feed.

Wolf-eels are perhaps the fiercest-looking of all the reef creatures encountered in California. Though capable of inflicting serious wounds with their caninelike jaw teeth, their looks belie a truly docile nature. Wolf-eels use their strong jaws to feed on market crabs and other small crustaceans, mollusks, and echinoderms, but certainly not on divers.

Blennies are small fish, and most California specimens are less than 6 inches long. They have a blunt head, a long thin body, and are often beautifully colored in a variety of hues. Almost all species are primarily benthic and feed on small crustaceans and fish found along the seafloor.

Upon first encountering a diver, blennies often dart back

into a hole. However, their curiosity usually gets the best of them, and before long they will come out to examine a diver who remains relatively still. They will dart back and forth, looking at the diver from a number of angles, and continually closing the gap.

Three species of blennies are frequently observed by divers who closely examine the cracks and crevices of California reefs: the rockpool blenny, found south of Point Conception; the mussel blenny, found south of Santa Barbara; and the bay blenny. Distinguishing one blenny species from the next within the blenny family is a difficult task, even with a detailed scientific key; in the field it is practically impossible for those who lack specific expertise.

Although there are many types of **gobies** in California waters, three species are frequently seen in rocky terrain by sport divers: the Catalina or bluebanded goby, the zebra goby, and the blackeye goby. **Bluebanded gobies** are among the world's most striking fish, their bright red-orange body covered with vertical blue bars that match the color of their iridescent head. These 2-inch-long fish are often seen in crevices with morays. Bluebanded gobies are extremely territorial, and males fiercely guard their eggs, which are usually

A Catalina goby.

laid in empty shells. Bluebanded gobies are a treat to see, but they are extremely skittish and can be difficult to photograph at close range.

Less brilliantly colored and less common than bluebanded gobies, **zebra gobies** have more and thinner stripes. The **blackeye goby** (sometimes called nickel-eye goby) is the largest of the three, reaching a length of 6 inches. Other than size, the blackeye goby can be distinguished by its whitish body and large black eyes, which really aren't as large as a nickel but which appear oversized relative to the rest of its body. The blackeye goby is able to clamp down on rocks with its pelvic fins, which are fused together and act as a suction cup.

Although zebra gobies are usually shy, males will heroically guard eggs from predators.

A sunburst lights up a seemingly barren sandy plains habitat.

CHAPTER 6

THE SANDY PLAINS

A sea pen.

Between the oases of California's rocky reefs and kelp forests are great expanses of sand that resemble terrestrial deserts. Some of these sand plains extend for hundreds of square miles, while others are only a few yards wide. Despite the proximity of the biomes, the marine creatures that inhabit the sand are considerably different from those of a rocky reef community, a kelp forest, or the open ocean. Perhaps the most unusual aspect of this seemingly desolate habitat is that you'll never even see most of the animals that call the sandy plains home. The majority of life in this habitat abides beneath the sandy seafloor. For example, many divers are never even aware of the existence of the amazing variety of polychaete worms that live within the sand (and that are prey to many more familiar animals), yet these hidden worms have the largest total biomass of any sandy plains animals.

The most interesting sandy communities are usually in areas where decomposing debris accumulates and continuous supplies of phytoplankton are available, providing food and some protective cover. There is a distinct lack of plant life in the sand, so the food web is based primarily on plankton and decaying debris that has drifted into the area. The variety of sand-dwellers usually increases with distance from the beach, as the water becomes deeper and the effect of surge is reduced. If the sand patch lies downcurrent from a nearby kelp bed, a greater variety of species can be expected.

Because there are no rocks for protection in the sandy plains, there are few places to hide other than in or on the sand itself or under and amongst debris. So, as you might suspect, most sand-dwellers have an extremely low profile. In order to survive, sand-dwellers must be at least one of the following:

- **Excellent burrowers**: Many clams are expert diggers. Clams spend a considerable amount of time buried in the sand with only their paired siphons exposed. These siphons enable clams to take in oxygenated and food-containing water and eliminate wastes without exposing themselves to danger.
- **Able to rebury themselves rapidly after they are exposed**: Sea pens spend their days buried beneath the sand, but at night come up to feed. If threatened or if uncovered during the day, sea pens can rebury themselves for protection.
- **Able to stabilize the substrate around them**: In many sites, groups of sand dollars are so thick that the association works to stabilize the sand. The same is true for several species of worms.

- **Experts at camouflage**: Flatfish such as turbot, halibut, sole, and sanddabs use their splotchy coloration to camouflage themselves in the sand. Flatfish are able to closely match both the color and the pattern of the sand around them. Experiments have shown that the fish must be able to see their surroundings, and then are able to alter the shape of special black pigments in the cells of their skin. This allows them to change the color and pattern of their own skin to imitate their surroundings.

    Even larger predators such as angel sharks are very adept at changing their color pattern to blend in with the sand. Like many sand-dwellers, they also frequently bury themselves so that little more than their eyes and spiracles are exposed. Observant divers find these hidden creatures by noticing their outlines in the sand.

The sandy plains are similar to terrestrial deserts in many ways. During the day these sand patches may appear barren and boring, but at night the same area can come bewilderingly alive. On some nights in the sandy plains, everywhere you look a pair of eyes is staring back at you; fish, octopi, crabs, squid, angel sharks, cusk eels, thornback rays, guitarfish, and more are all around you. Fascinating invertebrates such as clams, sea pens, sea pansies, sea stars, and tube

Dense communities of sand dollars help stabilize the sandy substrate.

Plankton
The Wanderers

Plankton is not a single type of plant or animal. It is a diverse group of both plants and animals, encompassing all floating organisms that are too small or too weak to fight the ocean's currents. Derived from the Greek word *planktos*, meaning "wanderer," plankton are the drifters of the sea.

Marine creatures generally belong to one of three categories: the plankton (drifters), the nekton (active swimmers), or the benthos (seafloor-dwelling creatures). Thus, although the term "plankton" is popularly used to refer to microscopic plants and animals, its members actually range from microscopic bacteria and single-celled protists to jellyfish whose tentacles may be over 30 feet long. Many animals pass through more than one of these forms over the course of their life cycle. Young fish are often planktonic until they grow large enough to swim freely with the nekton, and the larvae of many benthic creatures are planktonic until they settle to the ocean floor. Many plants and animals, however, are planktonic throughout their lives.

Plankton are generally divided into two groups: phytoplankton and zooplankton. Phytoplankton are photosynthetic creatures, gaining their energy directly from the sun and using it to convert raw materials into body mass; this is called primary production. Zooplankton are animals, obtaining energy and mass by eating other organisms. Some odd creatures fall into both categories—they both photosynthesize and eat other plants and animals.

Phytoplankton can survive only within the photic zone (shallower waters that receive enough sunlight to support growth by photosynthesis). Zooplankton are found throughout the water column, although individual species are often limited to a particular range of depths. Plankton have little or no ability to control their horizontal motion, but many zooplankton have a remarkable ability to adjust their vertical position. For example, tiny crustaceans known as copepods are often found in deeper water during the day, when they may be avoiding predation, and in shallower water at night, when they feed.

You may wonder why you should care about a group of creatures so small that you probably will never even see most of them. Some plankton cause the bioluminescence enjoyed by beach visitors at night, but these amazing light shows don't even scratch the surface of plankton's importance to humankind. Phytoplankton produce much of the oxygen we breathe each day. They are, even more importantly, responsible for the majority of the world's primary production. As the term implies, primary production is the basis of all food chains; without primary producers there is nothing for herbivores to graze on, and therefore nothing for carnivores to prey upon—and thus no food chain, or any life at all.

Zooplankton are also important members of the marine environment. Some animals, such as baleen whales and whale sharks, feed directly upon plankton, but other animals cannot eat anything so small. Zooplankton that do eat tiny phytoplankton are eaten by larger zooplankton, which are eaten by larger animals, which are then eaten by even larger predators. Zooplankton are thus an essential conduit for the energy of primary production to larger animals.

Although plankton are often ignored because of their small size, they are absolutely crucial to the existence of most other marine life, and to life as we know it on land. The next time you're out diving, remember to appreciate all the microscopic creatures around you for sustaining the wonderful diversity of life you do see.

anemones seem to be everywhere. Of course, there aren't always that many creatures to be found; sometimes there is simply no one home, and you can spend a lot of time just trying to find some living thing to look at. As in the open sea, conditions in the sandy plains tend to be feast or famine.

Sandy Plains Invertebrates

Sea pansies are purple, heart-shaped colonial cnidarians that anchor themselves into the sand with the stalk on the underside of their disc. Modified eight-armed polyps called siphonozoids on the disc create a water current that circulates through the colony, supplying oxygenated water and food. The food is taken in through a different group of modified polyps called autozooids. Sea pansies also secure food by secreting a mucous net that they swallow when it becomes full of entrapped food.

Like their close relatives the sea pens, the sea pansies typically appear to be a little on the drab side during the day, but at night they are often brilliantly luminescent. Sea pansies are frequently seen in southern California at depths of 20 feet and more.

A sea pansy.

Sea pens are colonial cnidarians that are closely related to sea pansies. They generally require quiet waters and are rarely found close to the surf zone. Sea pens are noted for their greenish bioluminescence, which can be activated simply by the gentle touch of a diver. At night, flashes of light are sometimes emitted when the polyps are disturbed.

Sea pens are supported by a central axis made from calcareous secretions, bordered by polyp-bearing lobes. They

Bioluminescence

If you have ever been swimming, diving, or boating in the open sea at night, you were probably thrilled by the way the water around you seemed to glow. The lighting effect was the result of a phenomenon called bioluminescence, a spectacle often witnessed by those who venture out into the Pacific after sunset.

Bioluminescence is an organism's ability to generate and emit light. Occurring in a wide variety of marine invertebrates and some vertebrates, representatives from more than half of all animal phyla display this rather curious ability. Bioluminescence is the result of the conversion of chemical energy to radiant energy (light) by one of a variety of reactions. The reactions are extremely efficient, with almost no heat produced as a by-product, so bioluminescence is often referred to as cold biological light. Some bioluminescence is produced by bacteria living within an animal's tissues, but other animals produce their own bioluminescence.

This fleshy sea pen is bioluminescent, giving off flashes of light when gently touched.

California waters are often lit by single-celled bioluminescent planktonic dinoflagellates. At night these animals glow when mechanically stimulated by wave action, the bow of a boat, the kick of a fin, or the swipe of a hand. When dinoflagellates are present in dense concentrations, their flickers of light are bright enough to outline a swimmer or diver.

Bioluminescent displays by sea pens and sea pansies in California waters can be induced by night divers who lightly touch the colony. The touch will often generate a wave of light that travels up and down the organism.

In many species of deepwater fishes and squid, bioluminescence has a distinct survival value. It may serve to frighten or confuse predators, or to attract prey or mates. The importance, if any, of bioluminescence in lower invertebrates is not well understood, but it may have evolved to help prevent oxygen poisoning. Whatever the purpose, bioluminescence is an endlessly fascinating phenomenon that can add an aura of magic to your night dives.

are attached to a bulb that is buried in the sand. During the day and in rough conditions the lobes retract and the stalk slides into the sand, leaving only a couple of inches exposed.

The two most common California species are the fleshy sea pen and the white or slender sea pen. **Fleshy sea pens** are the most visually striking, with the soft white axis bearing fluffy pink to orange lateral lobes that create a featherlike appearance. Generally inhabiting deep water with a coarse sand substrate, fleshy sea pens are found throughout the state's waters. Larger specimens stand 2 feet above the sand bottom and are common in central and northern California. As its name suggests, the **slender sea pen** is tall and thin, reaching a height of more than 1 foot but a width of only 2 to 4 inches.

Tube anemones are among the most striking of the sandy plains invertebrates. These anemones construct long, mucus-lined tunnels into which they retract when inactive or disturbed. The tubes are laced with stinging nettles, strategically deposited by the anemone for its own defense. Feeding tube anemones extend two rings of tentacles into the water column. The longer tentacles of the periphery, which typically extend 4 to 5 inches beyond the tube, are used to capture fish and other prey, which are then transferred to the shorter tentacles around the mouth for feeding purposes. The

When threatened, this tube anemone quickly withdraws into the protection of its casing.

tentacles, like the tube, are a light brown color, but their flowerlike appearance makes potentially interesting photographic subjects out of these rather blandly colored creatures.

Some tube anemones seem to be a bright pink underwater, but appear drab brown in photographs lit with an artificial light source. The apparent change in color is due to the intensity of the strobe lights that are normally used by underwater photographers. At depth when sunlight has been naturally filtered, tube anemones reflect a different wavelength of light than they do when lit from close range by a powerful strobe. In essence, at depth when lit only by sunlight, the wavelengths of the reflected sunlight create a pinkish hue. But when blasted by strobe light, the pink colors disappear because of the intensity and wavelengths of the artificial light.

The **sand-rose anemone** is another

A sand-rose anemone.

Blue siphons of a horse-neck clam next to an anemone.

like miniature versions of some prehistoric sea monster. Their pear-shaped body tapers to two prominent points at the leading edge of the carapace. Growing to 6 or 7 inches long, sheep crabs possess formidable claws, but when approached they tend to scuttle away on their surprisingly agile long legs. Juvenile sheep crabs habitually attach sponges, rocks, shells, algae, and other debris to their own carapace for camouflage.

The smaller **masking crab** (both the juvenile and the adult) is another local species that decorates itself with debris. As do all other crabs, sheep crabs and masking crabs must molt as they grow, shedding their old exoskeleton and forming a new and larger one. After molting, the crabs must begin their artistic endeavors all over again, although they sometimes salvage as many of their old decorations as they can. In addition to camouflage, decorating crabs may be afforded additional protection from predators by the stinging tentacles of small anemones and the noxious tastes of other attachments to their shells.

Dungeness crabs are the most important commercially harvested Pacific Coast crab south of Alaska. Easily recognizable by the "teeth" that line the edge of their carapace, these cancer crabs grow to about 9 inches in width and are considered to be a culinary delight. Dungeness crabs feed on small invertebrates and fishes and may occa-

beautiful inhabitant of the sandy plains. Its long whitish or pinkish tentacles give it the flowery appearance that inspired its name. The column of the sand-rose anemone is lined with rows of tiny projections covered with particles of shells and sand, and is usually at least partially buried in the sand.

Its large eyes, huge size (up to a foot in length), and patches of brilliant blues, reds, and yellows make the **mantis shrimp** distinctive among other sandy plains crustaceans. Whiling away the days in burrows as deep as 6 feet or more, these shrimp emerge at night to terrorize their prey. Bivalves and other small invertebrates are smashed with mighty blows of the shrimp's claws. Divers beware: the claws of the mantis shrimp are not to be trifled with.

Once you see a **sheep crab**, you will never mistake it for any other sandy plains inhabitant. These dramatic photographic subjects look

A sheep crab clambers through fields of squid egg casings to feast on dying market squid.

sionally dine on their own small young. **Yellow crabs** are another commercially harvested crab found in California waters. These yellowish-orange crabs sometimes clean parasites from the scales of sand bass.

Horse-neck clams are among the many species of clams that live beneath the sand. Like other clams, they have an incurrent and excurrent siphon that extends to the surface of the sand, through which they gather food and excrete wastes. The rest of the animal lives in a shell that is burrowed into the substrate. These large bivalves sometimes grow to greater than 8 inches long and weigh nearly 4 pounds. Their fused siphons are so large that they cannot be completely withdrawn into the animal's shell. Clams are amazingly fast burrowers, especially when disturbed. If you do not speedily dig a clam out of the sand or mud, you are unlikely to even see the shell. Upon first sighting the unburied siphons of a clam, many divers have no idea that the organism they are looking at is even an animal, because siphons have a somewhat plantlike appearance.

Considered by many to be the cleverest and most advanced of the invertebrates, **octopi** provide a constant source of entertainment for divers and snorkelers. Glimpsing a sucker-lined tentacle extending from a crevice is always a thrill, offering an exciting opportunity to peer into the den of a fascinating animal. The **red octopus** is often encountered in sandy habitats. (Octopi are also found in rocky reef habitats; see Chapter 5.) Because octopi can change the color and texture of their skin at will, it is

An octopus at rest on the sand.

very difficult to determine species in the field. Red octopi are almost always less than 1 foot from tentacle tip to tentacle tip and are primarily nocturnal, rarely encountered out in the

A red octopus swimming over the sandy plains.

open during the day. At night they emerge from the protective confines of their dens in order to hunt.

Red octopi are often discovered resting on the sand just outside the mouth of their dens. Normally their coloration is very similar to that of the surrounding sand, though when disturbed they can change the hue, shape, and texture of their skin in dramatic fashion. When stalking or pouncing on prey, an octopus often flashes red, whereas when frightened it may show dark stripes or spots to make itself appear bigger. The range of possibilities seems limitless, and the different modes are believed, at least in some instances, to indicate emotions such as anger and fear. Pigment-filled skin cells, called chromatophores, enable octopi to vary their color, while muscular contractions allow the changes in texture. Many times I have tried to film one of these camouflage artists and have lost the animal out in the open sand. To my astonishment, my diving buddy would point to the octopus, which had remained in the exact same place it was throughout my filming efforts—the quick-change artist had changed color, shape, and texture to blend in with the surrounding sand.

California octopi feed upon varied creatures, including lobster, a variety of clams, shrimps, and scallops. Several species of octopi readily prey upon tuna crabs when available. While up in the water column, tiny kelp scallops some-

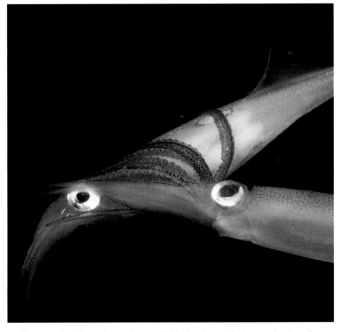

The tentacles of a male market squid blush crimson during mating in order to discourage competitors.

Locomotion Through the Ocean

A California sea lion demonstrates its mastery of aquatic maneuvers.

Have you ever wondered why many marine animals are able to swim so quickly and maneuver so well underwater? For me those moments usually come on the heels of a dive during which I have been constantly outmaneuvered by my photographic quarry. How was it possible for these creatures to be so much more efficient than I? Two events stand out in my mind as experiences that opened my eyes to how and why body design is so important in an animal's adaptability to its surroundings.

The first episode occurred as I was working with mako sharks that had been baited in for filming. A lone sea lion approached and I was certain I was about to witness an attack by the sharks. Instead, I watched in astonishment as the sea lion consistently outmaneuvered the sharks, nipping and chasing them until the sharks abandoned the bait for the sea lion to devour at its leisure. It's probably not accurate to conclude that sea lions are better swimmers than mako sharks, but they certainly are more maneuverable.

The second episode occurred in a kelp bed at San Clemente Island, where I encountered a squadron of bat rays. As I tried to approach them, I was constantly frustrated by their ability to keep a significant distance from me without even beating their mighty pectoral fins. Swimming as rapidly as I could, I couldn't close the gap as much as an inch. I suddenly realized that the bat rays, a picture of hydrodynamic perfection, are so perfectly designed for their life in the sea that they can easily glide faster than I can swim.

These events led me to think about the importance of body design to an animal's swimming abilities. Superb swimmers have bodies that minimize drag and pressure resistance from the water. The more streamlined and longer the body, for example, the smoother the flow of water over the animal, and therefore, the faster it can swim. Fish have a wide variety of body designs, including the following:

- **Fusiform**: more or less torpedo-shaped, with a slightly rounded head and a long, thin, tapered body (as seen in blue sharks, mako sharks, and barracuda). Generally speaking, these animals are the fastest swimmers.

- **Laterally compressed:** flattened from side to side (as in the case of garibaldi).

- **Dorsoventrally compressed:** flattened from top to bottom, thus creating a wide, flat profile (as in angel sharks, halibut, and bat rays).

- **Attenuated:** long and thin, with a body diameter that is very small in comparison to the fish's length (moray eels are classic examples).

- **A small selection of unusual shapes:** each with only a few representatives (such as seahorses and ocean sunfish).

Most fishes have a combination of characteristics from these basic body designs. Each combination provides its possessor with a different set of abilities that suit and determine its particular lifestyle.

Many of the fastest-swimming species—tuna, open-ocean sharks, and barracuda—are generally fusiform, but the fusiform shape has been altered by a slight flattening from side to side. This shape, combined with a powerful tail, creates an excellent design for the speed needed by open-water predators.

Fish with laterally compressed forms are extremely maneuverable, but less capable of the speeds attained by fish with more fusiform shapes. In reef areas filled with a latticework of hiding places, laterally compressed species like garibaldi and blacksmith fish are well designed for slipping into thin crevices to hide or to seek prey.

Dorsoventrally compressed animals, such as halibut and angel sharks, are capable of maintaining a low profile and moving almost unnoticed along the bottom, where they typically blend in so well. Their shape also allows them to better grip the seafloor, so that in most cases they can remain motionless even in current and surge. Bottom-dwelling rays such as bat rays and thornback rays have evolved unique methods of locomotion, cruising through the water by beating or undulating their large, powerful pectoral fins.

Attenuated fishes such as morays have long bodies that minimize the water resistance as they swim. They are also able to enter crevices inaccessible to wider animals, giving them a larger selection of potential hiding places as well as a greater ability to search out their prey.

Body design can tell you quite a lot about an animal. With a little practice, you'll be able to guess with some accuracy where an animal lives, how it feeds, and how it protects itself from predators, just by noticing its general shape.

times attach themselves to the tuna crabs, and as the scallops grow, the crabs become too heavy to support themselves and sink to the bottom. The octopus sits very still and waits for a careless, overweighted crab to stray too close. As the crab draws near, the octopus carefully extends a tentacle. When the crab gets within an inch or two, the octopus quickly reaches out with the tentacle and envelops it, then pulls the entangled crab under its mantle and bites it. I have seen octopi only 10 inches across capture and devour as many as five tuna crabs in twenty minutes.

In order to avoid being attacked by a potential mate, a male octopus signals his amorous intentions by flashing certain colors or patterns, or by curling back his tentacles. He may caress the female with a gentle tentacle in hopes that she will be receptive. He then places a sperm packet on a modified tentacle, offering it to the female. If she accepts his offer, she takes the sperm packet—and occasionally part of the male's tentacle as well. The female fertilizes herself with the packet when she returns to her den. Although the male may mate with other females, he will die at the end of the breeding season. The female

Coupling over vast fields of already planted squid eggs, these market squid will die soon after they mate.

A multitude of predators, including this young bat ray, feast on the dying squid.

A spiny sand star greedily ensnares two dying market squid.

underneath the mantle of the female, who uses it to fertilize her eggs.

Immediately after mating, the captivating color shows slow and cease, and the squid take on a sickly pallid hue as their tentacles become grossly disfigured. This rapid deterioration makes them easy prey to the animals that come to feed on the dying squid. Interestingly, the seemingly vulnerable egg casings are not heavily preyed upon. Some specialists suspect that this is due to the presence of proteins that are repulsive to potential predators.

lays strings of eggs and attaches them to the ceiling of her den, where she protects them until they hatch. She does not leave the den to eat, and refuses any food offered to her by well-meaning divers. Shortly after the young octopi hatch, she dies.

Common squid, or market squid, usually inhabit deep water, but they mate and lay their eggs in much shallower surroundings. Of all the phenomena that occur in the sand, squid mating is perhaps the most fascinating. During heavy runs, which can last for several weeks, millions of squid gather to mate in coastal canyons and along steep sand drop-offs at the offshore islands. After successful fertilization the females lay their eggs, and then the adults die.

Squid are capable of swimming forward, backward, and sideways with equal rapidity, jet-propelling themselves with a directable siphon and undulating tail fins as they seek out a mate. Most mating occurs at night, and is accompanied by rapid flashes of color as the squid pulsate from creamy white to purple to brown and green. When a male successfully latches onto a female, his tentacles immediately blush a scarlet warning to deter other males from attempting to woo his mate. He quickly and adeptly passes his packet of sperm

The eggs are laid inside of 4- to 10-inch-long white egg casings that are firmly attached to the sandy bottom. Each case contains close to 200 squid eggs; only a few of the

DID YOU KNOW?

. . . LIKE FIREFLIES, MANY MARINE ANIMALS CAN CREATE THEIR OWN LIGHT (BIOLUMINESCENCE). IN FACT, A MAJORITY OF THE JELLYFISH, CRUSTACEANS, AND FISHES THAT LIVE IN DEEPER WATERS ARE BIOLUMINESCENT.

White sea urchins swarm and consume a red sea urchin . . .

. . . leaving only the bare skeleton of their prey behind.

embryonic squid will become adults, as the hatchlings are heavily preyed upon by a variety of carnivorous fishes and crustaceans. In many places the casings are so thick that they completely obscure the bottom, and the once light brown sandy substrate takes on the appearance of a luxurious, creamy-white shag carpet for as far as you can see. After five to seven days you can see the bright red eyes of the unhatched squid within the egg casings. In another week or so, the eggs will hatch, and the newborns will instinctively head for deep water.

Along the egg- and dying squid–covered seafloor, a diversity of scavengers and predators gorge themselves. Bat rays, horn sharks, and angel sharks eat so many squid that they end up resting on the bottom with partially eaten squid dangling from their mouths, as if immobilized by their consumption. Rockfish, black sea bass, cabezon, sculpin, and a multitude of other fishes often join the feast. Lobster and crabs leave the protective crevices of the reef to forage on the dying adults. Even with all this activity, the squid die off so fast that in places they are stacked one on top of the other in piles up to 2 feet high.

High up in the water column, the feast continues for sea lions, harbor seals, pilot whales, and blue sharks that prey upon still-living squid. Blue sharks rarely come so close to shore, but the appeal of so much food sometimes brings these open-ocean sharks into shallow water to feed. At times the blue sharks are present in such large numbers that everywhere you look, you will sight a blue swimming, mouth agape, through the squid.

When the squid do mate at depths accessible to sport divers, it is generally during the middle of winter; however, I have witnessed heavy runs in August in

San Diego. The squid are driven by strong instincts and pay little attention to outsiders, whether predators or diving photographers, as they frantically search for partners. They are believed to live only one year, and the strong mating instinct ensures that they will make exhaustive efforts to reproduce before dying.

Many species of **snails** reside in the sand, their passing evidenced by distinct grooved tracks left behind as they make their way across the sandy bottom. One of the most common species is **Lewis' moon snail**, which attains a diameter of nearly 5 inches. Lewis' moon snails have a well-developed olfactory sense that helps them locate their favorite foods: clams and other snails. They are characterized by their large gray foot and a gray mantle that almost covers the shell. The shell is brown, gray, or off-white, with a very large aperture.

Sand dollars are echinoderms that are closely related to sea urchins. The spineless, disc-shaped body of dead specimens, with its characteristic five-petal flowerlike design, is familiar to almost everyone. Living sand dollars are typically 3 to 4 inches in diameter, purple, and furry in appearance. A solitary pink barnacle is found atop many specimens.

Orienting themselves with the prevailing current, sand dollars usually occur in numbers so large that their partially buried bodies almost obscure the bottom. In rough waters, sand dollars burrow farther under the sand to avoid being tumbled about and swept away. Adults are also able to resist the currents by growing heavier skeletons as they age, while juveniles may swallow sand grains to weigh themselves down.

Sand dollars are detritivores, feeding primarily upon decaying organic matter caught on their spines or entrapped by their sucker-tipped tube feet and a sticky mucus among their spines. Even larval sand dollars unfortunate enough to settle within an existing sand dollar bed are soon eaten by hungry adults.

The sweet potato cucumber looks more like a vegetable than an animal.

Among the most numerous of the sandy plains sea stars is the **spiny sand star**. This species attains a diameter of up to 10 inches. Almost always grayish in color, they can easily be recognized by the rows of spines along the margins of their arms. Amazingly, they can move either on or below the surface of the sand in search of their gastropod prey. The spiny sand star's cousin, the **sand star**, has thicker arms, longer spines, and a slightly narrower width.

The feeding habits of many species of sand-dwelling sea stars are fascinating to observe. A sea star often finds its prey

A bat ray forages for buried invertebrate animals.

buried deep in the sand, and to get to its desired quarry it extends its stomach far down into the burrows dug by its prey. It then envelops the hapless catch with its stomach, and the digestive process begins.

The **sweet potato cucumber** is an aptly named denizen of sandy terrain. Closely resembling its namesake, this sea cucumber is smooth, mottled with brown and yellow, and—unlike most other species of sea cucumbers—lacks tube feet. Sweet potato cucumbers partially bury themselves in the sand and feed on detritus extracted from the large amounts of sand that pass through their guts. Inhabiting southern California waters, sweet potato cucumbers grow to nearly 10 inches long.

From Santa Barbara southward, in deeper, cooler waters over sandy plains, divers occasionally discover large gatherings of small white sea urchins. This species is commonly called the **white sea urchin**. Although they can take on an orangish hue, they are often snow-white. Individuals attain a maximum diameter of about 2 inches. Sometimes spread out and solitary, these urchins will aggregate together in softball-sized groups when scavenging on a common source, including other urchins.

Another fascinating sand-dwelling urchin is the **heart urchin**, sometimes called the mouse urchin or sea porcupine. Heart urchins look like spiny balls of fur, with the longest spines generally curved back over the body. This species buries itself in the sand, usually exposing only its long, pliable spines. When uncovered, heart urchins can scurry across the bottom at a rapid pace. Once settled, they will quickly rebury themselves. When handling heart urchins, it is amazingly easy to get punctured by a spine. Although the wound is usually not serious, it can be irritating.

Rays and Sharks of the Sandy Plains

Stingrays are named for their formidable defense: they possess venomous spines at the base of their tail. When stepped on or threatened, a stingray can drive its spine(s) into the attacker with a whiplike action of its tail. However,

The face of a bat ray.

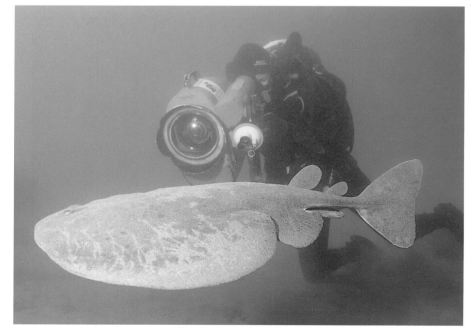

A diver films a torpedo ray, taking care not to come within reach of this shocking animal.

so long as swimmers and divers don't step on a sleeping stingray, they are highly unlikely to be threatened in the slightest. Most injuries occur when swimmers and waders in shallow water accidentally step on a stingray that is camouflaged against the sandy bottom. One way to avoid a wound is to do the "stingray shuffle": by shuffling your feet along the seafloor, you will scare away any hidden stingrays before you get close enough to step on them.

Round stingrays are the most commonly observed stingrays in southern and central California sandy plains habitats. Growing to about 22 inches in length, these small rays are brown or gray, round, and often marked with yellow spots. They mate in very shallow water in June, and females return in August and September. Younger rays prey primarily on worms and small crustaceans, while older larger rays also feed on clams.

Bat rays are among the most graceful of marine creatures in California waters. Watching these stingrays majestically soar through the water is a treat divers never tire of. Usually solitary, bat rays occasionally gather together in large squadrons to feed or mate. They are easy to distinguish from other rays by their relatively large size and fleshy, protruding forehead, and by the location of their eyes on the sides of the head rather than on the flat upper surface, as is the case with most rays. Bat rays are normally about 3 to 5 feet across, but 7-foot "wingspans" have been reported.

Bat rays are often encountered resting on the sand. When first approached by divers, they tend to rise up on their wing tips as if to give notice that if the diver continues to approach, the ray will depart. That is usually the case, but once in a great while you will encounter a bat ray that allows you to get within a foot or two. It is also quite common for divers with a catch bag full of abalone to turn around and find a hungry bat ray cruising curiously behind them—abalone, as well as clams, oysters, crabs, and tube worms, are the favorite prey of bat rays. When feeding on sandy bottoms, bat rays grub through the sand with their head and "wings," creating huge depressions in the sand in their effort to unearth prey. In areas of heavy feeding the seafloor may look like a crater field. Bat rays are also observed using their head to dislodge abalone from rocky reefs.

Electric rays are sometimes seen cruising ever so slowly or hovering over sand patches, but often hide themselves beneath the sand. An electric ray has a flat blue-gray upper body, a light underbelly, enlarged pectoral fins, and a short tail. True to their name, they are capable of generating enough voltage to stun prey or defend themselves—an unwary predator quickly learns to avoid these rays after receiving a painful electric shock instead of food. Unlike other rays, electric rays possess highly developed electrical organs composed of muscle tissue in which the normal electricity-generating capacity has been dramatically increased.

A thornback ray scours the seafloor for dead or dying market squid among egg casings.

The Submarine Canyons

If you were in an airplane and all the water suddenly disappeared from the Pacific Ocean off the coast of California, you would find yourself looking down at dramatic, canyon-filled mountain ranges resembling the more familiar terrestrial mountain ranges. This dramatic undersea topography is due to large submarine canyons that cut chasms through the sandy plains near shore in many areas of California. Coastal currents often enrich the canyon areas with a constant supply of nutrients that become trapped where the water flow is blocked by canyon walls, providing the foundation for an impressive diversity of life. Large numbers of invertebrates and a variety of fishes are found in these nutrient-rich sections of the canyon.

Burrowing flatfish such as this turbot contribute to erosion in submarine canyons.

Like the majority of submarine canyons, California canyons typically have V-shaped profiles with high steep walls, terracelike ledges, rock outcroppings, a constantly shifting substrate, and a number of tributaries along a winding course. The topography of individual canyons changes dramatically from gentle slopes to sheer cliffs that descend into the depths. In between the two extremes there are a variety of slopes and cascading ledges arranged in steplike fashion.

Several of these canyons are particularly noteworthy because of their massive size or their popularity with divers and fishers, including La Jolla Canyon, Scripps Canyon, Monterey Canyon, Redondo Canyon, Dume Canyon, Mugu Canyon, Carmel Canyon, Delgada Canyon, Mattole Canyon, Eel Canyon, Mendocino Canyon, and Sur-Partington Canyon. Perhaps the most notable are La Jolla Canyon and Scripps Canyon, off the coast of La Jolla in San Diego, and Monterey Canyon, which heads off Moss Landing near Monterey. La Jolla Canyon, which extends to approximately four-fifths of a mile south of the pier at the Scripps Institute of Oceanography, is a favorite night diving site for many San Diegans. Similarly, Monterey Canyon is a popular spot for divers in the Monterey area. More than 51 miles long and 2 miles deep, the three-branched Monterey Canyon is the largest undersea canyon on the West Coast, and is often compared to Arizona's Grand Canyon.

Diving in the canyons is very rewarding, but you must be very careful to monitor your depth and time and take careful bearings. It is all too easy to be lured into deep water when pursuing interesting creatures, and in some places the canyons plunge steeply to a depth of several hundred feet. Even if you stay in relatively shallow water, you may stir up the bottom so completely that you cannot find the canyon walls—"silt-outs" are a serious hazard to be avoided. If you have taken good compass bearings, you can relocate the canyon walls, but if not, you may lose the bottom and find yourself hovering over exceptionally deep water.

However, with a modicum of common sense and care, you can safely spend dive after dive playing with octopi, filming beautiful sea pens and sea fans, or discovering life-forms rarely found in other communities. Most submarine canyons border deep basins, so some animals that normally live in deep waters are more apt to visit the canyons than other areas accessible to sport divers. This is especially true at night, adding the excitement of the unexpected to nighttime exploration.

These organs, one on each side of the rounded body disc, are filled with more than 375 stacks of cells that work much like the electrical plates in batteries. The rays have voluntary control over these organs, and can generate electricity at will. They use their special ability to feed on fish, crustaceans, and mollusks, and have been observed feeding upon dying squid during squid runs.

Worldwide, there are approximately thirty species of electric rays, and the electricity they generate varies considerably from species to species. One nonlocal species has been documented to produce up to 220 volts at 20 amps! The shock of the electric rays that inhabit California is not strong enough to seriously hurt a swimmer or diver, but if you are hit, you will feel an unpleasant jolt similar to what you would feel when touching spark plug wires. Though not overtly aggressive, electric rays are not as wary as many other sea creatures. Their curiosity, or lack of fear, often leads them to hover near and follow divers.

Thornback rays, also commonly called banjo sharks, feature several rows of small spines that extend down the midline of their back. Thornback rays have a brown back and a white or cream-colored underbelly, and attain an overall body length of 2 to 3 feet. Ranging from San Francisco to Baja, they are common residents of many sand communities. They are generally seen resting on the sand and often turn away when approached by divers. Thornback rays feed primarily upon small crustaceans, mollusks, some echinoderms, and various fishes.

Almost every group in the animal kingdom has its eccentricities, and the cartilaginous fishes are no exception. Resembling a cross between a ray and a shark, the **shovelnose guitarfish** is essentially a flattened shark. Guitarfish are classified as batoids, a group of fishes closely related to sharks. Reaching a maximum length of about 4 feet, they are both carnivorous and cartilaginous like sharks, but their body is extremely compressed from top to bottom. Shovelnose guitarfish feed upon a variety of mollusks and crustaceans.

Not much is known about their life cycle, but these batoids are obviously well adapted for their life on the bottom. Breathing through a spiracle rather than a mouth, shov-

A shovelnose guitarfish.

elnose guitarfish draw water in through the valved spiracles located on top of their head and pass it over gill tissues before expelling it through ventral gill slits. The spiracle helps these bottom-dwellers with their lives in the sand; it is very likely that delicate gill tissues would be severely damaged by coarse sediment if oxygen-rich water had to be sucked in off the bottom.

Skates strongly resemble rays upon first glance, but there are at least four significant distinctions. First, skates lack the stingers or barbs found at the base of the tail of many rays. Second, the tail of a skate is lobed and fleshier and heavier than that of rays. Third, the broader tail of skates often contains many spines. And fourth, all skates lay eggs, whereas all rays are live-bearers. Many skates have electrical tissue in their tail, but the output of electricity is minimal.

At least eight species of skates have been reported in California waters. Of these, the **big skate** is the most common one seen by swimmers and divers. This skate is found in depths ranging from 10 to 360 feet from San Quintin Bay, Baja, to Alaska's Bering Sea. Although known to grow to 8 feet long, few specimens are longer than 6 feet. Like most benthic sharks, rays, and skates, big skates feed on a wide variety of mollusks, crustaceans, echinoderms, and small fishes. They are preyed upon by some bottom-dwelling sharks.

Angel sharks are characterized by their unusually flattened body, terminal mouth, and greatly enlarged pectoral fins. Their normal coloration varies from sandy gray to reddish-brown, with a white underbelly and dark spots above. Angel sharks attain a maximum length of 5 feet and weigh up to 60 pounds. They are generally observed resting on the bottom, either partially or completely buried. Because of their dorsoventrally compressed body, the nonthreatening appearance of their face, and their docile nature, angel sharks are often mistaken for skates or rays.

As lie-in-wait predators, angel sharks feed upon a variety of small fish, crustaceans, and mollusks. They do not readily come to bait, and are known to lie in the same place and position for extended periods of time. However, even when resting on the seafloor, angel sharks are ready to capture and engulf unsuspecting prey. When potential prey passes through a rather small zone immediately in front of and above the shark's head, the shark quickly rises up off the bottom and opens its cavernous mouth in an effort to capture it. Amazingly, a 3- to 5-foot-long shark can open its mouth as wide as 1 foot from lower jaw to top jaw. Although angel sharks are formidable predators, they are extremely particular about timing their attack; I have seen possible meals such as octopi and lobsters literally crawl over the top of a resting angel shark, and the shark didn't even move because the potential prey never entered its "feeding zone."

When frightened by divers, angel sharks flee along the bottom. Often, as one angel shark swims away, another previously unseen angel shark will also bolt, and then another and another in a domino effect, until as many as five or six sharks are gliding gracefully away along the seafloor. In the past decade, however, this majestic sight has become all too rare, as an angel shark fishery has been growing along the California coast. Angel sharks have small home ranges and are therefore extremely easy to find. Because of overfishing, angel shark populations have been severely affected along much of the California coast.

Flattened and colored like the sandy seafloor, a camouflaged angel shark waits to engulf unsuspecting prey.

Bony Fishes of the Sandy Plains

Spotted cusk eels are among the many fascinating bony fishes that inhabit the sandy plains. These small eels reach a maximum length of nearly 15 inches and are easy to identify by their barbels or chin whiskers, and the dark spots

The oddly twisted face of a flatfish.

The C-O sole gains its name from the pattern on its tail.

along their thin, almost translucent body. Ranging from northern Oregon to San Cristobal Bay in Baja, spotted cusk eels are usually encountered only at night on sandy bottoms, when they hunt octopi, small fishes, and various crustaceans. When threatened or alarmed, they can bury themselves in the sand by rapidly wiggling their way in tail-first. Spotted cusk eels are rarely seen during the day, when they remain buried in the sand several inches below the surface.

All **flatfishes** are born upright with one eye on either side of their head, but as they mature they lie on one side and one eye migrates over so that both eyes are located on the top side of the fish. As you can imagine, the faces of these fish look as though they were the survivors of a minor nuclear holocaust. Halibut and sanddabs are members of a family commonly called lefteye flounders, in reference to the fact that the eye on the right side migrates to the left side, although occasionally the left eye migrates to the right side. There are also twenty-two species of righteye flounders in California waters, including rock sole, starry flounder, C-O sole, and diamond turbot. In adults, both eyes are most often found on the right side of the head of righteye flounders. As with other flatfishes, their coloration patterns vary, and their eyes are occasionally found on the left side. Identification of flatfishes is therefore tricky without a detailed pictorial reference source.

The **California halibut** is easily distinguished from other flatfishes in state waters. By far the largest of the flatfishes, it possesses a large mouth, many sharp teeth, and a high arch in the lateral line above its pectoral fin. It is usually speckled brown on top and white underneath, although all-brown and all-white halibut are known. California halibut range from Oregon to Magdalena Bay, about halfway down the Baja Peninsula, but specimens show up north of Morro Bay only seasonally.

Of all the fish species that can be found in a sandy environment, the California halibut is the most heavily sought-after by fishers. Both experienced spearfishers and seasoned rod-and-reel enthusiasts are well aware that halibut are usually located in sandy areas in less than 60 feet of water. Sport fishers troll with large anchovies when possible, but halibut will hit a variety of live bait, dead bait, and artificial lures.

Halibut are slow-growers; five-year-old fish average only 15 inches long. Large females can reach a size of up to 50 inches and 50 pounds. Halibut feed on anchovies and other similarly sized fish, and are preyed upon by a variety of sharks, electric rays, sea lions, seals, and some inshore dolphins.

If you were to ask a group of scuba divers if they had seen a **sculpin** during a dive, odds are the answer would be "Yes, in fact we saw several." The term "sculpin" is a common name used to describe many different kinds of fish in two separate families. The family Scorpaenidae, the scorpion fishes, contains sixty-two species, the most species of common California fish belonging to one family. Included in this grouping is the California scorpionfish, often called the common sculpin or spotted sculpin. All rockfish are also found in the Scorpaenidae family, in the genus *Sebastes*.

However, fifty-six additional species that inhabit California waters are also usually called some type of sculpin. These fish belong to a family named Cottidae. Confusing? To well-schooled ichthyologists, no, but to fishers, divers, and other recreational enthusiasts it certainly can be. In general, the fish known as sculpin are united by their awkward appearance; their bulbous face, wide mouth, large lips, bulging eyes, and mottled colors make these creatures so ugly they're cute. Sculpin also have dorsal spines that can wound an unwary angler or diver.

Frequently observed species of the Cottidae family include the roughback sculpin, spotfin sculpin, lavender sculpin, buffalo sculpin, tidepool sculpin, grunt sculpin, and cabezon. Some of these species are found in both sandy and rocky substrates, while others show definite preferences for one habitat or another. For example, grunt sculpin are seen much more often in northern California than in the south, and cabezon are often observed in rockier areas where they prey on abalone (see Chapter 5).

A one-spot fringehead peers ferociously from its home.

Its widely flattened head, bulging eyes, and upturned mouth make the **plainfin midshipman** an unmistakeable, if somewhat unattractive, sandy plains bottom-dweller. These nocturnal feeders remain buried in the sand with only their eyes and mouth exposed until nightfall, when they come out to hunt. At the sight of a diver's light, a midshipman will dive headfirst back into the protection of the sand.

This endearingly ugly face is typical of sculpins.

The sarcastic fringehead has a face at least as odd as its name.

allows communication among them. Not all plainfin midshipmen are luminescent, however; the light-producing reaction requires a chemical produced by a small planktonic crustacean, and fish that live in areas where these crustaceans are scarce are not able to luminesce. Luminescence is a rarity among shallow-water fishes.

The **sarcastic fringehead** has a face to match its bizarre name. Growing to a length of just under 1 foot, sarcastic fringeheads are found in crevices, discarded shells, and holes in sandy or muddy bottoms, or even in discarded cans and bottles. Their bulbous eyes, heavily frilled face, enormous mouth, deep purple to brown coloration, and two metallic blue spots on the dorsal fin make positive identification easy. The sarcastic fringehead can be distinguished from its cousin, the **one-spot fringehead**, by the two spots on its dorsal fin, as opposed to one. Fringeheads, along with various kelpfish, are members of the Clinidae family.

During mating season, male plainfin midshipmen woo females with a monotone hum that can be quite loud (and, according to some reports, irritating) in areas where the fish are abundant. The males dig nests under rocks in the intertidal regions of northern and central California and in the shallow subtidal in southern California. Once successfully seduced by a male's serenade, the female lays eggs on the rock that overhangs his burrow. The male vigilantly guards his nest until the larvae hatch and develop, staying at his post even during very low tides when the hatchlings may be completely exposed.

Plainfin midshipmen are lined with rows of luminescent white spots called photophores. Scientists speculate that this luminescence is useful for camouflaging the fish against a light background, or that it

DID YOU KNOW?

. . . SQUID HAVE THE LARGEST NERVE CELLS OF ANY ANIMAL—UP TO A MILLIMETER IN DIAMETER. THESE GIANT NERVE CELLS HAVE BEEN INVALUABLE IN RESEARCH ON THE HUMAN NERVOUS SYSTEM AND TREATMENT OF NERVOUS DISEASES.

Mature male fringeheads are highly territorial and openly defiant even of divers when their territory is invaded. An incensed male will rise up from his burrow or borrowed shell, snapping what suddenly becomes an enormous, brightly colored mouth. Physical confrontations between competing males are often avoided by the superior display of one male, which drives the other away from the disputed territory.

Blue sharks are among the most graceful of animals encountered in the open ocean.

CHAPTER 7
THE OPEN SEA

A purple jellyfish.

With the exception of the beaches, environmental conditions change faster and more dramatically in mid-ocean than in other sectors of the sea. Life exists very ephemerally in any given area of the open sea. In such a feast-or-famine setting, it is difficult to predict the presence of specific animals on a particular day in a particular location.

Most boaters and divers rarely even notice planktonic life unless it is present in concentrations dense enough to alter the water color and reduce visibility. Yet the very existence of larger, more interesting animals—apex predators such as blue and mako sharks, gray whales, and dolphins—is predicated upon the availability of tiny planktonic plants and animals. The presence of plankton attracts small animals such as sardines and anchovies, which in turn are preyed upon by larger species such as mackerel, which attract yellowtail, albacore, and barracuda. These middle predators are sought after by pelagic sharks and marine mammals. The survival of animals at the top of the food chain directly depends upon planktonic life.

Local concentrations of plankton are controlled by many factors, such as currents. The currents, in turn, are significantly affected by several variable forces, including wind, tide, swell, and temperature. As a result, the presence of concentrations of planktonic organisms is very difficult to predict. Concentrations may occupy only an acre, or extend to thousands of square miles. Other drifting animals whose whereabouts are governed by winds and currents are jellyfish, salp, comb jellies, and by-the-wind-sailors; these animals also appear in enormous quantities at times, only to be nearly absent at others. Life in the open sea is truly "here today and gone tomorrow," as migratory animals constantly pursue those that drift with currents.

A rock scallop surrounded by *Corynactis* anemones.

The Seamounts

Seamounts are undersea pinnacles that rise dramatically from the deep ocean floor, creating sheer vertical walls, ledges, plateaus, caves, cracks, and crevices that are ideal living quarters for a great many marine animals. Oases of the open sea, seamounts are constantly awash with currents and nutrient-rich upwellings, creating an extremely prolific environment. The surface area provides a place of attachment for bottom-dwellers, and their presence attracts a diverse group of other species. There are several prominent seamounts in California waters that can be visited by both fishers and sport divers, and many are associated with the Channel Islands. Although you are unlikely to discover creatures that are not present elsewhere, the diversity and quantity of life you can encounter at a seamount are often staggering.

The seamounts are rocky reefs, though this is difficult to believe upon first sight. The rocks are often totally obscured by a carpetlike covering of invertebrates. Almost everywhere you look are aggregates of bright red, orange, and pink *Corynactis* anemones, and large white *Metridiums* with stalks that are often more than 2 feet tall.

Nestled amongst the anemones are chestnut cowries, sponges, barnacles, colonies of encrusting bryozoans, well-camouflaged crabs, worms, dinner-plate–sized rock scallops, nudibranchs, and a host of colorful sea stars, creating the enviable problem of what to admire or photograph first.

Some crevices are occupied by large lobsters, morays, and cleaner shrimp. Others harbor wolf-eels, cabezon, lingcod, and a variety of rockfish. Schools of mackerel, barracuda, and yellowtail are common sights at the seamounts. Many people believe that California fishes other than the garibaldi are rather drably colored, but nothing could be further from the truth. Some of the more striking examples of California fishes are vermilion, rosy, starry, copper, black-and-yellow, and china rockfish, as well as treefish, blue-banded gobies, and sculpin.

Ocean sunfish often hover around the pinnacles. Commonly referred to by their scientific name, *Mola mola*, these rather bizarrely shaped fish are always fun to encounter. On some days, the first exhaust of scuba bubbles sends ocean sunfish hurriedly on their way. On other days divers can swim right up to them, but if you touch them, you are likely to be sorry. They have very fine scales on their skin, coated with a thick layer of mucus that adheres to anything and everything it touches—especially divers.

Divers frequently see beautiful purple jellyfish and salp chains floating past in a mid-ocean current. And yes, blue sharks constantly cruise many seamounts, attracted by the presence of so much food.

One really can't say enough about the quality and excitement of diving on the seamounts. There just seems to be more life, both large and small, per square yard of reef. Visibility is usually considerably better as well. On good days the diving is superb, and on great days it is truly "off the scale." The only disadvantages are that strong currents are often encountered, conditions must be better than average in order to anchor safely, and it is very easy to be lured into deep water if you are not disciplined in your diving habits.

Open-Sea Invertebrates

Occasionally, great expanses of the surface of the open sea are covered by thousands of **by-the-wind sailors**. Large gatherings are the result of population density and prevailing winds and currents, and may occupy several acres. These cnidarians reach a diameter of nearly 4 inches, and have a clear body surrounded by a blue to purple border. The distinguishing feature is the small sail, which sits above the water surface. On days when there is very little wind and the surface is flat, positioning your head close to the surface and looking out into a dense concentration of by-the-wind sailors can reveal a truly remarkable seascape.

Made up of more than 90 percent water, graceful **jellyfish** seem more ocean than animal. These primitive creatures have no brain, employing only a simple system of nerve nets to control reactions, feeding, and the rhythmic pulsations used in swimming. They are able to detect changes in light, to sense which way is up, and to "taste" the water around them. Although they can use this information to adjust their vertical position to some extent, jellyfish are relatively poor swimmers; they are planktonic creatures that tend to go wherever currents, winds, and wave action take them. They are, however, remarkable predators due to their small stinging cells, called nematocysts, which all cnidarians possess. Nematocysts are located both in the tentacles and around the edge of the mouth, and are laced with a potent,

This large jellyfish is a member of the plankton, drifting through the open seas with water currents.

A purple jellyfish.

feeding tentacles before they begin their own independent pelagic existence.

Comb jellies look like jellyfish at first glance, but belong to an entirely different phylum: Ctenophora. Comb jellies take on a variety of shapes, including a common ribbonlike form, whereas jellyfish are generally bowl-shaped. Comb jellies lack the stinging nematocysts used by jellyfish, and have the distinguishing characteristic of eight rows of ciliated "combs," which appear as lines covered by tiny hairs on the body. The cilia sometimes catch and refract light into shimmering rainbows of color that ripple along the sides of these beautiful animals. Though capable of independent movement via the rowing motion of their cilia, comb jellies usually go wherever the current and wind take them. For this reason, you will usually see dozens or none on a given day, but rarely only a few.

fast-acting, paralyzing venom that quickly halts the struggling of most prey. The nematocysts of some jellyfish are capable of penetrating human skin, and the severity of the reaction to stings depends both on the species of jellyfish and on the physiology of the victim.

Worldwide, there are more than 200 species of jellyfishes, and though several species are seen in state waters, the most common and most striking is the **purple jellyfish**. Purple jellyfish have a silvery-white bell with brownish to purplish stripes radiating out from the center. They grow to slightly more than a foot in diameter, and the tentacles can trail more than 6 feet behind the bell. Purple jellyfish feed on plankton and small fish. Despite the deadly risk, however, juvenile slender crabs and small fishes often take refuge among their tentacles. These daring animals must be extremely wary and agile, because although they are sheltered from other predators, they are not immune to the jellyfish's poison—a moment of clumsiness or an instant's distraction may well cost an unfortunate victim its life.

Moon jellyfish are less colorful than purple jellyfish, but are no less beautiful. These jellies have a translucent snow-white bell, through which four horseshoe-shaped gonads are visible. Their tentacles do not trail beyond the bell, as do those of many other jellyfish, so that moon jellies look a bit like the cap of a mushroom made transparent. The embryos of moon jellies develop on special grooves in the mother's

Sharks of the Open Sea

Named for their beautiful coloration, **blue sharks** are the most commonly sighted of California's open-ocean sharks. Inhabiting temperate seas all over the world, blue sharks are easy to recognize by their royal blue color, long slender build, and comparatively long pectoral fins. Blues typically range from 5 to 8 feet, and at 8 feet weigh 70 to 80 pounds. There have been unverified reports of a 13-foot-long blue in California waters; on many occasions I have filmed blues that were at least 10 to 11 feet long.

The beautiful blue color of these sharks is most obvious on sunny days when they are near the surface. Their iridescent skin sparkles as shimmering rays of sunlight reflect off their backs. Like many open-sea predators, blue sharks are well countershaded, meaning they are more lightly colored on the underside. When you are looking up toward a blue that is near the surface, the whitish underbelly tends to blend

Blue sharks are named for the beautiful iridescent color of their skin in the sunlight.

in with the lighter water colors found there. And when you look down onto a blue from above, their darker topside tends to blend in well with the blue-black waters below. Counter-shading affords blues a better chance to go undetected by predators and prey alike.

Extremely graceful swimmers, blues glide rather effort-lessly at a speed only slightly faster than most humans can easily swim. They rarely seem to swim at full throttle, but make no mistake about it, blues can move in a hurry when they so desire. In fact, they are believed to be among the fastest of the sharks. Like most of the world's more than 370 species of sharks, blues use their long powerful tails

for thrust, controlling their attitude and turns primarily with their pectoral fins. These highly maneuverable animals give the impression of always being in total control while normally operating at a level well below their maximum capabilities.

Blue sharks tend to be sexually segregated, and in southern California one sees almost all males in the summer and almost all females in the winter. The two genders are believed to mix for brief periods of time in both spring and fall. The males can easily be identified by a pair of claspers on the underbelly, and the females by a lack of claspers. Claspers are part of the males' reproductive system, common to males of all cartilaginous fishes. Exactly where and how blues mate are still a matter of speculation. Females are often scarred with the imprints of the males' teeth. These scars are believed to be the result of bites during courtship and mating, and are thus referred to as mating scars. Females benefit from an interesting adaptation in that the skin covering their gut, pectoral fins, and head is up to three times thicker than that of males. This adaptation is found in many shark species, and probably protects the females from injury while mating.

A blue shark.

Blues are often accompanied by small fish called common **remoras**, also called suckerfish. Their behavior is not completely understood, and though it is clear that the remoras benefit from the presence of the sharks, scientists are not sure if the sharks benefit, are harmed, or remain unaffected. Larger remoras capture some of their own food, while smaller specimens are thought to clean parasites off their hosts. Certainly remoras feed on scraps dropped by a host shark. But there is no such thing as a free meal, even for remoras, and they are commonly found in the stomachs of blues and other sharks.

A blue shark's diet consists primarily of squid and small schooling fishes such as anchovies and sardines. Amazingly, they have also recently been observed feeding on tiny crustaceans called krill, after the krill were densely concentrated by swirling schools of hungry anchovies. Perhaps the most impressive display of blue shark predation occurs during the massive common squid matings, when blue sharks join other opportunistic animals that come to feast on the multitudes of dying squid. Blues gorge themselves on this easy meal, eating until their stomachs are grossly distended and squid hang out of their mouths. Rather than stopping at this point, they regurgitate some of what they have eaten and once again begin to munch their way through the densely schooling squid. Such a scene tends to make one think of sharks as wasteful eating machines, but in the wilderness there are no guarantees or free meals. When an opportunity to feed presents itself, blues must take maximum advantage. Some specialists maintain that when the sharks regurgitate, they are getting rid of parts of the squid that are difficult to digest and have little nutritional value.

The slender silhouette of a blue shark.

Testing a Shark Suit with My Own Flesh

A diver wearing an anti-shark suit
offers his arm to a riled-up blue shark.

Twenty miles out to sea in water several thousand feet deep, and everywhere I looked there were sharks. At least a dozen sleek, missile-like silhouettes were swimming over me. Most were blue sharks, although I had seen one big mako shark only a few minutes before. As I looked out into the cobalt blue, I saw a large blue shark descend and head toward me. As it neared, my mind replayed the grating and crunching sounds I had heard only moments earlier when I was bitten on the right arm by another blue shark.

This setting might sound like one's worst nightmare come true, but it was just what I had hoped for. Lots of sharks, clear water, me, and my camera. You see, the sounds were made by a blue shark's teeth raking over the stainless steel chain mesh of the protective Neptunic anti-shark suit I was wearing. Weighing 17 pounds, it is made of approximately 400,000 individually, electronically welded stainless-steel links, and was derived from products similar to those being used by butchers in meat markets. The Neptunic was codeveloped by San Diegan Jeremiah Sullivan and Australians Ron and Valerie Taylor. Although I had not been involved in the development, I had been fortunate enough to see the trio test and modify the suit from the early stages.

But seeing someone else's body in the mouth of a biting shark and putting yourself in that situation are two different things, no matter how much you like your friends. Being right-handed, the first time I ever tested the suit, I offered my left forearm to a rather small blue shark. The suit did a great job of protecting me, and the battle proved to be far more psychological than real. In short order I became completely confident in its ability to protect me, especially in the case of blue sharks.

So, what does it feel like to get chewed on? The idea behind the suit is to spread the bite pressure out over the surface area of the bite, not allowing the pointed, razor-sharp teeth to penetrate one's flesh. And it works. Most of the time what I feel is increased pressure—as if I were in a small vise—rather than sharp points. At times a single tooth has nicked me enough to draw blood. I have often described the situation as reminding me of when my father grabbed me when I was a child. He never hurt me, but he had a firm enough grip—not to mention the look on his face—to have my complete and undivided attention.

The real benefit of the suit is that it gives photographers like Howard Hall, Bob Cranston, Mike deGruy, and me the opportunity to work safely around a lot of sharks out in the open sea without putting safety divers in jeopardy. When Bob and I ran our shark diving trips for sport divers, we demonstrated the suit. It is of interest to a lot of divers and doesn't harm the sharks. They get a lot of mackerel for their trouble before the day is over.

Although blue sharks are considered to be opportunistic feeders, they are not indiscriminate about what they eat. When chumming for blues, it is imperative to use a bait source that is part of the sharks' natural diet. Rather bizarre items have been found in the stomachs of blue sharks, apparently due in part to the design of their mouth and teeth. Like many marine predators, blue sharks can extend their upper teeth well forward when feeding. In the act of closing their mouth, the sharks' teeth fold back toward the stomach, making it rather difficult for their natural prey—and any other odds and ends that might have been sampled—to escape.

Another migratory species of shark commonly sighted in California waters during late spring, summer, and fall is the **shortfin mako shark**, sometimes called the bonito shark. Makos are members of the family Lamnidae, which consists of a few fast-swimming species, including great white sharks. Many books will tell you that makos are easily distinguished from blue sharks by their conical snout, thick fusiform body, extremely large gills (which allow for highly efficient gas exchange), pronounced caudal peduncle (which forms the caudal keel), and homocercal, or almost perfectly lunate, tail fin. In the water, telling the two species apart is even easier. Simply put, blues are beautiful; makos appear frightening. A mako looks like a gaggle of teeth attached to the front end of a torpedo. Rows of long, narrow teeth are almost always exposed, giving the impression that the teeth are too large to fit in the shark's mouth. Excited or nervous makos move in a herky-jerky fashion, darting back and forth in a rather unnerving manner, in vivid contrast to the effortless, graceful movement of blues. Numerous parasitic copepods and their long thin strings of eggs are often attached to the dorsal fin; the parasites are also evident in the mouth of makos, where they cause nasty-looking sores. The combined effect of rows of exposed teeth, a thick body, wounds, and streaming parasites is a look that Hollywood producers would love to put on the face of any sea monster.

Despite their fearsome impression, makos are extremely careful about what they bite. While blues typically swim right up to a bait, makos tend to be more wary, and by the time they approach they are usually very excited. Makos feed upon a variety of fast-moving fishes such as albacore, swordfish, and other sharks, and are built for power and speed—as they must be in order to capture such speedy prey. Fishers are well aware that makos tend to follow albacore populations—when frustrated fishers catch only

Swimming with teeth exposed, mako sharks have a menacing appearance.

seas such as Mexico's Sea of Cortez, Ecuador's Galapagos Islands, and Costa Rica's famous Cocos Island. During certain times of the year, divers regularly see gatherings of several hundred scalloped hammerheads in these areas, but in California waters these sharks tend to be solitary. It is very unusual for apex predators (animals at the top of a food chain) to school. Because they lack significant numbers of natural predators, there is no reason to believe that scalloped hammerheads school based on the concept of safety in numbers. It is likely that mating or migratory behavior is at the heart of the issue, but to date no one is really sure.

Like many species of pelagic sharks, scalloped hammerheads prey primarily on smaller fishes, squid, and some pelagic rays when in the open sea. When hunting in reef communities, they are known to feed on a variety of fishes, crustaceans, and mollusks.

the head of an albacore, the culprit is often a contented mako.

In fact, almost everything about a mako indicates that it is built for power and speed. Their comparatively large gill slits enable these predators to metabolize large amounts of oxygen in a matter of seconds. Makos also have a large percentage of red muscle fiber, which has a higher rate of blood flow so more oxygen can be supplied to the muscles in a shorter period of time. A body temperature that is constantly maintained at a level a few degrees higher than ambient temperature allows their muscles to respond faster and increases stamina. The lunate tail and the thickness of the caudal peduncle, sometimes called the caudal keel, help generate speed as well.

On many occasions I have witnessed sea lions harassing makos, biting them repeatedly in a successful effort to chase them out of an area full of bait that our film crew had placed in the water. The sea lions return to the scene and feed to their heart's content, as if the whole encounter were simply "no big deal."

Scalloped hammerheads are occasionally seen in southern California waters during summer and fall, especially when surface temperatures are higher than normal. As their name implies, hammerheads are characterized by their flat, wide, hammer-shaped head. They can be distinguished from other hammerheads by pronounced ridges that create a scalloped effect along the leading edge of their head. When fully grown, scalloped hammerheads can be 10 feet long.

In recent years this species of shark has been the subject of many television documentaries and magazine articles because of their now famous schooling behavior in tropical

A scalloped hammerhead shark.

Common thresher sharks are characterized by their enormously long tail fin, which can be almost as long as the rest of their body. Like white sharks and makos, threshers maintain a body temperature higher than the surrounding water temperature. This adaptation allows them to live active lives and hunt successfully in colder deep waters. When they are hunting small schooling fishes such as sardines, anchovies, and herring, threshers are known to use their extremely long tail to herd and stun their prey. They are also known to prey upon squid, small tuna, hake, and other fishes. Common threshers range from central Baja to Canada.

Of all fishes, **basking sharks** are second in size only to whale sharks. Basking sharks can reach a length of 45 feet, though most individuals grow to less than 30 feet. A 30-foot-long specimen once caught near Monterey weighed 8,600

Blue sharks circle divers.

Shark Diving California Style

Sharks are to scuba divers what lions, tigers, and cheetahs are to those who go on big-game safaris in Africa and India. Seeing these animals in the wild is a special experience, one that almost any diver or trekker worthy of the name would enjoy. I had never set out to begin a business in taking other divers out into the open sea on shark diving expeditions, but in the late 1980s that is where I ended up.

For a decade or so prior to that time, I had been involved in a lot of California-based shark filming projects. Working primarily with Howard Hall, Bob Cranston, and Larry Cochrane, I had spent hundreds of hours out in the open sea trying to film blue sharks and mako sharks. When I told my diving pals about my adventures, many of them begged me to take them along. I understood this, as it was the same thing I had done to Howard and Larry a few years earlier. Thus, Bob and I began a business called San Diego Shark Diving Expeditions, working closely with Carl Roessler of See & Sea Travel.

For five or six years we took a hundred or so divers annually out into the open ocean, where they could see and photograph sharks from within the safe confines of a shark cage, and where they could watch us demonstrate the effectiveness of the stainless steel, chain mesh, Neptunic anti-shark suit. We had a great time and, for the most part, so did our guests. A few years ago we sold the business to Paul "Doc" Anes, who continues to operate such trips, as do other operators at Catalina Island, in Los Angeles, and in the Monterey area.

Blue sharks and makos generally inhabit the waters of the open sea, so it only makes sense that sharking takes place out in the open ocean, miles from the nearest land. Diving out in the blue, in the middle of nowhere, is a very different experience from diving on a reef. To my knowledge all the operators use shark cages and no divers work outside the cages. However, that doesn't mean that you won't get a good look at the sharks, especially blue sharks. Once attracted by bait (although chumming is no longer allowed in the Monterey area), blue sharks readily approach divers in a cage. Most of the time makos do so as well, but there are days when makos seem to keep some distance. Over the years we've also seen whales, albacore, ocean sunfish, turtles, pelagic stingrays, and myriad other open-sea inhabitants.

If you are curious about sharks and want to do something a little out of the ordinary, California shark diving is a great place to start. Safety is a priority and education is a big part of the overall program. Orientation, or practice, dives make up part of the classes, and no one is asked to do anything he or she isn't comfortable with. On the trips that Bob and I ran, most people experienced at least some pre-trip anxiety, but almost all had a great time and learned a lot about sharks. These trips are intended for divers of an intermediate experience level or beyond who have a sense of curiosity about sharks and the open sea.

Hopping Kelp Paddies

Floating clumps of kelp drifting on the surface in the open sea are referred to as kelp paddies. Diving, "jumping," or "hopping" the paddies is a favorite activity for many spearfishers and photographers. There's no telling what you will encounter. Hop enough paddies and you are likely to see just about everything that lives in the sea. Of course, sometimes there is nothing but floating kelp and empty blue water. At other times it is a virtual Noah's Ark. I suppose that is what makes hopping the paddies so exciting.

Almost anything that floats in mid-ocean, paddies included, will eventually attract some kind of crowd. Juvenile fishes often use the debris as a hiding place. But kelp paddies and other floating objects also attract the big boys. Spearfishers who want a crack at yellowtail are well aware that big yellows frequently cruise under kelp. So do schools of albacore, as well as an occasional blue shark or mako shark.

Ocean sunfish, also commonly referred to by their taxonomic name, *Mola mola*, often hang under kelp paddies. On some days *Molas* are extremely skittish and quick to flee. But on other days they readily approach slow-moving divers. They make great photographic subjects, and it is always fun to see animals in the open sea that you are unlikely to ever encounter while diving inshore.

If these big fish are not around, take a close look in the blades of the kelp and you are likely to find a variety of crabs, shrimp, and fishes that are not obvious at first glance.

pounds. Like whale sharks, basking sharks are filter-feeders. They swim, mouth agape, through dense concentrations of plankton, and continuously take in enormous quantities of water that is strained for food by their huge gill rakers.

The body of a basking shark is grayish-black above, shading to paler colors below; its skin is studded with densely packed, thornlike dermal denticles. Basking sharks are rarely seen by scuba divers, but they are often sighted in small schools by boaters in deep waters off the coasts of central and northern California. Typically these sightings are made on cloudy, windless winter and spring days when the sharks are near the surface. The range of basking sharks extends from the Sea of Cortez to Alaska.

The name **megamouth** describes a large deepwater shark whose very existence had been questioned until fairly recently. In 1984 the first documented megamouth was caught in a net off Catalina Island. It was confirmed that both a species and a family of sharks that were thought to be extinct for centuries do, in fact, still exist. Several other megamouths have been caught since 1984, two of them off the coast of southern California. Some experts believe that these behemoths' mouths have a bioluminescent lining that may attract zooplankton into the cavernous maws, while other scientists believe that the silvery lining may simply reflect bioluminescence that is produced by tiny animals on which megamouths feed. Although very little is known about the habits of megamouths, they are believed to feed in the deep scattering layer of plankton.

Bony Fishes of the Open Sea

Northern anchovies are the feeder fish of the open sea. Sought after by other fishes, squid, seabirds, sharks, mammals, pizza makers, and pretty much any other animal that can catch them, anchovies are crucial links in countless food chains. These small silvery fish reach about 7 inches in length and seem to grow more slowly in warmer waters. Their most noticeable characteristic is their huge mouth, which extends well past their eyes, causing them to resemble Grover from *Sesame Street*. Swimming through the water with mouth agape in an enormous "yawn," anchovies feed on smaller fishes and plankton.

Tight-knit anchovy schools are impressive displays of synchrony. Although it looks as though anchovies were pros

The gaping maw of a feeding basking shark.

at playing "follow-the-leader," in fact there is no leader. When the school suddenly reverses direction, the leader fish finds itself playing caboose. Instead, anchovies coordinate their movements by keeping a close watch on their neighbors, using visual cues and pressure waves to determine their direction.

Several species of **mackerel** play a vital role in open-ocean food chains. These include Pacific mackerel, bullet mackerel, and skipjack. **Pacific mackerel** (also called blue, chub, or striped mackerel) attain a length of up to 25 inches and a weight of 6.3 pounds. **Bullet mackerel** are slightly smaller, up to 20 inches long and 5 pounds, whereas **skipjack** can be up to 40 inches long and weigh as much as 35 pounds. These fishes are members of the family Scombridae, as are bonito, albacore, and other fishes commonly called tuna. Pacific mackerel, bullet mackerel, and skipjack feed mostly upon small fishes and shrimplike creatures called krill, but are also known to feed opportunistically on other bite-sized animals, especially juvenile squid. Porpoises, sea lions, yellowtail, marlin, sharks, black sea bass, and other large predators prey upon small mackerel and skipjack.

Schooling rapidly through the open sea, **tuna** challenge fishers and delight divers. **Albacore** frequent state waters in summer and fall. These highly migratory fish range from Clarion Island off the Pacific coast of Mexico all the way to Alaska and Japan. Albacore are attractive tuna with a dark blue back, silvery belly, and long pectoral fins. The largest documented albacore weighed 93 pounds and was 5 feet long. **Yellowfin tuna**, obviously named for their yellow fins, normally prefer warmer waters, but visit southern California waters during El Niño years. Young **bluefin tuna** are more permanent residents of California waters, although older specimens (three to six years old) depart to spawn in the western Pacific. Like yellowfin tuna, California bluefins grow over 6 feet in length and weigh up to 150 pounds or more. Bluefins have shorter pectoral fins than yellowfins or albacore, and their fins are bluish-colored. Tuna feed on a variety of prey, including squid, pelagic red crabs, some forms of plankton, and a variety of small fishes. In turn, tuna are preyed upon by swordfish, marlin, a variety of sharks, and even orca whales.

Schools of **Pacific bonito**, also commonly called boneheads or bonies, frequent California waters in late spring, summer, and fall. Reaching up to 40 inches long, bonito are dark greenish-blue above with dark slanted stripes and a silvery underbelly. Feeding fish sometimes also develop black bars on their sides. Bonito range from Chile to the Gulf of

Diving Blue Water

Blue water diving is an exhilarating and unpredictable experience. While diving the open sea, you will probably spend a lot of time in a combined state of suspense and boredom just staring into a void of blue water—but when something comes along, it is likely to be unusual, exciting, sometimes large, and occasionally dangerous. In the final analysis, it is worth the wait to watch golden rays of sunlight illuminate a majestic blue shark or to watch in awe as powerful mako sharks make a high-speed run on a bait.

Because the ocean is large and filled with comparatively small fish, some divers bait the water in order to attract a variety of open-ocean species. Baiting certainly increases the odds of encountering blue sharks, mako sharks, and even some pelagic stingrays, but a lot of animals, such as dolphins and whales, couldn't seem to care less. Beware, if you choose to bait the water, that the rules of the game will change dramatically. In fact, it's real life, not a game at all, for sharks and other open-sea predators. Don't fall into the trap of taking baited animals for granted—doing so can exact a high price.

No matter who you are or how much diving you have done, you are likely to feel uneasy the first time you step off a boat in the middle of nowhere. Diving the open ocean is not just a matter of motoring one's boat out of sight of land, cutting the engine, and going for a swim. Anyone who wants to dive midwater safely must be prepared. It is too easy to become disoriented in a sea of blue when no bottom is in sight. Many times, your only reference points are rays of sunlight (except on overcast days), the lighter colors toward the sun, and the blue-black color of the water below. It is often only the pressure change felt in your ears that indicates you are ascending or descending. Currents are impossible to detect without a reference point, and it is very easy to let your boat get away from you as it is pushed by the wind. Many blue water divers choose to use a tethering system—a safety line that connects them to the boat—in case of disorientation or emergency. Blue water diving requires that divers always pay attention, as the open sea has a reputation for being unforgiving of human error.

Despite the difficulties and careful preparations required for blue water diving, it can be well worth the effort. Blue water divers can see marine phenomena and explore a part of the ocean that very few divers ever see firsthand. In many ways that possibility is the essence of scuba diving—what more could an adventurous diver want?

Alaska and are usually encountered only well out to sea. Members of the tuna family, bonito are speedy swimmers that feed on squid, anchovies, and other fishes. They must swim in order to pass oxygen-rich water over their gills, and otherwise would suffocate.

Their round elongated bill, triangular dorsal fin, and movable pectoral fins distinguish **striped marlin** from other fishes in state waters. Striped marlin generally appear in southern California during summer and fall, ranging northward to Point Conception. Most specimens weigh less than 250 pounds, but the largest known individual was 10.5 feet long and weighed 465 pounds. Marlin prey on pelagic fishes, such as sardines, jackmackerel, bonito, and flying fish, and are also known to take squid and crabs. These remarkable fish are an extremely popular sport fishing catch.

Swordfish inhabit warm temperate seas all over the world. In California waters, they are most abundant south of Point Conception, and are most commonly observed from June through September. However, when the water is uncommonly warm, as it often is during intense El Niño currents, they have been known to travel as far north as Oregon. Swordfish are occasionally seen leaping dramatically out of the water, and have also been filmed as deep as 2,000 feet by camera systems mounted on submersibles.

The largest documented swordfish was nearly 15 feet long and weighed 1,182 pounds. Swordfish are easily distinguishable from other fishes by their flattened "sword," which forms their greatly extended upper jaw, and by their lack of scales and pelvic fins. Squid are one of their favorite prey, but swordfish also feed on fishes such as sardines and anchovies, which they sometimes impale or slash with their formidable snout.

Ranging from Cabo San Lucas at the southern tip of Baja to as far north in some years as Monterey Bay, **yellowtail** are a popular game fish in California. Yellowtail are schooling fish found close to shore, near offshore islands, and over offshore banks, but they are also attracted by mid-ocean kelp paddies. Yellowtail have been documented to attain a length of just over 5 feet. The West Coast record is listed at 80 pounds, and a 111-pounder was caught off New Zealand. Except during the short-lived height of the albacore season, yellowtail are the most highly sought-after game fish in the state.

Yellowtail feed primarily during daylight hours. Their preferred prey include pelagic red crabs, anchovies, squid, sardines, and small mackerel, though they are opportunistic feeders that often take whatever food is available. Yellowtail may be cooperative hunters; groups of them have been observed herding and surrounding their schooling prey before going in for the kill. They have also been seen engaged in the seemingly suicidal behavior of rubbing up against blue sharks, perhaps in an attempt to dislodge parasites on their own skin.

Ocean sunfish, also commonly called by their taxonomic name, *Mola mola*, are among the most bizarrely shaped fishes you'll ever see. Their long anal and dorsal fins, along with an

A diver eyes the bizarre form of an ocean sunfish.

DID YOU KNOW?

. . . **BLUE SHARKS ARE AMONG THE MOST NOMADIC OF SHARKS. BLUES TAGGED IN ENGLAND HAVE BEEN RECAPTURED AS FAR AWAY AS BRAZIL AND NEW YORK.**

oval-shaped, truncated, and extremely laterally compressed body, make these fish unique. In short, they strongly resemble frisbees with fins. This resemblance is unfortunate for the sunfish, which are occasionally caught up and tossed about as if they were frisbees by playful California sea lions, which also slap the hapless fish against the water and nibble off their fins.

Ocean sunfish cruise singly or in small groups near the water surface, often with the tips of their long dorsal fins breaking the surface. They seem to be fond of basking on their side at the surface. It has been hypothesized that parasitized sunfish bask in "request" of a cleaning from seagulls, which have been observed to pick at the sides of the fish. It has also been suggested that basking sunfish are simply unhealthy specimens.

Ocean sunfish have been known to reach 10 feet in length and weigh 3,000 pounds, but most specimens are much smaller. Inhabiting tropical and temperate open waters worldwide, they occasionally visit kelp forests, seamounts, oil rigs, and other underwater structures. Ocean sunfish prey upon various creatures such as jellyfish, salps, crustaceans, and some fishes. Although normally wary, once in a while a bolder fish will allow a human to approach surprisingly close.

Multitudes of other fishes inhabit the open sea in California waters, but they are far too numerous to mention as individual species here. Those described in this chapter are some of the more spectacular species and the most commonly seen and sought-after by sport divers and fishers. If you are either new to diving or inexperienced in the sport, you might wonder, "Who dives out in the middle of nowhere anyway?" Well, a surprising number of advanced divers do. "The middle of nowhere" has been the site of some of my most memorable dives.

A California sea lion basking in the sunlight.

CHAPTER 8

MARINE MAMMALS

A humpback whale.

Perhaps no one fully understands humankind's affinity for other mammals, but undoubtedly they occupy a special place in our view of the animal kingdom. Maybe we feel a common bond, finding kindred spirits in creatures so similar to ourselves. And we probably feel some collective guilt and sorrow for the cruelties we have wrought on so many mammal populations. In any case, being in the wild with marine mammals is a treasured privilege for all of us, and few places provide better opportunities than California.

From San Diego to the Oregon border, California waters are blessed with diverse marine mammals. Over the course of the year, state waters are frequented by whales, dolphins, porpoises, seals, sea lions, and sea otters. One or more of these fascinating animals can be seen in each of the previously discussed marine habitats. Sea lions and seals are especially wide-ranging and can be observed resting on rocky shores and on sandy beaches, swimming in kelp forests, over sand, and out in the open sea. Whales and dolphins are most often seen in the open ocean, but are also occasionally encountered in shallow water. Sea otters are commonly sighted in kelp

California sea lions visit kelp forests, rocky reefs, sandy plains, and beaches all along the coast.

forests and hunting in reef communities; I have even seen them feed by digging clams out of sandy bottom habitats.

Marine mammals are the descendants of creatures that once lived on land. Like their land-dwelling relatives, they breathe air and nurse their young. Some have body hair, and many possess at least skeletal remnants of the legs they gave up eons ago. As mammals evolved back to life in the sea, they developed characteristics that equipped them for survival in the aquatic environment. Because water conducts body heat away much faster than air does, one of the greatest challenges marine mammals had to overcome was keeping warm. Marine mammals are usually large, and therefore have proportionately less surface area exposed to the cold water than a smaller animal would, effectively trapping more heat within their body. Whales further combat the cold by insulating their body with a thick layer of fat, called blubber. Fat layers are also an important energy reserve for times when food is scarce. Seals and sea lions also have a fat layer, but have insulating body hair or fur as well. Sea otters and fur seals do not possess a significant fat layer, relying instead on a dense pelt of fur and oils that repel water, and the energy obtained from their voracious feeding habits.

DID YOU KNOW?

. . . **DOLPHINS ARE**

A TYPE OF WHALE.

Cetaceans: Whales and Dolphins

All whales and dolphins are cetaceans. This order is divided into two suborders: Mysticeti, the baleen whales, and Odontoceti, the toothed whales.

Baleen whales are toothless, and feed primarily on plankton and small fishes they strain from the water. They swim open-mouthed through dense concentrations of krill and other plankton, then close their mouth to expel the water. The plankton are trapped by tough, flexible, horny sheets of modified hair called baleen, which resembles a synthetic fiber. A mouth full of these "fibers" looks much like an oversized scrub brush. Baleen whales are also known to feed occasionally upon small fishes. California gray whales, blue whales, finback whales, minke whales, and humpback whales are all baleen whales.

The toothed whales of California include pilot whales and orcas (killer whales), as well as dolphins. Toothed whales are active predators that prey primarily upon squid, octopi, and fish, although some, including orcas, also feed on other mammals.

Of all the marine creatures that can be seen in California waters, few, if any, have captured the public's attention as **gray whales** have. Gray whales are easily observed in the wild along the Pacific coast of North America during their southward migration in late fall and early winter. On a good day, as many as seventy-five whales may pass a given coastal observation point, and whale-watching expeditions are well worth the price at this time of year.

Gray whales are named for their mottled coloration, a combination of natural black skin and large patches of white barnacles that attach to their body. Mature whales reach a length of nearly 50 feet and weigh more than 40 tons. As large as those numbers may seem, grays are relatively small whales; blue whales can grow up to 100 feet long and weigh more than 100 tons.

California gray whales migrate annually from the feeding grounds of the Bering Sea to the calving and breeding grounds in the lagoons of Mexico's Baja Peninsula. At a speed of 3 to 5 miles an hour, mature California gray whales swim 10,000 miles during this round-trip journey, the longest known mammal migration. Even more astonishing is that these whales cover the entire distance without any significant feeding, according to many experts.

These whales spend the late spring, summer, and early fall of the Northern Hemisphere feeding upon benthic amphipods in prolific northern waters. In late fall they begin their journey south. During the migration a gray whale normally takes a series of three to five breaths about twenty seconds apart before dipping its head and throwing its tail into the air to begin a three- to- five-minute dive that can easily reach a depth of several hundred feet. Groups of southbound whales number as high as fifteen, although smaller groups of two or three are more common. The southern journey extends well into the winter months and brings the whales close to land outcroppings all along the Pacific coast. Whale-watching is most spectacular during this portion of the migration.

The whales reach the lagoons along the Pacific coast of Baja in early winter. Most of them stop at Scammons Lagoon, San Ignacio Lagoon, or Magdalena Bay, a series of shallow bodies of water along the west coast of Baja, but some gray whales swim all the way to the Sea of Cortez. Scammons

A California gray whale soars through the water.

A diver with whales.

Diving with Whales

Over the years I have found myself in the water with a variety of whale species: grays, humpbacks, blues, orcas, southern right, and pilot whales, just to mention some. Every time I am in the water with a whale, three thoughts come to mind. First, I always feel humbled because of their size. Maybe if I spent a lot of time around elephants or even bears, I wouldn't feel so small.

Second, I am always amazed by their wonderful sense of coordination and how well they control their large bodies. I suppose it would be dumb to think that whales would be anything other than extremely capable swimmers. But because of their enormous size, their grace and power are remarkable. I have repeatedly come within inches of humpbacks and gray whales and yet they avoid bumping into me. At least that is true for the adults; calves can be a bit rambunctious, and getting bounced around on the nose of a gray whale calf can be a very painful experience, even if the calf is just playing.

Third, I always want to know what the whales are thinking. There is something surreal about looking into the eye of a whale and watching the whale watch me. There is no question that they are extremely intelligent, sensitive creatures. I wonder what they think about us.

Lagoon, San Ignacio Lagoon, and Magdalena (often called "Mag") Bay are large, well-protected areas tucked into the seclusion of the Baja wilderness. There, courting whales mate and the pregnant females give birth, normally to a single calf.

Mating usually occurs in groups of three: one female and two males. The role of the second male is a subject of some debate. He may be present only to learn the finer points of courtship, or he may be there to steady the female so the first male can achieve penetration. The courting ritual takes place on the surface and often lasts for several hours.

The calves are born in early winter after a thirteen-month gestation period. At birth, they are between 12 and 17 feet long and weigh more than 3,000 pounds. While that certainly seems large for starters, the calves are capable of gaining up to 220 pounds per day for several months following birth. Cows are highly protective of their offspring and keep their young close to their side for two or three months after birth. During the whaling days, gray whales earned the name "devil fish" for the violence with which they defended themselves and their offspring from attack.

In late winter and early spring, the whales begin their northern journey back toward the feeding grounds. This route takes them farther out to sea than does the southbound segment. Exactly how grays successfully navigate such great distances is not well understood, but a sense of the earth's magnetism may play a role (see the echolocation sidebar in this chapter). Visual cues and echolocation may also play a part in navigating the migration route. Gray whales are often seen holding their head out of water in an act called

A diving California gray whale.

California gray whales travel 10,000 miles annually,
the longest known mammal migration.

How Whales Avoid the Bends

Human divers face a unique risk: the higher water pressures at deeper levels of the ocean. When subjected to higher pressure, our bodies absorb far more nitrogen from inspired air than at the surface. Unlike oxygen, nitrogen is not metabolized by our bodies, so at depth we simply absorb more and more nitrogen over time. When we return too quickly to the lower pressures of shallower waters, nitrogen can come out of solution faster than we can get rid of it by the exchange of gases through our lungs. Nitrogen bubbles that come out of solution in our bodies can cause a dangerous and potentially fatal condition called the bends. In order to prevent the bends, scuba divers must make slow ascents and decompression stops to allow the nitrogen to outgas through the lungs. Yet marine mammals, particularly elephant seals and some whales, can dive deeper than 2,000 meters and rapidly ascend, safely and repeatedly, without making decompression stops. How do they do this?

Although we do not yet fully understand how marine mammals avoid the bends, we are beginning to learn some of the contributing factors. As a marine mammal descends, its heart rate slows dramatically and it can cut off circulation to nonessential body parts, adaptations that minimize the circulation of nitrogen to body tissues. Furthermore, marine mammals, unlike scuba-diving humans, do not breathe as they dive, so they are not constantly inhaling additional nitrogen to accumulate in their bodies. But the primary factor that allows deep-diving mammals to avoid the bends seems to be that their lungs collapse under high pressures. As this occurs, the air is forced into bony passageways, preventing most of the nitrogen from reaching the blood, particularly because nitrogen is more soluble in the oily lining of the passageways than it is in blood. As the animal surfaces, the nitrogen is simply exhaled.

A related question is, how are marine mammals able to remain submerged for so long without needing to breathe? The answer lies in the fact that their breaths are deeper and they extract oxygen more efficiently than we do, and thus do not need to breathe as often. Furthermore, marine mammals have proportionately more blood than we do, and a higher proportion of the red blood cells that transport oxygen. Perhaps most important, their muscles contain a much higher proportion of myoglobin. Myoglobin's affinity for oxygen is even higher than that of blood, so much of the oxygen needed by a marine mammal during its dives is stored in its muscles. Finally, the slowing of the animal's heart and the limitation of oxygenated blood to vital organs maximize the efficiency of its oxygen utilization.

spy-hopping, sparring, or spying-out. Some authorities believe the whales are trying to visually orient themselves with prominent landmarks, while others consider the grays' abovewater vision to be rather poor.

Throughout the migration, gray whales can be seen leaping almost entirely out of the water in a dramatic maneuver called breaching. Swimming at speeds of nearly 30 miles an hour before propelling themselves skyward, they spin around in the air before crashing and splashing back to the surface. This spectacular behavior is often repeated as many as ten times in succession within only a two- or three-minute span. The purpose of breaching is not known; it may help the whale dislodge parasites, be an elaborate form of communication, be a response to feeling threatened, or might simply just be fun.

Upon first consideration, it would seem to be a waste of energy to travel 5,000 miles annually just to calve and breed. However, the waters of the Bering Sea are too harsh for the survival of newborn whales, and the lagoons seem to offer a habitat in which the calves have the best chance for survival. In late winter and early spring, after the young have grown enough to tolerate colder waters, the whales return north in search of more plentiful food. Not long ago, grays mated and calved in more northern regions such as San Diego Bay, but heavy shipping traffic has forced them to seek quieter waters. How far they can be pushed without greatly endangering the species is a point of major concern.

Underwater encounters with these clever creatures are rare, especially with mature whales during their migration. In spite of their size, approaching gray whales will almost

The skin of California gray whales is often encrusted with barnacles.

always turn or dive to avoid an encounter with comparatively tiny divers. However, the calves are usually more curious than mature animals, and on occasion will approach and follow divers. To my knowledge, I am one of a small number of divers who has been fortunate enough to repeatedly swim eyeball to eyeball with wild gray whales. I have done so only twice in California waters, but have spent considerable time with grays in the waters of Baja while working on documentary film projects. During these dives I learned that I was more impressed by their incredible control and grace than by their size. Whales can swim repeatedly within inches of a diver without making contact. When threatened, however, they can and will accurately throw their powerful flukes at the offending target. Considering their size . . . well, enough said.

The size of a gray whale is overwhelming. Underwater, you soon realize that grays have body parts much bigger than you are. To see a gray approach while you are bobbing on the surface is to watch the horizon change shape as the top of the whale's head blocks out a portion of the sky. It is the diving thrill of a lifetime. Although most people will never see a gray whale while underwater, just knowing they are out there is somehow as comforting as it is thrilling.

The **blue whale** is the largest animal ever to have lived on earth. Up to three times bigger than the largest dinosaur, blue whales are reported to reach 111 feet in length and weigh in excess of 100 tons. At birth they are over 20 feet long and weigh almost 3 tons, and can attain a length of 50 feet by the time they are only eight months old. Like most of the ocean's largest creatures, blue whales are filter-feeders, subsisting primarily on krill and other planktonic organisms.

A blue whale mother and her calf.

Humpback whales communicate with bellowing songs that can be heard for miles underwater.

The folded ridges on the underside of their head allow them to open their mouth extremely wide, somewhat like an expanding accordion, as they swim through dense concentrations of food.

Blue whales are the only deep blue to jet-black whales with folded ridges on the underside of their jaw. Individuals that inhabit cold waters for extended periods of time sometimes become covered with a film of yellowish diatoms, giving rise to the common name sulphur bottoms. Despite their incredible size, they are sometimes hunted by packs of orca whales that repeatedly attack and eventually overwhelm their gargantuan prey. Blue whales have a worldwide distribution and, next to gray whales, are the second most commonly observed baleen whale in California waters.

A diver films a feeding blue whale.

Eyeball to Eyeball with the Biggest of Them All

It is easier to memorize statistics that describe animals than it is to truly appreciate what it is like to be in the water next to a wild animal that is as big as a school bus, or perhaps several school buses linked together. Take blue whales, for example. They are the largest animal on earth, reaching proportions of nearly 110 feet long and 120 tons. Use whatever word you like—enormous, huge, monstrous—you simply can't convey what it is like to be in the water with a large blue whale (as if there were such a thing as a small one).

Despite the fact that blue whales are somewhat rare on a worldwide basis, it is not uncommon for pods to be sighted in California waters. Even from the deck of a boat, it is difficult to comprehend how large these behemoths are.

I once had the pleasure of being in the water with a pod of feeding blue whales. It was an astonishing sight. For starters, when a blue whale swims by you, it just keeps on coming and coming and coming as if the body had no end. At first you see the head and face. They pass, and the body comes into view. After a few seconds you begin to look for the tail so you can be sure to avoid a collision, but the wall of animal continues to materialize. Imagine, even in 50-foot visibility, that if you were dead center on the whale's body, you couldn't see either the tip of its head or its tail. If you were lucky and the whale didn't change course, the tail would finally appear.

Even when I understood just how large a blue whale's body is, it was still impossible for me to believe how large its mouth and throat become when the animal feeds. If you were to look at a picture of a blue whale's head, you would notice that the throat is pleated. The throat expands somewhat like an accordion during feeding. How big are the mouth and throat? I am not sure how to quantify it, but I have the impression that a feeding blue whale could easily put two Volkswagens in its mouth. Of course, blue whales don't feed on large prey items. Like most of the ocean's larger animals, blue whales feed on dense concentrations of small planktonic creatures.

Being next to a feeding blue whale is simultaneously awesome and humbling. How else would you expect to feel if you were swimming next to an animal more than 1,000 times your size?

Once hunted to the edge of extinction, they are making a surprising comeback thanks to their protected status as an endangered species.

Finbacks, or fin whales as they are sometimes called, visit the California coast during the summer. They are similar in build to blue whales and are the second largest baleen whale, reaching a length of 76 feet. In addition to krill, these whales sometimes prey on small fishes as well as squid and other invertebrates. Thought to be the fastest swimmers of the larger whales, finbacks may be capable of short bursts of speed of 20 miles per hour.

Finbacks are easily recognized by their small dorsal fin, which is located quite close to their fluke. The distinct ridge that stretches from the dorsal fin to the fluke has earned these animals the nickname "razorback whale." Finbacks are unique among mammals in their asymmetrical coloration, with a blue-gray main body and left baleen plate, and a yellow-white underbelly and right baleen plate.

A pilot whale mother and her calf.

Finbacks became protected as an endangered species in 1970 after whaling seriously depleted their numbers. The worldwide population estimate as of this writing is 120,000 individuals; although finbacks have not yet recovered to pre-whaling numbers, they are believed to be the most abundant large whale species. They are still hunted at a subsistence level in eastern Greenland.

Minke whales look a great deal like miniature finback whales, but the largest minke ever documented was only 33 feet long. At birth, minkes are not much larger than a tall human, generally between 7 and 9 feet long. Although they

Echolocation

Most mammals have a well-developed sense of vision. Even most marine mammals are believed to have a very useful visual acuity underwater—although their ability to see in air is suspect. However, several groups of mammals, including some whales, dolphins, and pinnipeds, augment their visual ability to orient themselves with a sophisticated faculty called echolocation. In a sense seeing with their ears, these animals are perceiving reflected sound rather than reflected light, but may be receiving as much or even more detailed information about their surroundings than we do with our eyes. Approximately 20 percent of mammals are believed to possess the ability to echolocate, and they are quite capable of using echolocation to find even very small objects in total darkness.

Echolocating animals produce sharp sounds of variable frequencies and analyze the returning echoes to give them information about the size, shape, and location of an object. These sounds are very different from those used in "songs" of communication (such as the well-known song of humpback whales). The sounds most useful for echolocation are trains or pulses of very short clicks. Some of these clicks are well within the range of human hearing, while other clicks are of a higher frequency than humans can discern. It is generally believed that low-frequency clicks serve to orient in a general sense, and that higher-frequency clicks are used when finer discrimination is required.

For example, a bottlenose dolphin may produce a series of clicks, with each click lasting only a fraction of a millisecond. These clicks are often repeated up to 800 times per second, but each click must be received as an echo before it is useful to emit another. When the sound waves bounce off an object, the length of time

Whales and dolphins use echolocation to gain information about their surroundings.

before they return as echoes provides the dolphin with information that allows it to gauge the size and shape of an object, its distance, and the speed and direction of its movement. In captivity, dolphins have shown an incredible ability to distinguish between objects of the same shape and size but made of different materials.

Although different species have developed their own methods of producing and processing the clicks of echolocation, the principles are essentially the same. For example, all toothed whales have a large melon-shaped deposit of fat at the front of their head that apparently focuses the clicks into a narrow, directional beam of sound. The reflected echoes are received by another deposit of fat in their lower jaws; this organ transmits the sound to the animal's ear for processing by the brain. By using a series of clicks of increasing frequency for finer and finer discrimination, and by

moving its head side to side in the same way that we locate the origins of sounds, an echolocating whale can very precisely locate and identify its target.

Another fascinating, although less sophisticated, faculty thought to be possessed by at least some cetaceans is the ability to sense the earth's magnetic field. The bodies of some organisms (ranging from bacteria to mammals) contain magnetite crystals that constantly align with this magnetic field. These animals are believed to be able to perceive shifts in the orientation of the crystals, and use the information as a navigational aid, much as human navigators use a compass. The live strandings of many cetaceans are considered to be at least partially due to errors in using their magnetic sense for navigation.

are usually solitary and are only occasionally seen in groups of two or three, there are reports of hundreds of minkes gathering in the Antarctic, perhaps to feed on their prey of krill and small fishes. Minkes are heavily preyed upon by orca whales. Because they are slow swimmers and sometimes curiously approach ships, they also make easy targets for whalers.

Humpback whales are distinguished by their comparatively long pectoral flippers, which can be almost 15 feet long, while the entire animal reaches a length of just over 50 feet. These flippers stand out prominently during dramatic breaches as the humpbacks leap clear of the water, spinning and crashing back to the surface. Interestingly, the flippers of humpback whales that inhabit the Pacific are easily distinguishable from those of their brethren in the Caribbean: Caribbean humpbacks' flippers are white all over, while those of Pacific humpbacks are white underneath but dark on top. The breeding populations of these two groups of humpbacks are entirely separate, and although they are believed to belong to the same species, their different flipper colorations may be a preliminary indication of a slow divergence into separate species of whales.

Humpbacks are baleen whales, feeding on small fishes and enormous quantities of tiny plankton they

A young bottlenose dolphin swims protected at the side of its mother.

filter from the water. These fascinating whales sometimes trap their prey within a "bubble net," a curtain of bubbles created as the humpbacks slowly ascend and circle their prey. The schooling fish or krill become concentrated in the center as they avoid the bubbles, allowing the whales to charge through the middle to engulf their prey.

Humpback whales are most famous for their bellowing songs. Distinctive from the sounds of other whales, these songs are believed to help humpbacks communicate for distances of several hundred miles, and are also thought to explain how competing males attract females in the waters of Alaska and Hawaii, where they mate. The song of one male humpback is repeated by others in the area; the songs are regionally dis-

A pair of Risso's dolphins.

tinct and continually evolve over the breeding season. Recordings of the humpbacks' haunting songs were sent out on the *Voyager I* space explorer for possible discovery by life from another planet.

Pilot whales, sometimes called blackfish, are dark brown to black and have a bulbous, melon-shaped head. These whales grow up to 22 feet long. They typically school in groups of a few to hundreds of individuals, often in the company of bottlenose dolphins. Their favorite prey is believed to be squid, and during squid runs at the Channel Islands and in coastal canyons, large pods of pilot whales are commonly sighted. They sometimes dive to depths of 2,000 feet in pursuit of prey.

The **common dolphin** (also called the hourglass, crisscross, or saddleback dolphin) is uniquely identified by the white, hourglass-shaped marking on its belly. Traveling in large pods during late summer, fall, and early winter, common dolphins are often seen leaping entirely out of the water. They seem to enjoy riding the bow wakes of boats and whales even more than other species of dolphins do, and have even been known to stop feeding for this opportunity. These playful animals are among the most acrobatic of dolphins, displaying remarkable agility with joyful leaps and flips out of the water.

Common dolphins are relatively small, attaining a maximum length of 7 to 8 feet, but they are exceptional swimmers. In the wild they have been recorded swimming up to 18 miles per hour. These beautiful dolphins range from British Columbia to Ecuador. Like many other toothed cetaceans, they feed primarily upon small fishes.

As the name suggests, **bottlenose dolphins** have a prominent, bottle-shaped beak, with an upturned mouth that seems to smile a friendly welcome. Growing up to 12 feet long, they are generally larger than common dolphins. Bottlenose are an almost uniform gray color, and are stout-bodied, weighing as much as 800 pounds. Preying upon a

Common dolphins sometimes travel in enormous pods, playfully leaping through the water.

variety of fish, they are known to consume up to 20 pounds of mackerel per day in captivity.

Mature female bottlenose dolphins bear a single calf once every two or three years, and tenderly care for their offspring for as long as a year or more. Young dolphins are well tended by the dolphin pod as a whole, and observers have witnessed "babysitting," in which female dolphins care for several calves while the other mothers forage for food. Because of their social, playful nature and ability to do well in captivity, this species is one of the best known and most widely written about of all dolphins.

Partly because of their large, highly convoluted brains, dolphins are believed by some scientists to be the world's most intelligent animals next to humans. Having spent some time in the wild with bottlenose dolphins and some of their cousins, I wonder if this ranking is fair to the dolphins. They are truly remarkable animals that use complex patterns of whistling as well as body language to communicate.

Pacific white-sided dolphins dance through the water in pods of up to thousands of individuals. As they travel, they communicate with shrill whistles and calls to their neighbors, each dolphin with its own unique identifying call. These gregarious dolphins sometimes even seek out the company of other species of marine mammals. Pacific white-sided dolphins are talented aquatic acrobats, and are the only wild dolphins able to turn complete aerial somersaults.

The **Risso's dolphin** is a wide-ranging species that inhabits both the Atlantic and Pacific Oceans. The lightly colored head, which lacks a beak, and long white scars down the body make this dolphin easily recognizable. Although sightings are relatively rare in California waters, they are occasionally seen singly or in large schools. Schooling Risso's dolphins sometimes swim alongside one another at regular intervals in a formation that may be beneficial for hunting. They prey almost entirely on squid and octopi.

An orca whale pursues its prey.

Risso's and bottlenose dolphins are closely related and may, in fact, not be entirely distinct species. One Risso's dolphin kept in captivity in Japan mated with a bottlenose dolphin, producing a hybrid offspring. Dolphins that shared characteristics of both the bottlenose and the Risso's dolphin were once sighted off the coast of Ireland, and were also suspected to be hybrids.

A famous Risso's dolphin named Pelorus Jack accompanied ships passing through a particular stretch of water off Pelorus Sound in New Zealand for twenty-four years, from 1888 to 1912. His presence was considered lucky by many of the mariners who enjoyed his company.

Orcas, or killer whales as they are often called, are the largest members of the dolphin family. Without question, they have been the most widely misunderstood and misrepresented of all whales. Orcas are the only cetacean known to commonly prey upon other mammals, but attacks on humans remain virtually undocumented. Their misleading common name is actually derived from an errant translation of an Eskimo term. Years ago, the Eskimos referred to men that hunted orcas as whale killers. The English translation, "killer whales," mistakenly and dramatically altered the meaning.

Orcas are distinctly marked, with a black body, white underparts, and a large white spot just behind and above the eyes. Mature males possess a large, triangular dorsal fin that stands as high as 6 feet off their back, making them easy to identify when viewed from the surface. Males have been measured at more than 30 feet long, which is unusual among cetaceans in that mature males are much larger than females. Nevertheless, orca whale societies are matriarchal, and the pods are dominated by the most powerful female.

Orca pods are well-knit groups, and each pod has a unique set of calls. Scientists can even differentiate among pods solely by their vocalizations. Pods that interact with one another can apparently communicate, as they have some vocalizations in common. Within a pod, these whales seem to form special friendships, preferring to associate with certain members more than others.

California sea lion pups are amazingly energetic and constantly at play.

Orcas are known to feed upon seals, sea lions, walruses, birds, dolphins, and other whales, including blue whales. When preying on seals and sea lions, they sometimes come into water so shallow that they occasionally partially beach themselves as they make a run at their prey. While hunting, members of the pod often cooperate in a communal effort, a behavior that has been witnessed on numerous occasions as

Diving with California Sea Lions

Life at a sea lion rookery is like recess at an elementary school: highly chaotic, full of energy, at times out of control, and there are adults that appear to be more involved with performing some kind of task than they are with enjoying life. While bulls are busy defending their territory and females are tending to the tasks of motherhood, the pups' role in life seems to be playing and sleeping. They are either going all out or not at all.

If you catch the pups at the right time, when their energy level is high, your dive is guaranteed to be a great one. They constantly chase one another, darting around the rocks and in between stipes of kelp. I have never been able to determine exactly who is "it," and what the rules of the game are, but witnessing the scene is entertainment in its purest form.

Sometimes the pups swim right up to divers, nipping at their gear, and at other times they ignore them as if they could sense that

A California sea lion plays with a diver.

humans are so awkward that we would only slow things down. In other words, we offer no challenge. Boring, perhaps, to the sea lions, but not to anyone who has an appreciation for their sense of playfulness and their marvelous aquatic design. All of their play probably has a purpose and helps prepare them for the challenges of their lives, but whatever that purpose may be, it is certainly educational for any diver to spend a day around the pups.

But pay heed. Don't allow their aquatic superiority to humble you too much, and do not invade the territory of a bull. If you do so unwittingly, give ground if the bull barks at you or blows bubbles. And be careful not to get too close to pregnant females or mothers with pups. Keep your distance unless approached in a friendly manner, and you are likely to enjoy a dive you will never forget.

the orcas hunted both blue whales and sperm whales. They are also known to prey upon squid and fish.

With only the young, old, and sick being vulnerable to shark attack, orcas are the top predators of the ocean. However, having been in the open ocean with a killer whale, I am convinced (as are many others who have had similar experiences) that they are by no means indiscriminate killers. In fact, they generally prove to be somewhat shy and difficult to approach. In some instances these whales have demonstrated some curiosity about divers, but aggressive behavior in the wild toward divers is almost unheard of.

California sea lions glide through a kelp forest.

and are used as their chief means of propulsion in the water. Sea lions use their hind flippers as a rudder, while seals propel themselves with their rear flippers. Seals are unable to turn their hind flippers forward, and are therefore less mobile on land than sea lions.

- Sea lions have a harsh coat, whereas fur seals possess a dense soft undercoat protected by coarse guard hairs.

Pinnipeds: Seals and Sea Lions

California waters are inhabited by seven species of seals and sea lions, a group of animals collectively referred to as pinnipeds. The order Pinnipedia (meaning "fin feet") is subdivided into three families:

- **Otariidae**: the sea lions and fur seals
- **Phocidea**: the true seals (hair seals)
- **Odobenidae**: the walruses, found only in Arctic waters

Sea lions and seals share many common characteristics. All these animals have a thick hide with a heavy layer of fat underneath to protect them from their cold surroundings. Both groups have modified fore and hind limbs called flippers, which help them maneuver both in and out of water. However, there are significant differences between sea lions and seals. In fact, some experts maintain that seals are more closely related to cats and bears than they are to sea lions. Seals, cats, and bears are believed to have evolved from a common ancestor, whereas sea lions appeared later. Sea lions can be distinguished from seals by three characteristics:

- Sea lions possess small external ears, which seals lack. (Sea lions are correctly referred to as eared seals.)
- The fore flippers of sea lions are comparatively large,

Both seals and sea lions are highly social animals, gathering in large herds or colonies at many times during the year. Pups of both sexes and females without pups are more gregarious than breeding males and females that have recently pupped. It is quite common to see different species of seals and sea lions intermingling both in the water and on land. In fact, during the spring, Point Bennett on San Miguel Island is inhabited by upwards of 10,000 pinnipeds of at least three different species at the same time. This is the largest gathering of marine mammal species at one time anywhere in the world.

By far the best-known sea lion in California is, appropriately, the **California sea lion**. The bulls weigh as much as 700 pounds and attain a length of more than 10 feet. Males are generally much larger than females and have a noticeably larger head because of their pronounced sagittal crest, an arrow-shaped ridge extending from the forehead to the rear of the skull. Mature females are lighter in color than males, weigh close to 250 pounds, and reach a length of close to 8 feet.

California sea lions are quite gregarious throughout the year, preferring to gather in groups whether mating or not. On land, sea lions are most often found in either a rookery (a coastal region occupied by a breeding population) or a hauling-out site (a strip of land occupied by nonbreeding animals). They may appear awkward on land, but on the rocky and slippery terrain of the California coast, mature

Unlike seals, sea lions have external ear flaps.

breeding season, fighting is rare once territories are established and the females have arrived.

It is interesting that California sea lion bulls compete only for territory, making no attempt to prevent females from breeding with other bulls, so long as the act occurs outside their domain. Sea lions are polygamous, meaning that both sexual partners have more than one mate. Females tend to choose the most favorable territory in which to pup, but do not necessarily remain in this territory to mate. Copulation occurs both on land and in the water. A female bears her young approximately twelve months later during the next breeding season, although the gestation period is considered to be only nine months. The difference in the two time periods is due to a rather amazing phenomenon called delayed implantation, in which the fertilized egg lies dormant in the uterine wall for three months. Delayed implantation is common to all pinnipeds, conveniently enabling females to give birth at the rookeries where they breed.

animals can often move faster than humans for short distances. Bulls are highly protective of their territory, and based on their size compared to a human's size, no more need be said about approaching them too closely.

When on land, sea lions are usually found close to the water's edge, within splashing distance of the waves. They are extremely sensitive to heat, as their insulating layer of fat can quickly cause internal body heat to rise to a dangerous level. For that reason sea lions rarely stray far from the cooling water. Like other pinnipeds, they can also battle the heat by shunting blood to their extremities, hastening the loss of body heat.

At the beginning of the mating season in early May, mature bulls are the first to arrive at the rookeries. Before the females arrive, the bulls bluster and charge and fight one another in an effort to lay claim to the best territory. Fights involve plenty of chest-to-chest pushing and biting, all with the single purpose of shoving the other male out of the territory. Confrontations are intense, and breeding males often have extensive chest scarring. Once the territories are established, males bark incessantly to warn competitors against entering their domain. Although ritualized territorial displays continue throughout the

A California sea lion gives birth.

Mothers nurse their pups for one or two weeks before leaving for two or three days to forage. They will continue to nurse their pups for six months to a year or more, alternating a few days of foraging with a few days of nursing. Because mothers must be able to identify and find their young again after returning from a foraging trip, mothers and pups must develop a strong relationship within the first few hours of a pup's life. Sea lions in captivity have shown an ability to recognize their relatives for up to five years or more, preferring the company of their family to that of other sea lions, but it is not known whether this is true in the wild.

Mothers help their offspring learn to swim by the sink-or-swim method. The mother must usually drag a somewhat less than enthusiastic pup into the water, and then support and push the pup through the awkward stages. Although pups appear to be a little frantic for the first few minutes, they quickly take to the water. Soon they learn that the ocean is their playground, and begin to enjoy bodysurfing waves and wrestling with other young sea lions. It seems as if anything were a game to these playful youngsters; exuberant juveniles have even been seen chasing and swallowing their own air bubbles.

On land, California sea lions can be slowly and carefully approached quite easily from downwind. This does not mean that they are comfortable with humans, but more likely that their senses on land aren't keen enough to detect us easily. If startled by sudden movement or by approach from above, entire herds may stampede. The frantic sea lions tend to dash rapidly for water, sometimes suffering serious injuries or fatal falls in their haste.

Mature California sea lion bulls have a pronounced ridge on their skulls called a sagittal crest.

Some feeding habits of California sea lions have made them a center of controversy in California. They like to feed upon many species that are also pursued by both commercial and sport fishers, and will happily steal a fisher's catch whenever possible. Over the years some fishers have retaliated by shooting or bombing the sea lions, although this is strictly a short-term solution. California sea lions feed on and help control populations of other animals that prey upon fish populations. For example, in northern waters sea lions feed heavily on lamprey that can seriously deplete salmon populations, especially when their numbers are not naturally controlled. Recent studies have shown California sea lion populations to be increasing, so the conflict between fishers and sea lions is likely to intensify. But that is not the only conflict. In San Francisco and Monterey, sea lions have literally taken over valuable docks; chasing the animals away is a legally complicated issue. They are both bold and curious, moving into any area that seems appealing. A group of sea lions at Año Nuevo has even taken over an entire abandoned two-story house!

California sea lions are among the most fascinating animals to observe in the wild, but despite our interest in and observations of these mammals, many of their habits are still mysterious to us. For example, California sea lions sometimes carefully select and then swallow small stones. It has been suggested that the stones dislodge parasites or serve as ballast. In any case, we are far from knowing all there is to know about California sea lions.

Stellar sea lions also inhabit California waters, though they are not nearly as numerous as California sea lions. The

Never Take Wildlife for Granted

Sea lions are cute, cuddly animals, and their antics can entertain for hours. It's easy to fall in love with them. Unfortunately, it is also easy to fall into the trap of believing they have fallen in love with you. Although pups and subadults

A California sea lion bull charges full-speed at the photographer.

often display a sense of curiosity and at times readily approach divers, sea lion bulls, especially during mating season, should never be taken for granted. I once made the mistake of doing so, and it is only good luck that prevented me from paying a big price for it.

Sea lion bulls are highly territorial during their mating season. Interestingly, the males compete over territory, not females. Within its realm a mature bull is bound and determined to be the only male to mate with any female, but it couldn't care less if the same females mate with other males elsewhere, even in adjacent territories.

When defending their turf, bulls often bark at one another. They will also bark at and blow bubbles in the face of an encroaching diver. Once, I was at a rookery in which a number of divers, myself

included, had been around a bull that was barking and blowing bubbles at intruders. It was late in the season, and I made the mistake of thinking that the bull was all bluff and no bite. I was a cameraman on a shoot for *National Geographic,* and with those credentials to impress the bull, I decided the animal wouldn't harm me. Dumb—really dumb.

On my next dive I entered the bull's territory and in that instant the bull charged me and grabbed me by my left arm. I looked down in horror, realizing that the bull's head extended from my shoulders to my waist. I hate to think about what the bull could have done to me. Luckily all he did was shake me and let me go. No diver in the history of diving has ever retreated any faster or silently said more heartfelt thank-yous. Fortunately for me, the major damage was to my psyche.

If one gets three wishes in life, I have only two left. Never again will I take a wild animal's behavior for granted. Never.

---

largest colonies are in northern California at the Farallon Islands and at Año Nuevo. Stellar sea lions are much larger than California sea lions. Up to 13 feet long, bulls weigh as much as 2,200 pounds, whereas females reach 9 feet and weigh just over 600 pounds. Stellar sea lions are yellowish-brown in contrast to the darker brown of California sea lions, and lack the prominent sagittal crest of the latter. Stellars are

also typically much quieter than the constantly barking California sea lions. Sometimes foraging cooperatively, Stellars feed primarily on squid and fish species of little or no commercial value. Males, however, sometimes prey on other mammals, including juvenile northern fur seals, harbor seals, and possibly sea otters.

Like California sea lions, Stellar sea lion bulls battle for territory during the June and July mating season. Bulls often return to the same site for several consecutive years. In order to prevent the loss of their territory, the vigilant bulls do not leave, even to eat. Unlike California sea lion females, Stellar females sometimes flirtatiously initiate copulation, coyly swinging their necks and rubbing up against the bull of their choice. As soon as a female gives birth, she and her pup imprint on each other by nuzzling and vocalizing special calls. She will nurse her pup for a year or even much longer—in one instance, a large female was observed nursing a smaller adult female that was in turn nursing a pup.

Because of steadily declining populations, in 1990, Stellar sea lions were listed as a threatened species throughout their range. Sadly, to date, their numbers continue to decline.

One of the best known of seals worldwide, **northern fur seals** have been valued for years for their pelts. Preferring to congregate in large numbers at their rookeries, these animals were at one point hunted nearly to extinction. The original worldwide herd was estimated to be 2 million, but before the international treaty of 1911 that brought these seals significant protection, their population was only 125,000. Northern fur seals are still hunted, but have nevertheless made a remarkable comeback. More than a million northern fur seals are alive today.

Male northern fur seals are dark brown, with a gray neck and shoulders, while females tend to be gray. Males are considerably larger than females, reaching a size of 8 feet and 700 pounds; females peak at about 5 feet and 130 pounds. Unlike sea lions, fur seals lack a thick insulating layer of blubber, and depend on their lush fur coats to keep them warm. They are often seen "jugging" in the water, holding both fore flippers and one hind flipper out of the water to minimize heat loss. On land, however, the thick pelt can quickly cause fur seals to

Northern fur seals.

overheat, so these animals, like other marine animals, tend to stay very close to the water. When they do get too hot, fur seals sometimes pant like a dog.

When breeding season nears, the bulls are the first to head for the rookeries. As is the case with sea lions, northern fur seal bulls fight fiercely for their territory, announcing their claim with individually distinct trumpeting calls. Unlike sea lions, however, they most certainly *do* care if the females try to leave to mate with another bull. Bulls sometimes get quite rough with females in an effort to prevent them from leaving their territory.

Like most pinnipeds, northern fur seals almost always bear only one pup. Twin northern fur seals have been observed on three occasions, and each time one of the pups was rejected by the mother. Because of the energy drain of nursing for long periods without eating and the demands of protecting a pup, females are apparently unable to successfully raise more than one pup at a time. One week after giving birth, the new mothers are willing and able to mate again.

Northern fur seals prey upon a wide variety of food sources, including anchovies, squid, hake, herring, and an occasional seabird. They are sought after by sharks, orcas, and humans, and lose many pups to parasitic worms.

Like so many pinnipeds that inhabit California waters, **Guadalupe fur seals** have been hunted almost to extinction. Once they ranged from San Benitos Island off the coast of Baja to the Farallons in central California, but they were so heavily sought after that for some time they were thought to be extinct. Guadalupe fur seals have been sighted in recent years at the Channel Islands, and their population is slowly increasing.

Not as much is known about Guadalupe fur seals as about other pinnipeds, though they are believed to have a great deal in common with northern fur seals. Both the males and females are dark brown to blackish-gray, with a lighter gray head and neck. Males can grow up to 6 feet long, while females are slightly smaller. The long pointed muzzle and the silver mane of long guard hairs bordering the neck and shoulders make these fur seals easy to identify.

Harbor seals are small chunky seals with small front flippers and beautiful, dark-spotted creamy or gray coats. Males reach a size of up to 6 feet and 300 pounds, and females are slightly smaller. Groups of harbor seals can sometimes be seen relaxing on beaches easily accessible to the public. Although you are required by law to keep your distance from the seals, it can be very entertaining to watch these endearing animals surf up to the beach on a convenient wave, then inch their way farther onto the sand to sleep or bask in the sun.

A famous harbor seal named Hoover at the New England Aquarium amazed the public with her parrotlike mimicry of human language. Found as an orphaned pup, Hoover apparently learned human vocalizations instead of, or along with, seal sounds, and was able to clearly say words and small phrases such as "Hoover," "Hello," "How are you," and even laugh. Hoover did not use the words with any apparent intent to communicate, often speaking to no one in particular and stringing together nonsense phrases. Nevertheless, Hoover's "talking" gave scientists new insight into the way seals learn and communicate.

Harbor seals are more wary of intruders than are sea lions.

A harbor seal glances curiously at the photographer.

Male elephant seals' noses become raw and cracked from bashing into opponents.

DID YOU KNOW?

. . . DIVING ELEPHANT SEALS CAN HOLD THEIR BREATH FOR UP TO AN HOUR.

While they usually keep their distance from scuba divers and snorkelers, they occasionally curiously approach and follow their human visitors. The hide-and-seek antics of playful harbor seals can entertain divers and snorkelers for hours on end.

Californians typically refer to **northern elephant seals** simply as elephant seals, although another similar species called the southern elephant seal inhabits portions of the Southern Hemisphere. The male northern elephant seal is the largest of all seals, reaching a length of 16 feet and weighing up to 5,000 pounds. Males develop a large, bulbous snout, which, along with their size, is the origin of their name. Females lack the large snout, but like the males are brownish to silver-gray. The females attain a length of up to 11 feet, and a weight of just under a ton.

Elephant seals are the champions of deep-diving animals, going as deep as 4,100 feet and remaining submerged for up to an hour at a time. While at sea, elephant seal females dive almost constantly, on average to depths of 1,500 feet for about twenty minutes, and surfacing for only two or three minutes before the next dive. (Male elephant seals have yet to be monitored during their dives.) One female was observed diving constantly for eleven days straight. Because diving lowers their metabolic rate, elephant seals may actually expend less energy diving as they travel and forage than they would if they spent time resting or swimming at the surface. Elephant seals may even sleep deep underwater, but this hypothesis is still being investigated.

Northern elephant seals are heavily preyed upon by great white sharks, which seem to have a taste for the seals' substantial layer of fat. The seals are particularly vulnerable during high tides, when loss of hauling-out space forces more of them into the water. In order to minimize the risk they face as they go to sea, elephant seals dive quietly and quickly to the seafloor, following the contours of the bottom as they head directly out of the high-risk zone near the hauling-out or breeding area. Juveniles learn to swim at night, when the danger of attack by great white sharks is lowest. Males, on the other hand, tend to be oblivious to danger during the breeding season.

Unlike sea lions and fur seals, breeding elephant seal bulls fight for dominance, not territory. A dominant bull will be able to mate with most of the females in a breeding area, while the most subordinate bulls are unlikely to mate success-fully at all. Because of the constant vigilance required to maintain dominance and prevent upstart males from mount-ing his females, a dominant bull does not eat or drink for the duration of the breeding season, fasting for up to three months. Only large and healthy bulls can survive the drain of the fast and the incessant fighting, and all bulls look like ghostly remnants of their old selves at the end of the season.

An elephant seal barks out a warning.

A Photo Op Missed

One day I was diving in the kelp beds off Monterey when I was approached by a lone sea otter. I was on the surface and had my camera in hand. I had recently returned from a long shark-filming project and I flippantly commented to my dive buddy that I sure was glad to be in the water with an animal that wouldn't bite me.

The next thing I knew, the otter ducked down and swam toward me. "Perfect photo op," I thought, until it swam right over the top of my camera and perched atop my head. At first I thought it was rather comical, but I soon realized that I couldn't get the otter off my head. (I am well aware that it is illegal to pursue otters, but I don't think the reverse is true.)

Every time I reached up to try to push the otter away, the animal bit my hands or my head. Yes, hard enough to hurt. I didn't bleed, but I am not sure why. Finally, after about five min-utes, it let go and swam away. In the entire time, I never exposed a single frame of film, for the otter was always between the back of my camera and me. Never once did it give me the opportunity to point the lens in its direction.

My guess is that the animal had escaped from captivity, but as far as I could tell, the sea otter was not tagged and never had been.

Interestingly, elephant seals metabolize mainly fat, rather than protein, during the long fast.

Desperate for a mate, subordinate males often try to sneak past the vigilant alpha bull, hiding their nose and creeping cautiously low to the ground in an effort to blend in with the females. When they approach a female, however, she almost always hollers and squirms, creating a commotion that brings the dominant male charging over with vicious intent. Even if the subordinate male is lucky enough to find a receptive female, it is likely that she is quiet only because she has already mated. Females that have already mated and are heading out to sea are mobbed and often injured by groups of hormone-driven subordinate males, which attempt to mate with anything that even slightly resembles a female, including inanimate objects. Pups are sometimes killed by young bulls that mount them.

The noisy protest a female makes toward an amorous male helps ensure that she is mating with a strong bull, maximizing her odds of getting good genes for her offspring. When her pup is born she will nurse and protect it for about a month before she leaves it to fend for itself. While she nurses, she will not eat or drink. The enormous energy drain of reproduction is reflected in the fact that females that first reproduce at a young age also die at an earlier age.

Northern elephant seals were once quite abundant along the California coast. But like many other pinnipeds, they were hunted to near extinction. For years, in fact, northern elephant seals were believed to be extinct. The current population is descended from fewer than 100 elephant seals that managed to survive on a remote island off the coast of Mexico. Although their numbers continue to grow, there is essentially no genetic variability among individuals, so a single disastrous disease or dangerous change in their environment could easily wipe out the entire population. Breeding colonies of northern elephant seals can now

be found at the Channel Islands, the Farallon Islands, and at Año Nuevo.

Sea Otters

Members of the weasel family, **sea otters** are unquestionably among the most fascinating of California's marine mammals. The ancestors of sea otters returned to the sea much more recently than those of other marine mammals (5 to 7 million years ago), making otters more closely related to their terrestrial cousins than are other marine mammals. Although otter populations are much more heavily concentrated in the northern part of the state, they are occasionally seen as far south as the Mexican border.

Because otters do not have a thick layer of blubber, while they are at the water surface they constantly and vigorously rub their lush, reddish-brown to black fur in order to trap an insulating layer of air within the pelt. Sea otters sport the thickest fur coat of any animal in the world, with up to a million hairs on a postage stamp–sized area. Many older males are white-headed, but specimens of both sexes and varying ages also have this feature. Males grow to nearly 4.5 feet, including the 12-inch-long tail, and can weigh close to 85 pounds. The females are considerably smaller, reaching a length of up to 4 feet and weighing only 60 pounds.

Although more than fifty kinds of invertebrates are eaten by sea otters, each otter tends to stick to a few personal favorites. Sea otters often use rocks to gain access to their prey, bashing hard-shelled food sources such as crabs against a rock on their chest or punching holes in abalone to free them from the rocky substrate. Not only do these fascinating animals use tools, they are even equipped with pockets in their fur coats. Foraging sea otters can collect their prey and keep their forepaws free for more searching by stashing their finds in handy

A feeding sea otter.

flaps of skin under each front leg. They always return to the surface to feed, but must guard their meals well—unscrupulous otters greedily steal another's food whenever they can seize the opportunity.

Although they usually stick to shallow foraging dives, sea otters are quite capable swimmers and occasionally make dives of up to 300 feet that last more than four minutes. However, they spend most of their time at the surface in kelp beds, either resting on their back or swimming at a leisurely pace. While relaxing at the surface, they carefully hold their forepaws and hind flippers curled up out of the water, which keeps these poorly insulated limbs as warm as possible. They often roll themselves up in long strands of giant kelp floating at the surface, tethering themselves so that they will not be carried out to sea.

For thousands of years otters inhabited waters between Alaska and the lower portion of the Baja Peninsula. Their most viable natural predator is believed to have been sharks, but studies show that otter populations were once quite prolific. Then, in the late 1700s, hunters and trappers from Europe, Russia, and America began to pursue otters in quest of their valuable pelts. Throughout the 1800s and early 1900s the pressure continued as they proved to be an easy prey. It is estimated that in 170 years of hunting, more than a million otters were killed, and populations declined almost to the point of extinction. In 1911 the international Fur Seal Treaty was signed, protecting sea otters in international waters, and in 1913, sea otters gained full protection within the Alaskan territory and the region governed by the State of California.

At the time of this writing, California's sea otter population is concentrated in a 200-mile stretch of the state's central coastline. While most individuals remain within a home territory, the range has been expanding at about 2.5 miles annually, and the total population within California waters has been increasing by approximately 5 percent per year. However, it is estimated that the current worldwide sea otter population is only a tenth of its original size.

Sea otters can regularly be observed in a number of locations in northern California, especially along the Monterey Peninsula. If there is a lot of bull kelp in the area, spotting the otters is more difficult than when giant kelp is predominant. The dark brown floats of bull kelp bear a strong resemblance to otters. A good way to locate otters is to watch carefully as the swells roll through; when they reach a high point, the bull kelp is often submerged, but the otters remain on the surface. Binoculars are helpful, as is the presence of gulls and other seabirds that hover over feeding otters.

Sea otters wrap up in kelp to anchor themselves close to shore while they rest.

The Sea Otter Controversy

Sea otters play a vital yet quite controversial role in California's ecology. They are voracious eaters, feeding on a wide variety of invertebrates, including abalone, lobster, sea urchins, crabs, snails, mussels, squid, octopi, scallops, and (rarely) fish. Lacking a fat layer to assist in maintaining their 100°F body temperature, young otters often consume up to 35 percent of their body weight in a day's feeding in order to combat the effects of cold water. Adults eat closer to 15 percent of their weight every day. That means an adult otter devours nearly 5,000 pounds of food a year, and the entire otter population consumes in excess of 6,000 tons. It is easy to deduce that large otter populations limit the numbers of abalone, lobster, and other shellfish through their heavy feeding. Obviously, this presents a potential threat to commercial fishers, many of whom lobby strongly against the reintroduction of otter populations.

However, otters also feed heavily upon sea urchins, limiting the numbers of urchins in healthy kelp forest communities. During the late 1700s and through the 1800s, humans hunted sea otters to near extinction in pursuit of their highly valued pelts. With the demise of sea otter populations came a corresponding increase in the number of sea urchins, a problem that was exacerbated by the harvesting of

The health of California's lush forests of giant kelp is partially dependent on predators such as sea otters that keep sea urchins in check.

other natural predators of urchins, such as sheephead and other fishes.

The urchin population explosion created intense competition among them for food. Although urchins normally prefer to feed on kelp shed, they will readily feed on the kelp's living holdfasts when competition for food increases. Kelp plants quickly perish as they are torn loose from the bottom when the holdfasts are eaten. Once adrift, these stipes become entangled with other kelp plants, tearing them free as well. Scientists have documented the demise of thousands of square miles of kelp forests due to the unchecked explosion of sea urchin populations. The denuded areas left in their wake are aptly called urchin barrens.

Without kelp, the mainstay of the kelp forest ecosystem, the entire food chain suffers. In the long run, sea otters promote the health of kelp communities, and therefore that of the commercially valuable fish and invertebrates within the community, by limiting the numbers of urchins. Sea otter populations have made a substantial comeback, owing in part to their protected status, foraging abilities, and varied diet. However, because of new threats and the fact that the population has not recovered to its original size, sea otters continue to be classified as threatened under the Endangered Species Act.

GLOSSARY

This glossary is a quick reference source for some terms used to describe the marine environment or the plants and animals found within it. The following definitions are given for practical purposes, and are not intended as definitive, all-inclusive scientific definitions. Instead, they should help readers understand these terms as they are likely to apply to topics discussed in this book.

A

aboral. Away from the mouth or head.

abyssal. Of or relating to benthic regions in deep waters, beyond the continental slope.

air bladder. (1) Swim bladder in bony fishes that expands or deflates to allow the fish to hover at its chosen depth. (2) A pneumatocyst; a gas-filled chamber that buoys plants such as kelp.

alga. A type of simple plant that does not reproduce by flowering, including kelp.

algin. A natural product derived from giant kelp and other brown seaweeds. Algin has a high affinity for water and is used as a thickening, emulsifying, and gel-producing agent.

alternation of generations. The alternation of a sexually reproducing generation and an asexually reproducing generation in the life history of an organism.

amphipod. Small animals of the class Crustacea, most commonly noticed on beaches and often mistaken for insects.

Ampullae of Lorenzini. Sensory organs in the snout of elasmobranchs that detect electrical fields.

annelid. A member of the phylum Annelida. Annelids are also known as segmented worms.

anterior. Toward the forward end or head.

anthozoan. Any member of the class Anthozoa, including sea anemones, sea pens, jellyfish, and corals.

aperture. An orifice, as in the opening in the shell of abalone.

aphotic. Without light. The aphotic zone of the oceans is that region that does not receive enough light to support plant growth by photosynthesis.

armored. Having a protective covering of scales or bony plates.

arthropod. Any invertebrate described in the phylum Arthropoda, including marine examples such as lobsters, crabs, shrimp, isopods, amphipods, copepods, and other crustaceans.

ascidian. A member of a class of benthic tunicates.

asexual reproduction. Reproduction that does not involve the union of sperm and egg. Sporulation, budding, fragmentation, and fission are methods of asexual reproduction, which results in clonal offspring.

attenuated shape. Long and thin with a gradual taper.

autozooid. A feeding polyp found in some colonial anthozoans such as sea pansies. See **siphonozooid**.

B

baleen. A flexible horny substance that grows from the upper jaw of filter-feeding whales. Baleen is used as a sievelike filter to trap food.

bathyal. Of or relating to the benthic region of the continental slope.

benthic. Bottom-dwelling. Benthic animals live on or near the seafloor. See **pelagic**.

bilaterally symmetrical. Able to be divided into equal halves on only one plane.

binomial nomenclature. A naming system for organisms in which each life-form is given a taxonomic name consisting of two words, the first designating the genus and the second designating the species. When correctly printed, both the genus and species are italicized, and the genus is capitalized.

biological clock. An innate physiological rhythm that is often synchronized with environmental factors such as the rising or setting of the sun or the cycle of tides.

bioluminescence. The biological production of light by living organisms. See **phosphorescence**.

biomass. The total mass of organic matter per unit of area. This term is often used when explaining how much food is required to support predators.

bivalve. A mollusk that has a shell consisting of two halves.

bladder. A sac used as a reservoir for a gas or fluid.

blade. The leaflike appendage of a kelp plant.

blowhole. The nostril or spiracle on the top of the head of whales and dolphins through which respiration occurs.

C

calcareous. Made of or containing calcium carbonate ($CaCO_3$).

carapace. The part of the exoskeleton that covers the cephalothorax of some arthropods.

carnivore. An animal that devours the flesh of other animals. See **herbivore** and **omnivore**.

caudal fin. A tail fin.

cephalization. The process during which sensory nerves and organs become concentrated at the anterior end of an animal.

cephalopod. Any mollusk in the class Cephalopoda, including octopi and squids.

cerata. Club-shaped respiratory structures on the back of nudibranchs.

cetacean. Any animal that belongs to the mammalian order Cetacea, including whales and dolphins.

chordate. Any animal described in the phylum Chordata, including tunicates and all vertebrates.

chromatophore. A pigment cell used to alter colors in octopi, squids, some crustaceans, and other animals.

cilia. Minute hairlike processes found along the edge of a cell, used for locomotion or for creating a current.

circadean rhythm. An innate cycle timed to a biological clock, in sync with the rising and setting of the sun.

circalunadian rhythm. An innate cycle timed to a biological clock, in sync with the cycle of the tides.

clasper. One of a pair of reproductive structures located on the underbelly of males of all cartilaginous fishes.

class. A taxonomic category below a phylum and above an order.

classification. The systematic scientific categorization of plants and animals according to commonly shared characteristics.

cleaner. An organism that removes parasites and dead tissue from the surface of another animal.

clone. Having an identical genetic makeup.

cnidarian. Any animal described in the phylum Cnidaria, including invertebrates such as sea anemones, sea pens, jellyfish, and corals.

cnidocyte. A stinging cell that produces a nematocyst. Found only in cnidarians.

coelom. A fluid-filled body cavity that cushions and protects the internal organs. Found in chordates and higher invertebrates including bryozoans, mollusks, annelids, arthropods, and echinoderms.

cold biological light. Light produced by bioluminescent organisms.

cold-blooded. Having a core temperature that varies with ambient temperature. Most fishes, amphibians, and reptiles are cold-blooded. Also called ectothermic or poikilothermous.

colony. A group of living organisms that share a common skeletal case or test.

comb. A row of cilia found on ctenophores.

commensalism. A type of symbiotic relationship in which the symbiont benefits but the host does not; however, the host is not harmed.

continental shelf. The slightly sloping region of the seafloor that extends from the sublittoral zone to approximately 600 feet.

continental slope. The steeply sloping region of the seafloor beyond the continental shelf.

coralline. (1) An animal that bears a strong resemblance to coral. (2) A type of red algae containing lime.

countershading. A type of coloration that is light on the bottom and darker on top, allowing the animal to blend in with surface waters when viewed from below and with darker water when viewed from above.

crayfish. A freshwater crustacean closely related to lobsters. Most crayfish are smaller than most lobsters.

crustacean. Any arthropod in the class Crustacea, including lobsters, crabs, shrimps, copepods, isopods, and amphipods.

ctenophore. Any member of the phylum Ctenophore, including comb jellies.

D

decapod. Any crustacean classified in the order Decapoda, including lobsters, crabs, shrimps, amphipods, copepods, and isopods. Decapods have five pairs of walking legs.

delayed implantation. The phenomenon in which a fertilized egg remains unplanted in the uterine wall for an extended period of time, making the gestation period of shorter duration than the time between copulation and birthing. In some marine mammals with a gestation period of less than one year, delayed implantation helps allow females to give birth in the same area where they breed.

dermal denticles. Toothlike projections that comprise the skin of sharks. Sharks lack scales, but do possess dermal denticles that align in one direction, making sharks feel very smooth if rubbed in one direction, but very rough if rubbed in an opposing direction.

desiccation. Elimination or deprivation of moisture; a major threat to creatures that live in tidepool habitats.

detritivore. Any animal that feeds on dead organic matter, including refuse.

deuterostome. A group of animals, including echinoderms and chordates, that share a common pattern of embryonic development. See **protostome**.

diatoms. A plantlike, one-celled microorganism that makes up an important component of plankton.

dinoflagellate. A type of one-celled microorganism that is an important component of plankton. A species of dinoflagellate is responsible for the red tides that occasionally occur in California waters.

disc. A flat circular structure; used to describe the colonial body of sea pansies and the central section of brittle stars.

distribution. The range or area that a species normally inhabits.

diurnal. Pertaining to the day, as opposed to nocturnal. Occurring daily.

dorsal. Of or relating to the back or upper surface of the body of an animal.

E

ecdysis. The process of molting in arthropods, in which an arthropod grows by discarding its exoskeleton, experiencing a period of rapid growth, and then forming a new, hard exoskeleton.

echinoderm. Any marine animal described in the phylum Echinodermata, including invertebrates such as sea stars, brittle stars, sea cucumbers, and sea urchins.

echolocation. The biological sonar used by many species of marine mammals. The animals send out a series of sounds that reflect off objects back to the sender. The sender then analyzes the reflected sounds to gain information about its surroundings.

ecology. The portion of the discipline of biology concerned with the interrelationships among organisms and between organisms and their surrounding environment.

ecosystem. A natural system consisting of an interconnected community of organisms and their environment.

ectoparasite. See **ectozoan**.

ectozoan. A parasite that lives on the skin of its host. See **entozoan**.

elasmobranch. Any animal that is a member of the class Chondrichthyes, including cartilaginous fishes such as sharks, skates, and rays.

entozoan. A parasite that lives within another organism. See **ectozoan**.

epifauna. Benthic animals that live on the surface of bottom materials.

epizoan. An animal that lives on the surface of another organism. See **ectozoan**.

estuary. A body of seawater that is measurably diluted by fresh water, as at the end of a river.

evolution. The process of genetic change over extended periods of time. The process by which species change, adapt, and develop.

excurrent. Outflowing. In sponges the excurrent siphon helps to eliminate wastes and unwanted water. See **incurrent**.

exoskeleton. A protective external skeleton.

extant. Not extinct; describes a species with currently living representatives.

extracellular. Occurring outside of a cell.

F

family. A taxonomic category between order and genus.

filter-feeder. Any animal that feeds on tiny particulate matter that it filters from the surrounding water.

fingerling. A fish; describes the age between the time of the disappearance of the yolk sac and the end of one year.

finlet. A small fin located on either the dorsal or ventral side near the tail of tuna and other fishes. Finlets serve to reduce drag.

fitness. The ability of an individual creature to survive and reproduce in its environment. Sometimes measured as the number of the creature's offspring that survive to have offspring themselves.

flatworm. Any member of the phylum Platyhelminthes.

flower. A reproductive structure found in some plants, but not in algae such as kelp.

fluke. A horizontal lobe on the tail of a whale. In casual conversation the terms "tail" and "fluke" are used interchangeably.

food chain. A grouping of organisms in which energy is transferred from one trophic level to the next as members of each trophic level are consumed by members of a higher trophic level.

food web. A group of interconnected food chains.

frond. The blades, pneumatocysts, and stipe of a kelp plant.

fusiform. Tapered at both ends. Fishes such as giant barracuda, albacore, and blue sharks are said to have a fusiform shape.

G

gamete. Any cell capable of developing into a complete individual upon union with another compatible sex cell.

gametophyte. A plant that produces gametes. The gamete-producing generation of plants that reproduce by the method of alternation of generations.

gastropod. Any mollusk described in the class Gastropoda, including abalone, snails, limpets, nudibranchs, and sea hares.

genus. A taxonomic category between family and species.

gestation period. The period of time between the implantation of a fertilized egg in the uterine wall and birth.

gill. A respiratory structure in nonmammalian aquatic animals through which gaseous exchange occurs.

gill rakers. The projections on the gill arches of some fishes that serve to prevent food particles from passing through the gill slits.

gill slit. One of several openings in the wall of the pharynx. In marine animals the gill slits are separated by arches that bear gills.

girdle. The mantle of a chiton.

gorgonian. A coral described in the order Gorgonacea, including sea fans. The skeletal case of gorgonians is composed in part of a hornlike substance known as gorgonian.

H

habitat. The natural environment of an organism (for example, tidepools, kelp forests, and sandy plains).

haptera. Structures that serve to attach plants to the substrate. The haptera of a giant kelp plant collectively form a holdfast that secures the plant to the rocky bottom.

harem. A group of female animals that mate with and to some extent are controlled by a single male.

herbivore. Any animal that feeds solely or primarily on plants.

hermaphrodite. An animal that at some time over the course of its life possesses both male and female reproductive organs.

heterocercal tail. An asymmetrical tail in which the upper lobe is usually significantly larger than the lower lobe, as in the tail structure of blue sharks and many other shark species.

holdfast. A structure that attaches or anchors many marine plants to the substrate. The holdfasts of giant kelp plants consist of numerous haptera.

homocercal tail. A symmetrical or nearly symmetrical tail. A lunate tail. Mako sharks, great white sharks, and tuna have homocercal tails.

I

ichthyology. The science that deals with the study of fishes.

implantation. In mammals, the process through which fertilized eggs become embedded in the uterine wall.

incurrent. Flowing inward. In sponges the incurrent siphon brings in water containing oxygen and food. See **excurrent**.

indigenous. Native to or naturally found in an area.

ink sac. A rectal gland found in cephalopods that serves to produce and store ink.

intertidal. The region of the beach that is sometimes but not always submersed. Littoral. See **sublittoral**.

intracellular. Occurring within a cell.

invertebrate. An animal that does not possess a backbone or spinal column.

iridocytes. The specialized cells found in the skin of flatfish that enable the fish to closely match the color and pattern of their skin with that of their surroundings.

isopod. Any crustacean described in the order Isopoda.

J

juvenile. A young or sexually immature organism.

K

kelp. Any of several large brown seaweeds described in the order Laminariales.

kingdom. The broadest of taxonomic categories.

L

lamprey. A jawless fish described in the class Marsipobranchii. Lampreys prey upon other fishes by sucking their blood and other body fluids.

larva. The immature form of an organism that is unlike the adult form.

lateral line system. A series of sense organs in fishes that extends from the head to the tail along the sides of the body.

life cycle. The complete life history of an organism.

life history. The complete series of events displayed by an organism, encompassing every stage between its origin and death.

littoral. Of or relating to the seashore. The littoral area is the region between the tide lines; intertidal. See **sublittoral**.

longitudinal. Lengthwise or extending along the axis. Markings that are longitudinal run the length of the body, as opposed to across the body.

lophophore. The feeding structure of bryozoans.

luminescence. The production and emission of light without the accompanying production and emission of a significant amount of heat. Bioluminescent organisms create luminescent light.

lunate tail. A symmetrical or nearly symmetrical tail. A homocercal tail.

M

macroplankton. Planktonic organisms that can be recognized with the naked eye without any magnification.

mammal. Any vertebrate described in the class Mammalia, with marine representatives including whales, sea lions, seals, otters, dolphins, and manatees. Female mammals possess mammary glands that produce milk to nurse offspring. Mammals have hair, breathe air, have lungs, are warm-blooded, and most bear live young.

mandible. In general usage, the jaw. In arthropods, one of a pair of mouth parts used to cut, crush, or grind food.

mantle. The part of a mollusk that covers the visceral mass, controls respiration, and secretes a shell (if present).

margin. An edge or border.

medusa. The jellyfish-like, pelagic form of many cnidarians.

metabolic rate. The rate of chemical or energy changes that occur within a living organism as calculated by the amount of food consumed, the heat produced, or the oxygen used.

metabolism. The chemical and energy changes that take place within a living organism because of the activities involved in being alive.

metamorphosis. A process in which animals such as crustaceans undergo a change in shape or form as the animal develops from a fertilized egg into an adult.

microplankton. Members of the plankton that cannot be seen by the naked eye without magnification.

midden. A pile of debris often found in front of an octopus's den. Also called a midden heap.

migration. The extensive mass movement of populations of animals to and from feeding, breeding, and nesting areas.

mollusk. Any animal described in the phylum Mollusca, including invertebrates such as chitons, abalone, limpets, octopi, squids, nudibranchs, sea hares, clams, mussels, and scallops.

molt. The complete cycle of shedding and developing a new exoskeleton or outer covering.

mother-of-pearl. The lustrous inner layer of the shell of abalone.

mutualism. A type of symbiotic relationship in which two organisms of differing species live in close association with each other, to the advantage of both organisms. The relationship between moray eels and cleaner shrimp is described as mutualism.

N

narcosis. A state of confusion or stupor induced by a drug or foreign element. In the case of diving, nitrogen narcosis refers to a feeling that ranges from confusion to euphoria caused by the increased partial pressure of nitrogen in the human system at depth.

natural history. The study of or description of the life of various organisms. A complete discussion of the natural history of an organism would include information concerning its classification, habits, predator/prey relationships, life cycle, and distribution.

natural selection. The process through which natural events determine which members of a population will survive and which will perish, over time resulting in the survival of those specimens that are most fit for their environment.

nektonic. Actively swimming; often used in reference to large animals.

nematocyst. A specialized cellular capsule that contains a stinging nettle that can be used to paralyze prey or for defense; found only in cnidarians. Not to be confused with the pneumatocyst found in plants.

neritic. Of or relating to the waters that lie over a continental shelf.

nettle cell. A stinging cell found inside the nematocysts of cnidarians.

notochord. In chordates, a dorsal rod of cartilage that runs the length of the body and forms the primitive axial skeleton in the embryonic stage of all chordates. In most adult chordates, the notochord is replaced by the spinal column, whereas in tunicates the notochord forms the axial skeleton.

O

oceanic province. Ocean waters beyond the continental shelf.

omnivore. Any animal that feeds on both plants and animals.

operculum. A plate that covers and protects the gill openings in some fishes.

order. A taxonomic category below a class and above a family.

organic. Biologically produced; also describes biological compounds.

osculum. The large excurrent opening in a sponge.

osmoregulator. An organism that maintains a constant concentration of various salts within the body in spite of the concentrations of salts in the organism's immediate surroundings.

osmosis. The passage of water through a tissue or membrane as a result of different concentrations of salts.

oviparous. A specific type of reproduction in which females lay eggs that hatch outside the body of the female. See **ovoviviparous** and **viviparous**.

ovoviviparous. A specific type of reproduction in which females produce eggs encased in a shell that develop inside the body, but the young receive nourishment only from the yolk sac, not directly from the mother. See **oviparous** and **viviparous**.

P

paleontology. The study of plants and animals that lived during previous time periods, according to what can be learned from fossil remains.

parasite. An organism that lives on or in a host organism from which it takes some nourishment, to the detriment of the host.

parasitism. A type of symbiotic relationship in which one organism, the parasite, is dependent at least in part on another organism, to the detriment of the host.

pectoral. Of or relating to the chest or breast area of a body.

pectoral fin. One of the paired, laterally oriented fins of a fish. Pectoral fins are generally forward of the mid-body of fish.

pedicellaria. Small organs found on the body surface of some echinoderms such as sea stars, used to clean debris off the body surface. Under a microscope pedicellaria look like miniature pliers.

peduncle. The stalk of a barnacle.

pelagic. (1) Of or relating to the open ocean. (2) Living up in the water column as opposed to on the bottom. See **benthic.**

pelecypod. Any mollusk described in the class Pelecypoda, including mussels, scallops, clams, and oysters.

pharyngeal slit. In members of the phylum Chordata, one of a series of openings between the throat (or pharynx) and the surrounding environment.

pheromones. Chemical substances used for communication between members of the same species. Pheromones are used to induce the simultaneous release of sex cells in many invertebrates that reproduce via external fertilization.

phoresis. A type of symbiotic relationship in which the host provides transportation for the symbiont. The relationship between barnacles and California gray whales is correctly described as phoresis.

photic. Having to do with light.

photic zone. The region in the marine realm where sunlight is able to penetrate in an amount sufficient to support photosynthesis.

photophores. Light-producing organs found on some marine animals, especially deep-dwelling species.

photosynthesis. The process through which plants convert radiant or solar energy into chemical energy that is used for growth.

phylogenetic. Pertaining to the assumed evolutionary histories and relationships of organisms.

phylum. The largest taxonomic subcategory of a kingdom. A phylum is subdivided into classes.

phytoplankton. Plant plankton; members of plankton that are able to photosynthesize.

pinniped. Any aquatic mammal described in the order Pinnipedia, including seals and sea lions.

planktivore. An animal that feeds on plankton.

plankton. Aquatic organisms that have only limited control over their movement and drift passively with water currents.

pneumatocyst. The air bladder or float found on various marine algae. The pneumatocysts of kelp serve to buoy the plants toward the surface and sunlight.

pod. A group of whales, porpoises, or dolphins.

poikilothermous. Cold-blooded; having a core temperature that varies with the surrounding environment.

polychaete. A type of annelid worm, including all the annelid worms discussed in this book.

polygamous. Having more than one mate during a short period of time.

polyp. A small, benthic form of various cnidarians, in which the animals are attached at the base and have a mouth surrounded by tentacles. Colonial cnidarians are composed of groups of polyps that share a continuous skeletal case.

posterior. At or toward the tail or back end of the body.

predation. The act of seeking out and capturing other animals for food.

predator. An animal that practices predation.

prey. An animal that is captured and eaten by another animal.

proboscis. The elongated snout of various animals such as male elephant seals.

process. (1) A series of interconnected activities. (2) A projecting outgrowth on a body.

protostome. A group of animals, including mollusks, annelids, and arthropods, that share a common pattern of embryonic development. See **deuterostome.**

R

radially symmetrical. Able to be divided into equal halves on any plane that passes through a central axis.

radula. A tonguelike structure that bears rows of tiny teeth. A radula is found in many mollusks and is used as a tool for rasping and chewing.

red tide. An occasional water condition in which there is a high concentration of toxin-releasing microorganisms, causing local filter-feeding creatures such as shellfish to become poisonous to eat. During a red tide, the water is not always red.

regeneration. The regrowth of lost tissues or body parts. In some lower animals, such as sea stars, some lost body parts can regenerate into new individuals.

respiration. The exchange of gases between an organism and its surroundings.

rhinophore. A sensory organ located on the head of nudibranchs.

rostrum. A body projection extending forward from the head in manta rays and other animals.

S

sagittal crest. A pronounced arrow-shaped ridge in the midline of the skull in some marine mammals.

salp. The common name for members of a class of free-swimming marine tunicates.

scientific name. The taxonomic classification known as the genus and species of a given organism. The first letter of the genus name is always capitalized and both words appear in italics.

sea squirt. Another name for benthic tunicates.

sea star. A term that is replacing the word "starfish" in some educational circles, to reflect the fact that these animals are invertebrates and not fish.

seawater. Saline water found in ocean basins. Salt contents vary, but average close to 3.5 percent.

seaweed. Any of several large plants that grow in seawater, including kelp.

sediment. The matter that settles to the seafloor or other substrate.

sessile. Attached to the substrate; not capable of free movement.

sexual generation. In plants that reproduce in a cycle known as alternation of generations, it is the generation that produces gametes.

sexual reproduction. Reproduction involving the union of a sperm and egg. This type of reproduction results in offspring that are genetically different from each other and from their parent(s).

siliceous. Of or relating to silicon dioxide, also known as silica, which is the basis of sand.

siphon. A tubelike structure used to draw in or expel fluids. Siphons are found in many bivalves, cephalopods, and tunicates.

siphonozooid. A modified polyp that serves to create water currents in some colonial anthozoans. See **autozooid**.

speciation. The process by which new species are naturally formed.

species. The most exclusive of taxonomic groups. Creatures belonging to the same species are extremely similar to one another.

spermatophore. A packet of sperm transferred by a male to a female in cephalopods, various crustaceans, and other animals.

spicule. A needlelike structure contained in sponges.

spiracle. One of a pair of openings on the top of the head of rays, sharks, and skates, through which water is drawn in before passing over the gills. The term is also used to describe the blowhole of a cetacean.

splash zone. The area above the high tide line that is often moistened with spray from breaking surf but is only rarely, if ever, completely awash.

spongin. A protein contained in sponges.

sporophyte. A plant that produces spores. The spore-producing asexual generation of plants that reproduce by the method of alternation of generations.

stipe. A stemlike stalk or supporting structure, as in the stipe of a kelp plant.

stony coral. A cnidarian described in the order Madreporaria. In California waters, solitary corals are often referred to as stony corals.

sublittoral. Shallow ocean waters beyond the intertidal region, extending from the average low tide depth to approximately 150 to 200 feet.

subspecies. A subdivision of a species in which interbreeding is possible, but in which slight physiological differences are present.

substrate. The solid material on which organisms live, such as sand or rocks.

swimmeret. One of a pair of slender, branched appendages on the abdomen of crayfishes and lobsters. Females carry eggs on the swimmerets.

symbiont. Any organism living in a symbiotic relationship, or in symbiosis.

symbiosis. A lifestyle in which two organisms of different species live in close association with each other, including mutualism, commensalism, parasitism, and phoresis.

T

taxon. A taxonomic classification of any size such as a phylum, order, family, or species.

taxonomy. The arrangement and classification of plants and animals into categories based on commonly shared characteristics.

teleost. Any fish with a bony skeleton, a member of the class Osteichthyes.

tentacle. Any of a number of long, thin, flexible, unsegmented appendages that serve in a sensory, feeding, locomotive, defensive, attaching, or reproductive capacity.

terminal. Of or relating to the front or forming end of a body. The mouth of a garibaldi is located in a terminal position, while the mouth of a blue shark is not.

territory. An area to which animals normally confine their activities. In many cases the animals vigorously defend the area from intruders.

test. Another name for a shell.

thermocline. The depth at which water temperatures suddenly and noticeably change.

threshold. The lowest limit at which a given event will occur. A survival threshold describes the limit to which an animal or species can be pushed before dying.

tide. The periodic, cyclical, predictable rise and fall of the sea along the coast.

trinomial nomenclature. An extension of the binomial system in which a subspecies or a variety is scientifically named using a total of three words, two of which combine to comprise the species name. When properly written, all three words are italicized, but only the genus is capitalized.

trochophore. The first stage of a mollusk larva.

trophic. Of or relating to growth or nutrition.

trophic level. A place in a food chain defined by the number of times the energy of the primary producers (plants) has been transferred up the chain. Plants comprise the first trophic level, herbivores the second, animals that eat herbivores the third, and so on.

U

uniparous. Bearing one offspring at a time.

univalve. A mollusk whose shell has only one valve or plate that makes up the shell, such as a snail or a limpet.

V

veliger. The second stage of a mollusk larva.

ventral. Of or relating to the lower surface or underside of a body.

vernacular name. The common or nontaxonomic name of an organism.

vertebrate. Any animal that has a spinal column; described in the subphylum Vertebrata.

visceral mass. The main portion of the body of a mollusk, located above the foot and including the internal organs.

viviparous. A form of reproduction in which the eggs of undeveloped young hatch inside the body of the mother, and obtain further nourishment from her as development proceeds. The young are born at a later point in time when development has been completed. See **oviparous** and **ovoviviparous**.

W

warm-blooded. Able to maintain a core body temperature independent of ambient temperature. Also called endothermic.

whorl. A spiral turn or twist in the shell of a gastropod mollusk.

X

xenology. The study of parasitic relationships.

Z

zooid. An individual organism in a colony or closely associated group of animals.

zooplankton. The animal members of the plankton; plankton that consume other organisms. See **phytoplankton**.

SPECIES INDEX